This book may be kept
Twenty-one days
A fine of $0.20 per day will
be charged for each day it is overdue

Christian Heritage College Library
2100 Greenfield Dr.

...thence round Cape Horn

THENCE ROUND CAPE HORN

*The Story of United States
Naval Forces on Pacific
Station, 1818–1923*

by Robert Erwin Johnson

UNITED STATES NAVAL INSTITUTE
Annapolis, Maryland

Library of Congress
Catalogue Card No. 63-13587

PRINTED IN THE UNITED STATES OF AMERICA
BY KINGSPORT PRESS, INC.

For my Mother,
Agnes Sandquist Johnson

Preface

This is the story of the United States naval forces in the eastern Pacific Ocean, an area known to the Navy as the Pacific Station during most of the period 1818-1923. Just as the United States attained the status of world power in the course of that period, so the Pacific Station increased in importance until it became the cruising ground of the United States Fleet in the years following World War I. The growth of the nation and that of the station were not unrelated; the Pacific Squadron, later the Pacific Fleet, was one of the agencies contributing to the rise of national power, although its role was often unspectacular.

It was found convenient to follow a chronological arrangement in large part, but this work is not an operational history in the strict sense. Rather I have endeavored to reveal the policies responsible for the assignment of an American naval force to the eastern Pacific and for its maintenance there. Because the warships influenced, and were influenced by, the political, economic, and diplomatic conditions prevailing in the lands bordering on their station, an account of this relationship has been included. Some narration of actual operations was necessary to illustrate the discussion of policy and practice, but the reader must not expect to find all of the events which occurred on Pacific Station chronicled herein. The inclusion of technical aspects, baffling as they may be, was essential for my purpose. An effort has been made to define adequately the more mysterious terms.

The introductory chapter contains a consideration of the factors which led the United States Navy to adopt the distant-station policy, with especial emphasis on the conditions which caused the eastern Pacific to become one of its cruising stations. Most of the major problems faced by senior officers on distant stations are described also.

I have chosen to relate the events of two early cruises in some detail so that the reader may become familiar with the nature of duty on Pacific Station. Most of the more important occurrences of other cruises have received consideration, and attention has been given to events which seem to have been virtually unnoticed by other historians.

It is difficult to write of ships without frequent use of their names; this repetition may be tiresome to one who does not feel their enchantment. I am not among this group; therefore, I invite the reader to share with me the pleasure of such ship-names as *Fairfield* and *Brandywine,* names which have disappeared, I hope not for long, from the United States Navy.

In large part, of course, this is a story of the sea, of an ocean space so wide as to be almost beyond comprehension. Those who share my interest in "the way of a ship in the midst of the sea" perhaps will find in the following chapters more than a modicum of the attraction that the Pacific Station and the men-o'-war which cruised over its vast expanse have had for me.

A number of people assisted with research; among them my especial thanks must go to the following: the staff of the Navy Section, War Records Branch, National Archives, particularly Thomas C. Coleman, Jr., and Elmore A. Champie (both now employed in other governmental agencies); the staffs of the Manuscript Division, Library of Congress, and of the New-York Historical Society; Rear Admiral John B. Heffernan, U.S. Navy (Ret.), formerly Director of Naval History; Admiral Arthur J. Hepburn, U.S. Navy (Ret.); and Mrs. Harriette Saxton of Pasadena, California. The John Randolph Haynes and Dora Haynes Foundation of Los Angeles, California, was responsible for the grant which enabled me to do the research for this study, and my sister, Mrs. John Menegat of Arago Route, Myrtle Point, Oregon, lent additional financial aid. I am grateful to Mrs. Wilburt Scott Brown and John Fraser Ramsey who read the galleys, and to my wife, Vivian, who helped to read proof and prepare the index.

Finally, I can only acknowledge my debt to Professor John Haskell Kemble of Pomona College and the Claremont Graduate School, my good friend and adviser, who offered sound counsel at every turn. His admirable library on maritime history was open to me during the original writing of this work, and his knowledge of manuscript collections was of much value.

R. E. JOHNSON

Tuscaloosa, Alabama
28 March 1963

Contents

Illustrations   *xiii*
". . . and here must be our Navy. . . ."   *xv*

Chapter
1. *Distant Stations*   1
2. *The Cruise of the* Macedonian . . .   17
3. *From Ship to Squadron*   27
4. *Aground on Her Own Beef Bones* . .   43
5. *The Flying Welshman*   59
6. *Too Many Commodores*   77
7. *The Gold Mania*   93
8. *Guarding the Gold Steamers*   113
9. *Economy and Decline*   124
10. *A Stagnant Station*   143
11. *The Armored Cruiser Squadron* . . .   164
12. *Pacific Fleet in the Atlantic Ocean* . .   179
13. *"And Here Our Navy Is"*   189
    Notes   200

Appendix
  I *Sailing Orders to Captain Downes* . .   207
 II *Officers Commanding United States Naval
      Forces on Pacific Station*   209
III *Annual Composition of United States
      Naval Forces on Pacific Station* . . .   211
 IV *Characteristics of Ships Serving
      on Pacific Station*   230

     Bibliography   250
     Index   263

Illustrations

Following page 128

1. USS *Macedonian* under a jury rig, September 1818.
(*The National Archives*)

2. Captain John Downes. (*U.S. Naval Academy Museum*)

3. USS *United States.* (*The National Archives*)

4. Commodore Isaac Hull. (*U.S. Naval Academy Museum*)

5. USS *Peacock* in the Antarctic, 1839-40. (*U.S. Naval Institute*)

6. Lieutenant Charles Wilkes. (*U.S. Naval Academy Museum*)

7. USS *North Carolina.* (*Official U.S. Navy Photograph*)

8. American flag being raised at Monterey, California,
7 July 1846. (*Official U.S. Navy Photograph*)

9. USS *Vincennes* and USS *Columbus* departing from
Tokyo Bay, July 1846. (*Naval Historical Foundation*)

10. USS *Camanche,* launched at Union Iron Works,
San Francisco, 1864. (*The Bancroft Library*)

11. USS *Ohio.* (*Painting by Rear Admiral J. W. Schmidt, USN (Ret.)*
From the collection of R. E. Cragg, former Lieutenant Commander, USNR)

12. Commodore Thomas ap Catesby Jones.
(*Official U.S. Navy Portrait*)

13. Commodore Robert F. Stockton. (*U.S. Naval Academy Museum*)

14. Commander Robley D. Evans. (*U.S. Naval Institute*)

15. USS *Yorktown.* (*U.S. Naval Institute*)

16. Figurehead of USS *Trenton.* (*Official U.S. Navy Photograph*)

17. Apia Harbor, 17 March 1889, following the hurricane.
(*The National Archives*)

18. USS *Wateree* after a tidal wave at Arica, Chile,
in August 1868. (*Official U.S. Navy Photograph*)

19. USS *Pinta* in Juneau Harbor, 1889. (*Official U.S. Navy Photograph*)

20. Pago Pago, Samoa, 1908, with destroyers and armored
cruisers at anchor. (*The National Archives*)

21. USS *Monadnock,* Mare Island Navy Yard.
(*Naval Historical Foundation*)

22. USS *South Dakota* in her 1916 rig. (*Official*
U.S. Navy Photograph)

Illustrations

Following page 128

1. USS Macedonian under a jury rig, September 1818.
   (Navy Department archives)
2. Captain John Downes, USS Macedonian (Mariners Museum)
   USS United States (U.S. Naval archives)
4. Commodore Isaac Hull, USN, Naval Academy Museum)
5. USS Savannah in the Atlantic, 16-20-40 (U.S. Naval archives)
6. Lieutenant Charles Wilkes, U.S. Naval Academy Museum)
7. USS North Carolina (U.S. Navy Photograph)
8. American flag being raised at Monterey, California,
   7 July 1846, (original U.S. Navy Photograph)
9. USS Vincennes and USS Columbus departing from
   Tokyo Bay, July 1846. (Naval Historical Foundation)
10. USS Constitution launched at Union Iron Works,
    San Francisco, 1864. (Mariners Museum Library)
11. USS Osage. (Photos by _____ _____ and _____ _____ Smith, USN (Ret.)
    (From the collection of R.E. Gregory, former Lieutenant Commander USNR)
12. Commodore Thomas ap Catesby Jones.
    (Official U.S. Navy Portrait)
13. Commodore Robert F. Stockton. (U.S. Naval Academy Museum)
14. Commander Robley D. Evans. (U.S. Naval Institute)
15. USS Lackawanna. (U.S. Naval Institute)
16. Launching of USS Trenton 1876 (U.S. Navy Photograph)
17. Apia Harbor, 17 March 1889, following the hurricane.
    (The Navy and the Nation)
18. USS Watauga after a tidal wave at Arica, Chile,
    in August, 1868. (Official U.S. Navy Photograph)
19. USS Petrel in Tongau Harbor, 1890. (Official U.S. Navy Photograph)
20. Pago Pago Samoa, 1905, with destroyers and armored
    cruisers at anchor. (U.S. National Archives)
21. USS Nanshan, Mare Island Navy Yard.
    (Naval Historical Foundation)
22. USS South Dakota in her 1916 rig, coast.
    (U.S. Navy Photograph)

*E*verything conspires to render the Pacific of great interest to the people of the United States at the present time. Our future sea fights are as likely to take place here as on the Atlantic Ocean, for here we are acquiring a preponderating commercial interest, and here must be our navy also.

—*Commodore John Downes in 1833.*

1. Distant Stations

A small frigate rounded Cape Horn from the east, on one of the Cape's rare, quiet days in the summer of 1819, then squared her yards and ran off to the northward. The USS *Macedonian,* originally commissioned in the Royal Navy, but now flying the United States colors at her mizzen peak, had arrived in the Pacific Ocean to protect American commercial interests. While she was not the first of her country's warships to round the Horn, neither of her predecessors— the *Essex* and *Ontario*—had been assigned the specific mission of commerce protection. Moreover, Captain John Downes's sailing orders definitely stated that further ships would be sent to the Pacific; in short, it was to be one of the regular cruising stations for United States naval vessels.

The American flag had first been shown in the Pacific Ocean by merchant vessels soon after the founding of the North American republic. In 1784, the New York ship *Empress of China* arrived at Macao, China, by way of the Cape of Good Hope. This pioneer voyage was repeated by other American merchantmen, and four years later the ship *Columbia,* John Kendrick, master, and the sloop *Lady Washington,* under Robert Gray, became the first United States vessels to enter the Pacific Ocean by way of Cape Horn. Standing north from the dreaded cape, they traded for furs at Nootka Sound on Vancouver Island. The *Columbia,* commanded by Gray, took her furry cargo to Canton in 1789, traded the furs for tea, and returned to Boston via the Cape of Good Hope, thus becoming the first of her nation's ships to sail around the world. Once the way had been shown, there was no lack of vessels to follow, and New Englanders especially became familiar with the schedule of trade goods for the northwest coast of North America, peltry for China, and tea for the United States.

1

Later variations on this theme were furnished by ships sent out for cargoes of sandalwood from the Hawaiian, or Sandwich, Islands and by sealers which found the Pacific waters a rich source of sealskins and oil. Other vessels found it profitable and not unduly dangerous to ignore Spanish regulation by trading with the Spanish colonies on the west coasts of North and South America. The rigors of the passage around Cape Horn commonly gave adequate excuse for ships to stop at Valparaiso or Callao for repairs and for replenishment of water and provisions; once in port, it was not difficult to engage in contraband trade without official Spanish notice. Farther north, the rule of Spain was even less effective, and after 1796 Monterey and other California ports became the scene of clandestine fur-trading by American vessels.

While these ships were discovering most of the coastal and island areas in the eastern Pacific where fur-bearing animals could be hunted profitably, an even more lucrative occupation was luring other American vessels to Pacific waters. Whaling had been a flourishing industry long before the Stars and Stripes replaced the Union Jack over the east coast of North America. Beginning in the waters contiguous to the colonial coastline, whaling activity had been extended throughout the Western Ocean as the number of whales along the shore dwindled. South and east the hunt led the sons of Nantucket and New Bedford until they too found themselves in the vicinity of Cape Horn and the Cape of Good Hope. American whaleships, seven in number, first rounded Cape Horn in 1791, four years after a British ship had been the first to pursue the huge marine mammal in the Pacific Ocean. From the Chilean coast, the chase spread out just as it had in the Atlantic. Northward across the Equator and into the far reaches of the Pacific, the relentless hunt continued until the Pacific whaling industry was more valuable to the United States than was the earlier established fur and China trade.

Such widespread commercial activity was a national weakness as well as a strength, however, for neither whalers nor merchantmen were able to protect themselves against regular or irregular armed force. Trouble with the inhabitants of the various areas was frequent; and Spain, the power which considered itself the ruler of most of the Pacific, occasionally was responsible for interfering with the illegal (and, sometimes, legal) activities of American vessels. No real alarm was felt until the outbreak of the War of 1812, when some of the British whalers were given comparatively heavy armaments and letters of marque authorizing them to add American whalers to their legitimate prey. The presence of the United States frigate *Essex* in the Pacific in 1813 was sufficient to meet this threat, and Captain David Porter so well carried out his mission that the British whaling industry never recovered from his depredations. The *Essex* did not survive her triumph, succumbing to the overwhelming fire of His Majesty's Ships *Phoebe* and *Cherub* in neutral waters near Valparaiso in 1814, but American commercial interests in the Pacific region were relatively safe for a time.

The return of peace to the United States did not give a long respite to the Navy. Squadrons were sent out to protect American interests in the Mediterranean Sea and the West Indies soon after the Treaty of Ghent was signed in 1814, and then affairs in South America called for attention. A sort of chain reaction started by the French Revolution had reached the Spanish colonies in that area, and virtually the entire continent was in revolt against the authorities sent out from Madrid. The restored Bourbon monarchy in Spain had no intention of sitting by quietly while the richest portion of its overseas empire detached itself, and open conflict resulted. Neither side was overscrupulous in its observance of neutral rights. American interests seemed not to be seriously threatened, but it was thought prudent that the United States flag be shown in the disturbed waters by a warship.

The active force of the United States Navy, somewhat reduced at the conclusion of the War of 1812, was taxed to maintain a squadron on the Mediterranean Station while operations were being carried on against the Caribbean picaroons; consequently, the South American mission was entrusted to Captain James Biddle of the sloop-of-war *Ontario* which was under orders to sail to the Pacific Ocean and take formal possession of the land on both sides of the Columbia River mouth in the name of the United States. American claims to that area were based on the discovery of the river by Gray's *Columbia* in 1792 and on the subsequent Lewis and Clark Expedition. The American Fur Company had established the trading post of Astoria in 1811, but during the War of 1812 sold it to the British North West Company to prevent its seizure. Nonetheless, the United States flag was still flying when HMS *Raccoon* arrived a month later to demand the post's surrender. Thus the area was considered to have been captured, and although the North West Company continued to hold the post by right of purchase, the land in its vicinity reverted to the United States in accordance with the terms of the Treaty of Ghent, the *Ontario* being sent out to complete the formalities.

Captain Biddle sailed in October 1817, touched at Rio de Janeiro to deliver dispatches, and then rounded Cape Horn. Stopping at Valparaiso for supplies, he found that the situation was serious indeed. The Chileans had risen and had driven out their Spanish rulers. The latter were attempting to reassert their sovereignty from Peru while Spanish warships blockaded the port of Valparaiso, through which most of the supplies for the rebels (or Patriots) had to pass. This blockade supposedly had been proclaimed by the Spanish government on 17 March 1817, but no news of it had reached the United States by the following October. Under American interpretation of international law, sufficient time must elapse between the proclamation of a blockade and its enforcement so that all merchant ships bound for the blockaded port will have been notified. Obviously this practice had not been observed by the Spaniards; therefore, Biddle held that the blockade was illegal and that all American shipping seized by Spanish cruisers while attempting to enter Valparaiso should be released.

On the other hand, the Patriot forces had been guilty of confiscating American ships and cargoes, and had impressed American seamen for military and naval service as well. With the assistance of John B. Prevost, a diplomatic agent of the United States who was embarked in the *Ontario* for passage to Callao, Biddle undertook to obtain the release of ships and men detained by the Patriots. When little progress was realized in this effort, Prevost was left to continue negotiations while Biddle sailed to Callao to protest against the Spanish blockade. The viceroy at Lima, probably impressed more by the American captain's tact and bearing than by the *Ontario*'s twenty-two guns, acceded to most of the American demands. In return, Biddle agreed to act as mediator to arrange for the exchange of prisoners between the combatant forces. He was unsuccessful in this role and prepared to sail for the Northwest Coast, against the wishes of Prevost who felt that the *Ontario*'s presence on the troubled South American seaboard was of paramount importance.

American sovereignty over the land on both sides of the Columbia River was proclaimed by boat crews from the USS *Ontario* on 19 August 1818, Captain Biddle having been one of the first, but not the last, of the seamen who declined to hazard their vessels by crossing the treacherous bar at the mouth of the Columbia. Sailing south again, the *Ontario* touched at Monterey for provisions, thus becoming the first American naval vessel to visit the three future Pacific coast states.

Homeward bound, the sloop stopped at Valparaiso for three days and found the situation more menacing than before. Previously, the only naval force which had preyed on neutral shipping had been that of Spain, for the Patriots had had no navy worthy of mention. However, with foreign assistance and the dynamic leadership of the Scottish adventurer Lord Cochrane, a Chilean squadron was formed. Captain Biddle did not intend to remain at Valparaiso any longer than necessary, but he was forced to postpone his departure for the United States at the request of Patriot authorities. They feared that Biddle might warn the Spaniards of the sailing of Cochrane's ships, so the *Ontario* did not weigh anchor until the Chilean squadron had cleared the harbor and was standing to the northward.

Captain Biddle had carried out his mission in the Pacific, but it required no acute observer to see that the interest of the United States Navy in that ocean was just beginning. The American flag, unsupported by naval guns, would be no protection at all for the ships which called at ports on the west coast of South America.

A clearly established need for American naval forces in the eastern Pacific—and in other remote areas—led to a distant-station policy which was applied in the Mediterranean and Caribbean, as well as in the Pacific.

This policy of dispersing the warships in commission on widely separated and far-distant cruising stations was adopted by the United States Navy soon after the War of 1812. The Mediterranean Sea, where the embryo navy of the young republic had early shown its mettle, was the first of these foreign stations. The Barbary states had taken advantage of American preoccupation during the war against

England to renew their depredations on United States shipping, and Commodore Stephen Decatur had led a squadron out in 1815 to end this semipiratical activity. It was obvious that only the continued presence of warships could ensure the safety of American commerce, and the Mediterranean Squadron remained the strongest single naval force maintained by the United States for many years.

Second of these cruising stations to be established was that in the eastern Pacific. The events which led to the assignment of American warships to cruise in the Pacific have been described, but it may be well to consider the reasons which cause the beginning of the Pacific Station to be dated in 1818. Most naval historians state that the Pacific Squadron was established in 1821 when Commodore Charles Stewart was sent to those waters with the line-of-battleship *Franklin* and the schooner *Dolphin*. This is correct in that previously only a single ship had been present, although it is stretching the point a bit to dignify two vessels with the title of squadron. However, for many years the official name for the men-o'-war cruising in the eastern Pacific was "United States Naval Forces on Pacific Station," and this could be applied either to one ship or to a squadron. The more valid criterion would seem to be the duty to which the force was assigned. Captain Biddle was sent out primarily to take possession of the Columbia River area, and his orders contained no intimation that other warships were to follow the *Ontario;* consequently, his mission, no matter what it developed into, did not mark the beginning of the Pacific Station. The USS *Macedonian,* on the other hand, sailed in 1818 for the express purpose of protecting American interests in the Pacific Ocean, and Captain Downes's orders made it clear that the sloop-of-war *Hornet* was to have joined his command had not later events caused a change of assignment. The orders under which Commodore Stewart commanded his squadron differed only slightly from those given to Captains Downes and Charles G. Ridgely, his predecessors on Pacific Station, and the primary mission remained the same. Therefore, the United States Navy's Pacific Station may be said to have been established in 1818.

Third of the distant stations was that in the West Indies and Caribbean Sea. Even before the War of 1812, American naval vessels had operated in those waters, but they did not become a regular station until 1822. Again piratical activity drew warships to the scene. The

Spanish government in this area was too weak, and perhaps un-willing, to curb the brutal assault of the picaroons on defenseless merchant shipping; therefore, the United States Navy undertook the task. Once again it was apparent that the beneficial results of this intervention could be realized only so long as naval guns and landing parties were on hand to enforce them; thus, the West India Station was added to those already existing.

The afore-mentioned stations were followed by others: the Brazil Station in 1826, the East India Station in 1835, the Home Station in 1841, and the Africa Station in 1843. Not all had the same purpose; for example, the last-named was meant to deal with the illegal slave trade, while the Home Squadron was established to guard the Atlantic coast of the United States from any sudden foray by a fleet of war steamers belonging to a European power. For the most part, however, the United States naval forces on distant stations were maintained primarily to guard American commerce in those regions against interruption and annoyance.

This policy of dispersal of force has been criticized strongly on the ground that it made impossible the creation of an efficient fighting fleet. The various squadrons never met for combined maneuvers; indeed, the ships which made up these squadrons rarely operated in company, and if they did so occasionally, the group thus composed was usually so heterogeneous in nature as to preclude any semblance of tactical unity. It may be said that this remained a navy composed of single ships.

Yet it is not readily apparent that any other course was open to the United States Navy in the early nineteenth century. If all of the warships in commission had been gathered together to form an efficient fleet, which would have required that they be kept together, the extremely important merchant marine would have been left at the mercy of pirates and the unpredictable whims of local officials all over the world. The country was unable, or at least unwilling, to support a naval force which could maintain cruising vessels on distant stations in addition to an effective fleet in home waters, as did Great Britain. There was no immediate threat to American national existence which called for the presence of a fleet on the Atlantic coast. Moreover, all of the American warships then in commission could not have hoped to engage successfully the British fleet which dominated the Atlantic at that time. A government which had to face the demands of the extremely powerful shipowners that their interests be protected, might well be forgiven if it ignored the requirements of sound strategy, especially since much of the political support for any naval force was given by those same shipowners and the areas which they represented.

Far better, then, to adopt the practical course—rely upon diplomacy to keep the British lion in a good humor, knowing full well that he would not stand idly by to see his best market taken over by a third power, while the United States Navy spread its thin, sometimes nonexistent, protective net over the waters of the world where American ships and citizens traveled. Probably the system of distant stations with its dispersal of force was continued for too long a time, but for the early nineteenth century it is difficult to believe that a seemingly sounder strategic policy would have proven so successful and beneficial for the United States.

No doubt the greatest of all the problems attendant upon the distant-station policy was that of communications, and this difficulty was probably felt more on the Pacific Station than on any of the others. In 1826, Secretary of the Navy Samuel L. Southard informed the Chairman of the House Committee on Naval Affairs that the passage from the United States to Valparaiso required from 80 to 120 days, while the time could be reduced by half if the messenger traveled to Chagres, on the Isthmus of Panama, by fast schooner, crossed the Isthmus, and proceeded to Valparaiso in another schooner. These were optimum estimates; the sailing vessel could make no guarantee of such passages, and the time would be correspondingly greater if the commander in chief were at one of the more remote points of his command. It had been expected that the whalers going and coming to and from the Pacific would furnish a reliable means of communication between the United States and its Pacific Squadron. But few of these vessels were noted for their speed, and their leisurely cruising habits, added to the fact that whales generally did not frequent the shortest shipping routes, made them an extremely unsatisfactory means of communication.

Years later the clipper ships did reduce the time required for passage from the American Atlantic coast to the Pacific, and in 1851 the aptly named *Flying Cloud* romped in through the Golden Gate less than three months out of New York. But even the lovely *Cloud* made only one more such passage, and of all the other clippers, the *Andrew Jackson* alone rivaled the record on a single occasion. However, correspondence for the Pacific Squadron was passing across Central America by this time, so the clippers did not facilitate communications for the Navy.

The completion of the first transcontinental telegraph line in 1861 facilitated communication with the Pacific Squadron considerably, but it did not solve the problem with regard to a ship which was at sea or in a remote harbor. Only with the installation of radio in warships during the period just before World War I, did the communication difficulty become negligible.

Almost from the beginning of the Pacific Station, its commanders in chief pointed out the desirability of maintaining fast schooners to carry dispatches from the usual cruising ground of the squadron to Panama. Congress considered the proposals on several occasions, as well as a plan to keep a few such vessels running between Baltimore and Chagres; however, the cost of such a service was sufficient to ensure that it would not be approved. At least one officer took it upon himself to improve communications by having two small vessels built at his own expense and manned from his flagship, but the personal means of his successors on the station would not allow the continuation of this policy.

The difficulties resulting from this communication delay hardly need to be pointed out. At best, the officer commanding in the Pacific could expect an answer to his letter six months after it was sent, and it was not uncommon for the interval to be extended by two months or more. Dispatches usually were prepared in duplicate, each copy being sent by a different route or ship—a necessary precaution, for often only one copy would be received by the addressee. In short, the commander in chief could expect no advice from his government until long after the event. The responsibility thus entailed was tremendous, even in a day when all occurrences tended to develop much more slowly than at present. The flag officer had to meet all requirements with the force at hand, for reinforcement could not reach him in less than half a year after it was requested, and this makes no allowance for the time required to outfit and commission the vessel sent out to join his flag.

Communications were very uncertain even within the limits of the station. An order might take a matter of weeks to reach Valparaiso from Callao even if the sender were so fortunate as to find a vessel on the point of sailing to that port when his dispatch was ready. The more distant parts of the station were very nearly as remote as the moon—if the commodore wished to communicate with a vessel which had been sent to cruise among the islands of the eastern Pacific, he could do no more than to send copies of his letter to all ports at which the ship was expected to touch and hope that she would receive one of them. This was complicated by the fact that it was not always possible to find a merchant ship bound for the desired points. As soon as the departing warship saw the flagship disappear below the horizon, her captain was almost as independent of his commodore as was the latter of the Navy Department in Washington.

Yet another major problem involved in the distant-station policy was that of bases from which the squadrons could operate. It might be expected that the Pacific Squadron would base on the only Pacific coast area owned by the United States—the Columbia River and its environs. But this area was completely undeveloped and lacking in most of the supplies required by the squadron, and it was removed so far from the cruising ground of the warships as to be useless for this purpose. Instead, the major ports in which the men-o'-war were bound to spend some time were utilized. Valparaiso and Callao both served as rendezvous and supply depots for the Pacific Squadron in its early years, and other ports also became supply depots as the cruising area expanded. At first the necessary supplies had to be purchased on the station, but it became the practice to send out all but fresh provisions from the United States in merchant vessels chartered for this purpose. In addition, every warship sent out to the station was required to carry articles thought to be in short supply. That the goods so transported were subject to damage by dampness and rats was one of the unavoidable hazards of the system. More than once the commander in chief was forced to buy on the open market supplies which should have reached him from home, but the difficulty of justifying such purchases to the Navy Department made most officers extremely reluctant to adopt such a course except as a last resort.

Later the supply depots maintained ashore were supplemented or replaced by storeships which were moored more or less permanently at the ports frequented by the squadron. These might be either worn-out sloops-of-war with most of their batteries removed and crew spaces converted for storage of supplies, or merchant vessels purchased and fitted out for this duty. They were manned by a few officers and men whose most important task was to care for the stores embarked. The lieutenant in command was normally appointed a naval storekeeper while so assigned. Considering the boredom which must have accompanied such duty, it is not surprising that many of the officers and men of the storeships turned to drinking to relieve the monotony. Commodores on Pacific Station had frequently to intervene to maintain harmony between storeship officers.

The Board of Navy Commissioners, under whose jurisdiction came all matters of supply during the period 1815-1842, tried to provide for an adequate replenishment of supplies for the Pacific Squadron by sending out two ships each year. Reports from the commander in chief were supposed to include a statement of supplies on hand and those required. However, the inevitable communications difficulty and the spoils system in naval contracts combined to prevent the smooth operation of this plan. Commanders in chief denounced Navy Commissioners for shortages and defective or unwanted shipments, and the latter responded vigorously. Only more rapid transportation and communication could solve the problem of supply.

Obviously the vessels cruising from foreign ports had to have money on hand to purchase necessary fresh provisions. It was impractical to supply each warship with enough specie to last for her entire cruise on the distant station; hence, her captain was given authority to draw sight drafts on an international banking house, usually Baring Brothers and Company, the Navy Department's London bankers.

Fortunately, the sailing warship was much more nearly a self-sufficient entity than is the steel-hulled, steam-propelled man-o'-war. Even major damage could be repaired by the ship's company, and carpenters from the flagship often assisted the crews of smaller vessels with important repairs. Dry docks were unknown in American navy yards until 1833; therefore, repairs below the waterline were no more difficult on the Pacific Station than at home. The ship was simply eased onto a sandy beach at high water and her bottom planking was exposed as the tide ebbed. If a sufficiently smooth beach could not be found, the vessel might be hove down to a barge by means of tackles on her masts and by shifting guns and other weighty objects from one side to the other. Care had to be taken that her stability was not reduced unduly, or she might heel over too far and sink, as did the USS *Enterprise* in 1838.

One of the subjects stressed in the sailing orders of successive commanders in chief of the Pacific Squadron was that of relations with the authorities of the countries which they would visit and with the officers of the foreign warships certain to be encountered. In every case, the flag officer was urged to show the utmost courtesy in all such contacts. Promptness in rendering the usual salutes and honors was required, and no partiality or unneutral action was condoned. Commanders in chief were cautioned against too-zealous support of American nationals; any action on their behalf must be preceded by a thorough investigation into the circumstances surrounding the infringement of American rights. If United States diplomatic officials were present, they must be consulted and their recommendations considered by the senior naval officer present, although even diplomats of ministerial rank had no authority over naval personnel.

Relations with these diplomatic officials were not devoid of problems of their own. Generally, the naval officers co-operated in full agreement with the more responsible ministers, but the actions of the officers often did not please the consuls who represented the government of the United States at the seaports and more important inland cities. In common with the ministers residing at the various capitals, the consuls were supposed to report all occurrences and recommendations to the State Department in Washington. If the Secretary of State and his aides felt that the situation demanded the presence of a warship, they communicated this recommendation to the Secretary of the Navy, who, in turn, would send orders to that effect to the commander in chief of the Pacific Squadron. By the time all of these letters had been sent and received, the whole problem would have to be evaluated again by the senior naval officer before a ship could be dispatched.

Since this process would require a period of several months, State Department regulations allowed the diplomatic and consular representatives to apply directly to the commander in chief if the situation was considered to be sufficiently grave. Again the minister or consul could only request, and the responsibility rested entirely on the naval officer. What might seem an emergency to the man on the scene could easily appear to the flag officer in a different light, especially since the latter had to consider the needs of the entire station, so the whole situation was fraught with possibility of disagreement.

Ministers sent out to the various capitals by the United States government generally were men of high cultural and political attainments, and they usually found it easy to get along with the naval officers, but not so the consular officials. Often it was necessary for the latter to engage in private business for their livelihood; therefore, they were bound to become involved in local political affairs to some extent, although like the ministers, the consuls were supposed to remain aloof from domestic politics. In many cases, the consular appointments were given to men already prominent in the economic activities of the city. This had the advantage of giving the duties into the hands of men well acquainted with the local conditions and well known to local authorities, but they were the more likely to be parties to the factional wrangling which was so common in Latin American countries.

On the other hand, consuls sent out from the United States too frequently were mere political hacks who had neither understanding of, nor sympathy for, conditions in the regions where they were the sole representatives of their country. The reports of the naval officers on Pacific Station abound in instances where the intolerant and arrogant behavior of the American diplomat was responsible for the situation which demanded the presence of a warship. Consuls in remote areas sometimes asked that a vessel be sent merely to remind the inhabitants of American interest in the region, and often one suspects that they really wanted the company of their fellow-countrymen more than anything else.

The revolutions which so frequently inflamed the Latin American republics presented yet another problem for the Pacific Squadron. Often the senior naval officer on the scene did not know which of the factions had the approval of his government—sometimes it was difficult to know which was the established and recognized government. Of course, the arrival of the warship would be followed immediately by communication with the American diplomatic representative, but as has been stated, that individual was likely to be involved with one of the factions, and full reliance could not be placed on his report. Complete responsibility for any action was vested in the naval officer. He could only proceed with caution, trying to decide the case on its merits and knowing very well that his conduct might become the subject of an official inquiry, followed by a general court-martial, if he had not been successful in anticipating the desires of his government many thousands of miles distant.

Another of the problems inherent in the distant-station policy was that of deciding the force each station should receive. Opinion was divided as to the types and numbers of vessels to be assigned, but almost without exception commanders in chief on Pacific Station felt that they did not have enough ships effectively to perform the multifarious duties assigned them. The geographical area was so vast that several vessels were necessary. This fact and the shallow waters of many of the harbors made a few large ships rather less effective than a greater number of smaller vessels.

Only four ships-of-the-line served on Pacific Station during the days of sail, and each of these was sent out to meet a special emergency. For the most part, the squadron consisted of one or two frigates, a like number of sloops-of-war, and a schooner. The number, especially of sloops, increased as the station gained in relative importance. It was the opinion of most officers that the sloop-of-war was the type of vessel best adapted to the distant-station policy. Relatively inexpensive to maintain (an 1825 estimate of the annual expense of maintaining a vessel of each class at sea, exclusive of the pay and rations of commissioned and warrant officers: ship-of-the-line, $162,196.25; 44-gun frigate, $107,815.75; 36-gun frigate, $88,-146; sloop-of-war, $37,935.75; brig, $23,664.50; schooner, $16,-408), these ships possessed respectable batteries and crews large enough to furnish landing parties when the occasion required. Moreover, they had storage space for enough supplies to enable them to sail on extended cruises, and they could enter almost any port safely. The little twelve-gun schooners were handy and economical, but their crews were small and only with difficulty could they operate far from bases of supply. The presence of at least one frigate was necessary because an officer senior enough to command the station could hardly be expected to endure the hardships of life in a smaller vessel. Almost every South American republic on the Pacific seaboard could commission one or more frigates in its navy, and the British and French squadrons in the area always contained frigates and often ships-of-the-line, as well.

No evidence has been found to indicate that any of the warships of the United States Navy were designed for use specifically on the Pacific Station.[1] Rather, the vessels were designed with a view to operating efficiently on any station to which they might be assigned —the arguments in favor of ship-sloops might apply to almost any of the distant stations. Indeed, one group, the third-class sloops-of-war of 1838, was considered almost useless for service in the Pacific Squadron by one commander in chief because the ships could not stow sufficient supplies for extended cruising among the islands of the Pacific.

The ships which succeeded the *Macedonian* on the Pacific Station usually were fitted out for a three-year cruise, and their crews enlisted for this term of service. Navy Department regulations forbade the discharge of American seamen at any point outside the continental United States; consequently, the vessel had to return home within that period. Theoretically the crew could be re-enlisted while on the station, but could not be compelled to do so. Quite understandably, the men were extremely reluctant to carry out their duties after their terms of service had expired, so it was important that the ship arrive at a home port before this date.

Desertion was always a problem, not only because there were no American citizens to enlist in the deserter's place, but also because he was likely to become a burden upon the country in which he deserted. The latter's government often would demand that the United States assume responsibility for his well-being or for his transgressions against the laws of the country. Shipboard life was made even harder by naval discipline, and the Latin American countries, as well as the exotic Pacific islands, presented many inducements for the man-o'-warsman to remain after his ship got under way. An early annoyance was the impressment of deserters into the Patriot armed forces in South America, and later experienced seamen were in great demand to man the numerous small vessels which traded along the South American coastline. None of these allurements, however, could compare with the discovery of gold in California soon after the Navy won that area for the United States.

These general problems continued to worry every commander in chief of the Pacific Squadron right up to the Civil War. Technological advances and political developments presented solutions for some, but brought new difficulties in their wake. Almost every cruise was marked by its own specific problems which must be considered in their chronological settings. While this account is in no sense an operational history, the following chapters will be devoted to the story of these general and especial problems and the way in which they were met by the officers and men of the United States Navy who served on Pacific Station.

2. *The Cruise of the* Macedonian

The cruises of two American warships on Pacific Station have been chosen for narration in some detail, for they were so different that some mean between these two extremes will fairly represent an average cruise with the Pacific Squadron.

Captain Biddle's reports made it perfectly clear to the Navy Department that a man-o'-war would be well employed protecting American interests in the Pacific Ocean. The ship selected for this task was the small frigate *Macedonian* which had been bested by Commodore Stephen Decatur's *United States* in 1812. Almost alone of the British warships which surrendered to American vessels during that conflict, the *Macedonian* had eluded the British blockade and received repairs at New York. She was smaller and weaker than most American frigates, but was thought worthy of retention in the United States Navy and was recommissioned under her original name.

To command the *Macedonian* on her Pacific cruise, Secretary of the Navy Benjamin W. Crowninshield chose Captain John Downes. This officer had been Porter's first lieutenant in the *Essex,* and had commanded two of that ship's prizes which were commissioned as cruisers, so he knew the Pacific Ocean as well as any officer of the Navy. Moreover, Downes possessed other qualities essential in an officer selected to command on a long cruise in remote waters. His sense of humor and love of practical jokes made him a favorite of the enlisted men, and he was an able seaman as well. His performance of varied duties during the *Macedonian*'s cruise made it evident that Crowninshield had chosen well.

The little frigate, deeply laden and trimmed by the head, departed Boston on 20 September 1818. A week later she was battling a full gale under storm staysails. During the evening of 27 September, a flapping sail knocked the captain of the mizzen-top overboard, and he was soon engulfed by the heavy seas which made it impossible to lower a boat. By the next morning it seemed probable that he would soon be joined by the ship and all her company. She was laboring frightfully in mountainous seas, and her three masts were sprung.

In an effort to ease the vessel, Downes ordered the mizzen rigging cut and the mast soon went over the taffrail. Preventer shrouds failed to save the fore and main topmasts, and they too carried away. Flying jib boom and spritsail yard went next, and the captain decided to cut away his remaining masts and ride out the storm to a sea anchor. To this end a hawser was bent to part of the broken mizzen mast, but no sooner was a strain taken on it to bring the ship's head to the wind, than the hawser parted. Therefore the fore and main masts were made as secure as possible by preventer shrouds and fishing (fastening "splints" over the weakened places), and the wind died enough to allow the vessel to live. Clearly, however, she was a wreck; all hands got her under a jury rig and Downes set a course for Norfolk.

The *Macedonian* arrived in that port on 10 October. A month later the lost spars had been replaced, and once more she stood to sea under orders to proceed to the Pacific Ocean with utmost dispatch. Southeast to the Cape Verde Islands she went, far enough to the eastward to ensure weathering Cape San Roque, easternmost promontory of Brazil. Then she turned to the southward with the trade winds filling her sails, and it was noted that she seemed to sail somewhat sluggishly as compared with her performance before she was dismasted. Downes had shifted stores while at Norfolk so that the vessel trimmed by the stern in the approved manner; probably the *Macedonian* was one of those ships which sailed well when drawing slightly more water forward than aft. However, her captain was new to the ship, and so could hardly have known this.

The normal routine of a man-o'-war at sea was broken on 25 December when some of the sailors presented the play "Weather Cock," together with an afterpiece entitled "Sailor's Fortune." The moving spirit behind this presentation was a carpenter's yeoman who had written the second feature. The performance, in Lieutenant Charles Gauntt's words:

. . . was presented for the treble purpose, in the first place, of giving amusement to the Officers & Crew of the Ship, Secondly of his *faculties* or *powers* of the mind as an author, and thirdly, to show his merit as an actor, in all of which except the former, he failed most egregiously.[1]

Nevertheless, the enjoyment of all seemed to be great. It should be noted that Captain Downes was well aware of the value of such diversions for the morale of his men. Both in the *Macedonian* and in the *Potomac,* his flagship on Pacific Station at a later date, amateur theatricals were encouraged. He may not have been directly responsible for the performances, but they could not have been staged without his permission. Not a few of his contemporaries would have refused even this.

As the *Macedonian* stood to the southward, preparations were made for encountering the dreaded Cape Horn seas. Her commanding officer was no stranger to these, for the *Essex* had nearly foundered off the Horn in 1813. Nevertheless, the haste enjoined by his orders must have led Downes to carry sail too long, for New Year's Day of 1819 saw the main-topgallant mast go over the side in a squall. It did not really matter because the top hamper had to come down anyway. The long topgallant masts were struck below and replaced by stump masts, boats were secured as well as possible, the jib boom was rigged in, double breechings were fitted to the great guns, ammunition was sent below, and preventer shrouds were set up to support the masts. The anchors were struck below to relieve the bows of their weight, but Downes seems not to have followed the later practice of dismounting the guns at the extreme ends of the ship and stowing them on the berth deck.

Despite her reduced rig, the *Macedonian* lost no chance to carry sail. Captain Downes kept his studding sail booms aloft and, whenever possible, he gave the gods of that inhospitable region the very unusual sight of a vessel in Cape Horn rig scudding along with these fair weather sails set. But the gods were kind; the *Macedonian* experienced unpleasant but not severe weather. She was off the Horn on 14 January in airs so light that a boat could be lowered to check the force of the current, and Lieutenant Gauntt recorded the information that no sign was found of the presumably prevailing easterly current. Succeeding days brought more gales, but only one studding sail boom carried away although Downes cracked on sail at every opportunity.

Two weeks after leaving the Horn, the *Macedonian* rounded to in

Valparaiso Harbor, and her starboard bower anchor splashed to the bottom in twenty-eight fathoms of water. She was seventy-nine days from Cape Henry in Virginia, a short passage for that day. Soon afterward the American vice-consul came on board to consult with Downes, and a few days later the captain and some of his officers visited Santiago, the Chilean capital. American and British merchants residing there opened their homes to the visitors, and the Valparaiso citizens proved themselves equally gracious hosts.

In return for this hospitality, Captain Downes decided to celebrate Washington's Birthday by giving a gala ball. For this purpose, the after part of the frigate's gun deck was transformed into a ballroom decorated with flags, illuminated transparencies, and whatever other ornaments the ingenuity of officers and men could suggest. The whole received the hackneyed description of "fairy palace," and while it seems that the scene was somewhat less ethereal than a Titania might have desired, the guests were well pleased. Waltzes and Spanish dances were followed by a banquet with numerous toasts given and received. When at last the boats were called alongside to transport the guests to the shore, it was observed that many had difficulty in retaining their equilibrium, but this was easily explained by the revolutionary fervor which had inspired many of the toasts. And if some of the officers were "under a full press of sail," it was, after all, Washington's Birthday.

While captain and wardroom officers thus recovered from the rigors of the Horn, it must not be supposed that others shared in these delights. Fairy palace or no, the *Macedonian* was still a warship and there was work to be done if she were to retain her efficiency. Warrant officers and enlisted men were occupied with the tasks of replenishing supplies of wood, water, and provisions; recaulking portions of the hull and upperworks which had been strained; blacking the guns; and all of the myriad details that kept a sailing vessel's rigging efficient and dependable. Routine drills had been suspended off Cape Horn, but neglect of these would soon result in a loss of efficiency. As soon as the minor repairs had been completed and the necessary supplies were on board, gun crews resumed their wearisome great-gun drills, or seized pikes and cutlasses to repel imaginary boarders.

For the warrant officers, there would be permission to go ashore when the essential duties had been performed, but the enlisted men could expect no such relief. The delights of the "vale of Paradise" were apt to be too great a temptation for the seaman when he looked back on the hardships of naval life, and there was no place in the Pacific from which an American warship could obtain replacements for deserters. Moreover, the Patriot armed forces were delighted to impress the well-trained men from a foreign warship when the opportunity offered. Even if the sailor returned on board when his liberty expired, the chances were more than good that he would soon be on the binnacle list with one or more of the venereal diseases prevalent in Valparaiso. Thus the enlisted man's only contact with the beach came when he was a member of a boat's crew.

It must be realized that the United States Navy was not unique in this treatment of the enlisted man; no common seaman was immune to the temptations mentioned, and the simplest way to avoid trouble was to keep the men safely on board. Nevertheless, Captain Downes did grant liberty to his crew at Callao in December 1819, but this port was in Spanish hands and one of the dangers, that of impressment, was almost nonexistent.

The *Macedonian*'s first Valparaiso sojourn ended on 15 March 1819. She investigated conditions at Coquimbo, returned to Valparaiso, and then stood to the northward once more. Off Arica, a seaman fell from one of the bow ports and was drowned before a boat could reach him. Lieutenant Gauntt noted regretfully, "We have been peculiarly unfortunate in not recovering a single man who has fallen overboard, this being the fourth. . . ."

On 28 May, the frigate anchored in the Tumbes River and sent a boat with two officers to call on the governor at the city of Guayaquil, some sixty miles away. While awaiting the boat's return, other officers explored part of the shore adjacent to the anchorage. A messenger from the city arrived on 3 June with news that the officers and boat's crew had been detained by the governor who could not believe that an American man-o'-war was in that remote area. After a further exchange of messages and a small gift for the suspicious official, Downes got his men on board and sailed a week later.

Most of the summer was spent in visits to the Mexican ports of

Acapulco and San Blas where information relating to pilotage and port facilities was gathered. Sailing to the southward once more, the *Macedonian* arrived at Valparaiso in October.

The Chilean seaport was the scene of feverish activity as Lord Cochrane was fitting out an expedition to wrest Peru from the Spanish grasp. Some days after the Chileans sailed, the *Macedonian* weighed anchor and stood out for Callao where American shipping was likely to be endangered by Cochrane's activities. His Lordship was blockading the port with a frigate and a corvette when the American warship arrived off Callao.

It was rumored that Cochrane had sworn to capture the *Macedonian* if she came to Callao, and Downes, while doubting this, had his frigate cleared for action when the two Chilean ships bore down. Their movements seemed menacing, but a boarding officer returned to the flagship with the report that American gunners were standing beside loaded eighteen-pounders with slow matches smoldering. Probably Cochrane had had no intention of fighting at all; at any rate, he hailed to wish Downes a pleasant visit, and the Chilean ships made sail once more.

At Callao, as mentioned above, the "Macedonians" had their run ashore while some of their officers visited Lima, the Peruvian capital. At Downes's instance, the viceroy agreed to release an American citizen who had been captured while fighting in the Patriot army. This man and several Spaniards were embarked in the *Macedonian* as passengers, and she sailed on 6 December to escort two American brigs through the Chilean blockade.

Less than three weeks later, she anchored at Panama and sent four sailors across the Isthmus to join two American merchant schooners detained by want of men. Two more were sent on board the brig *Macedonian,* which was sailing almost in company with the like-named frigate. The two stood north to San Blas, and here the smaller vessel shipped two of Downes's midshipmen, one as first officer and the other a passenger. Naval vessels on Pacific Station frequently sent men from their large complements to serve in merchant vessels which had lost hands by desertion or other causes. Sometimes junior officers were even ordered to command merchantmen whose masters had died.

After the transfer of personnel, the two *Macedonians* parted com-

pany, with the brig bound for the East Indies while the frigate returned to Panama. A number of the frigate's invalids were landed to
proceed across the Isthmus of Panama on their way to the United
States, but the Spanish governor of Panama refused to permit their
passage. He claimed that several English prisoners had been given
refuge in the *Macedonian* on the occasion of her earlier visit, and so
they had, although Downes had known nothing of it at the time.
Now, however, the American officers were unable to find the erstwhile prisoners, and the invalids had to return to the ship. For Chaplain Azariel Wilson this was particularly unfortunate. Later he was
landed at Valparaiso in the hope of being restored to health, but
died there before the *Macedonian* returned to the United States.

The frigate had returned to Valparaiso when her Panamanian visit
had been cut short. In this Chilean port, on 24 July 1820, her company was re-enlisted for a period of ten months. Only ten of the
more than 370 men requested discharge, and their requests were denied. Probably the knowledge that they would not be put ashore at
Valparaiso deterred others from asking for discharges, but Captain
Downes ran a happy ship and there seems to have been little discon-
tent among the crew at being detained after their original enlistments had expired. Almost no other American warship on Pacific
Station was so fortunate.

After a month at Valparaiso, the *Macedonian* coasted to the
northward, touching at Coquimbo and then sailing on to Callao,
where neutral shipping was again endangered by Cochrane's cruisers.
Downes went to Lima to consult governmental officials and was there
when, on 6 November 1820, Lord Cochrane led a daring boat expedition which cut out the Peruvian frigate *Esmeralda*. The *Macedonian* was anchored nearby, with a small number of American merchant vessels close aboard, and she received several hits and some
slight damage from the fire of the forts. Feeling on shore ran high
over Cochrane's coup, and the Americans were suspected of having
helped him to achieve it. Therefore, when the *Macedonian*'s first
lieutenant somewhat unwisely sent the usual market boat ashore, the
American flag proved no protection whatever. Soldiers fired into the
boat, killing two men and wounding five. The survivors were rescued
by the British frigate *Andromache,* and later she recovered the boat.

More trouble followed three days later. The American merchant schooner *Rampart,* standing in to an anchorage under the *Macedonian*'s guns, drifted close to shore batteries which opened fire immediately. She was quickly abandoned by her crew and the Spaniards took possession.

This seemed almost to be the final provocation. The junior officers, already angered by the attack on the *Macedonian*'s small boat, now were furious over this added insult to their flag. Some seem to have felt that Captain Downes should have been on board his ship instead of visiting in Lima. Perhaps, but Downes's protests at the capital resulted in the return of the *Rampart* to her crew. Moreover, he had arranged for the release of sixteen American prisoners held by the Spaniards, so his time had not been entirely wasted. And desirable as his presence was on board the *Macedonian,* it would have been foolhardy for him to have undertaken any punitive action. The frigate was the only American warship within thousands of miles. Had she been lost or damaged seriously, no other could have arrived for a period of months. Moreover, there was little that one vessel could do alone. Lord Cochrane had no less than eighteen ships off Callao at one time, but did not feel strong enough to attempt more than the blockade. In this instance it seems that Downes was correct in acting as he did.

Meanwhile, the lives of American and British citizens residing at Lima were imperiled, so Captain Downes led a group of them to a small port south of Callao where they were embarked by the *Macedonian*'s small boats and taken on board the frigate. On 20 November, she put to sea to escort seven American and British merchant vessels through the Patriot blockade. This was in accordance with an agreement whereby Downes and the commanding officer of HMS *Andromache* undertook to protect the interests of one another's countries when possible.

With the merchantmen safely at sea, the *Macedonian* visited several smaller ports. At one of these, Huacho, she found the American *Louisa* detained for carrying contraband. At Lord Cochrane's order, the Chilean frigate *Lautaro* was watching her until his government ordered her seizure. After consulting *Louisa*'s master, Downes concluded that her detention was unwarranted and escorted her to sea. The heavier *Lautaro* followed for a time, but made no effort to interfere. Captain Downes could play a bold hand when it seemed necessary, but in this case he incurred the displeasure of the American consul at Valparaiso and of Chilean officials, as well.

The *Macedonian* anchored at Mollendo, Peru, on 14 January 1821 and here learned that the USS *Constellation* had arrived at Valparaiso to relieve her. Accordingly, Downes steered to the southward, touched briefly at Coquimbo, and arrived at Valparaiso on 4 March. While his men made preparations for the long passage to the United States, Downes undertook to acquaint his successor, Captain Charles G. Ridgely, with the problems and conditions prevailing on Pacific Station. The two officers journeyed to Santiago to consult the American chargé, and Ridgely was introduced to Chilean officials.

The *Macedonian* weighed anchor and sailed for home on 19 March. As usual, the eastward passage around Cape Horn was much easier and quicker than the outward rounding, and no untoward incidents delayed her progress. Downes took his ship into Rio de Janeiro for water and fresh provisions, and sailed again on 13 May, after an eleven-day visit. The USS *Macedonian* anchored in Boston Harbor off the Charlestown Navy Yard on 19 June 1821, two years and nine months after sailing from that port.

During her Pacific cruise, she had logged some 58,878 miles, and had lost twenty-six of her original company of a little over four hundred officers and men. Four were lost overboard, two were killed by Spanish fire at Callao, a midshipman was killed by a shipmate in a duel at Valparaiso, and nineteen died of various ills. This was not an abnormal death rate for a cruise of such duration; considering the conditions of life on board a small frigate, it must surprise us that so many survived.

Captain Downes had performed his various duties very well, and his diplomatic skill had averted serious trouble without exposing his country to disrespect. With a single ship, he had visited more ports and cruised a greater distance than would many of his successors who commanded squadrons. His feat of maintaining good relations with both Spanish and Patriot authorities was almost unbelievable, and if he failed to get along well with Lord Cochrane, that daring individual must have held the American officer in some respect, for Downes consistently bluffed him although Cochrane always had the stronger force.

It must be stated once more that the *Macedonian*'s cruise was unusually active, and lest there be a distorted impression of duty on the Pacific Station, the cruise of Commodore Henry E. Ballard in the USS *North Carolina* will also be related in some detail. But nearly two decades separated the cruises of the *Macedonian* and *North Carolina,* and to the events of the intervening years attention must first be given.

3. *From Ship to Squadron*

Captain Ridgely's *Constellation* had sailed under orders to await the summer season in the Rio de la Plata before standing south for Cape Horn. But, at Montevideo, Ridgely received a report that led him to order a survey of the frigate's main mast. A majority of the inspecting board decided that the spar could be fished securely enough to round the Cape, but felt that it should be condemned. Well aware that main masts were not available either at Montevideo or on the west coast, Ridgely returned to Rio de Janeiro where the Royal Dockyard made and stepped a new mast. This was merely the first in a series of instances where warships departed on protracted cruises in remote waters only to find that the navy yards whence they had sailed had done their work very poorly.

During the enforced delay at Rio de Janeiro, Captain Ridgely took action to cope with a problem which often confronted American commanding officers at the time. He noted with concern that a number of his midshipmen had been involved in duels, either as principals or seconds, at both Rio de Janeiro and Montevideo. The dangers of this practice were obvious, and the captain required the "young gentlemen" to pledge their honor that they would abstain from dueling before allowing them to go ashore. Three of the ship's twenty-nine midshipmen considered this unwarranted tyranny, and were sent back to the United States to resign their appointments. The Navy Department did not approve of Ridgely's action and allowed the midshipmen to remain in the service, if they so desired. It must be remarked, however, that the "Constellations" avoided duels thereafter. The Navy Department offered no alternative method for discouraging this demoralizing practice, and one's sympathies remain with Captain Ridgely.

After the afore-mentioned meeting with Captain Downes at Valparaiso, Ridgely lost no time in requesting that another frigate and a sloop-of-war be sent out to join him. Until they could arrive, he decided to follow Downes's example of co-operating with the British squadron in the area. He was soon a close friend of Commodore Sir Thomas Hardy. Anglo-American friendship prospered to the extent that a Board of Survey ordered to inspect the *Constellation*'s fore and mizzen masts included the carpenter of Hardy's flagship *Creole* and the master and carpenter of HMS *Owen Glendower*. It is apparent that the co-operation was more advantageous to the United States than to Great Britain, since the latter's squadron consisted of a ship-of-the-line, two frigates, and a sloop, while Ridgely had only his frigate. Hardy followed the practice of keeping one of his ships at Callao and another at Valparaiso constantly. In the *Constellation*'s absence, these ships watched American interests as well as their own.

Captain Ridgely had sailed from Boston in the belief that his personal sympathies would be with the gallant Peruvians and Chileans who were fighting for independence from Old World tyranny, but this feeling did not long survive his arrival at Valparaiso. He found the Patriots to be "base and vulgar" men almost without exception. This attitude was furthered by the arrogant manner of Lord Cochrane. Ridgely was not alone in his opinion of this adventurer; on one occasion Hardy had threatened to remove the Patriot admiral from his flagship and send him to England to be tried on charges of piracy.

On the other hand, the American captain was soon on cordial terms with the cultured Spaniards who were fighting to maintain a political system that he loathed. The Patriots, sure of the sympathy of their North American brethren, were aghast when Ridgely offered General Don Joaquin de Pezuela, the exiled viceroy of Peru, accommodations on board the *Constellation* while arranging for his passage to Spain in the American merchantman *General Brown*. The Patriots charged that Ridgely had acted in bad faith in this matter.[1] He had persuaded General José de San Martín to release the detained American vessel, and in her the Spaniard was given passage. The American consul at Valparaiso joined in denouncing this action, but his impartiality was not beyond suspicion. Whether or not Ridgely broke his word is not important here, but it is significant that this was the first example of political asylum being offered a refugee by an American warship on Pacific Station. In time this custom came to be authorized by naval regulations, but it had no basis in international law. Seemingly Pezuela was not allowed to carry on political intrigues from the safety of the *Constellation,* so it is difficult to judge Ridgely harshly for his humanitarian act.

One of the most serious threats to American shipping in the Pacific was presented by the semipiratical depredations of one Vicente Benevedes, a Spanish naval officer who had a commission of doubtful validity for operations against Patriot vessels. Basing at Auranco (location uncertain, probably Arauco), he showed little respect for any flag, and had captured American ships and imprisoned their men. Ridgely attempted to trap him, but the wily Spaniard escaped. A later effort by the commanding officer of HMS *Conway* was no more successful. The waters of the Spaniard's lair were too shallow to permit the approach of warships. Only boat expeditions could be sent against him, and these were always detected in time for their quarry to escape. Benevedes was never captured, but the foreign naval forces were able to limit his activities and most of his prisoners eventually made their way to Valparaiso.

Captain Ridgely's request for additional ships was answered by the news that he would be relieved by Commodore Charles Stewart, who was to leave the United States with the ship-of-the-line *Franklin* and the schooner *Dolphin* in September 1821. As Ridgely had reported, the British and French squadrons in the Pacific both included capital ships, and Cochrane had a vessel of sixty guns; consequently, the Navy Department felt it desirable to send the *Franklin* out. Her size made it necessary that she be accompanied by a smaller vessel which could do most of the active cruising, and for this purpose the *Dolphin* was assigned.

Stewart had received the courtesy title of commodore while commanding the Mediterranean Squadron. Any officer of the United States Navy who commanded a squadron was addressed by that title thereafter, regardless of his future employment. The ship in which he sailed flew a blue broad pennant at her main truck; he was accorded the courtesies due the same rank in foreign navies; and yet he was officially only a captain, for that was the senior naval rank which had Congressional sanction. But official or not, the Pacific Station received its first commodore commanding an American squadron in April 1822.

Commodore Stewart found the *Constellation* awaiting him at Valparaiso. Captain Ridgely took the new commander in chief and Mrs. Stewart, who had accompanied her husband in the relative comfort of the flagship, to Santiago for the usual introductions and consultations. They spent four days at the capital, but Stewart would accept no civilities from the government, nor did the latter show any great desire to offer them. Stewart's coldness undoubtedly offended the Chileans, but their attitude must have been due in part to their dislike of Ridgely.

Early in his command of the Pacific Squadron, Stewart came to grips with the problem of communications. He was unwilling to accept the delay incidental to sending dispatches by way of Cape Horn, especially since this delay could be cut by half if the messenger traveled the shorter Isthmian route. But few merchant ships sailed from Valparaiso and Callao to Panama, and the *Dolphin* could hardly be used as a dispatch boat to the exclusion of all other duties, more especially because the *Franklin* had gathered much marine growth while in ordinary at New York, and so was no longer the swift sailer that Stewart had commanded in the Mediterranean.

The American commodore solved the problem in his own way. When the merchantman *Pearl* arrived at Valparaiso from the United States with the dismantled frames and timbers of three small schooners which she hoped to sell in the Hawaiian Islands, Stewart entered into an agreement with her master. Carpenters from the *Franklin* assembled all three; Stewart purchased two for a nominal sum, and the master of the *Pearl* disposed of the other. The three were the *Peruvian* (sometimes called *Peruviano*), launched at Arica in August 1822; the *Waterwitch,* built at Quilca about a month earlier; and the *Robinson Crusoe,* assembled at Juan Fernández. The first two were manned from the *Franklin* and served as dispatch boats until they were sold in 1824 prior to Stewart's return to the United States.

The exact status of the two schooners was very uncertain. Stewart himself considered them to be his private property; certainly he had paid for them although they were assembled and manned by naval personnel. With one brief exception, neither was employed on private business. However, there was no Departmental sanction for their acquisition and use, and neither was commissioned as an American warship. Therefore, it seems best to regard them in the light of private vessels maintained by the commander in chief solely for the purpose of facilitating the performance of his duties.

These little schooners proved to be most useful. They kept the commodore in fairly close contact with events at Guayaquil and Panama, then the northern limits of his station, and hurried the passage of letters and dispatches to the United States, as well. Although they were not public vessels, they were not ineffective in showing the flag because both were so obviously manned by naval personnel. The *Franklin*'s lieutenants eagerly sought the active service offered by command of the schooners. However, Stewart's effort to provide better communication with the United States had one result that he did not foresee and that did not become evident until the completion of his tour of duty in the Pacific.

Commodore Stewart had arrived in the Pacific Ocean to find that the newly created Patriot government of Peru had recently proclaimed a blockade of the entire coastline still under Spanish control. This supposedly was enforced by a squadron commanded by Admiral Guise, who had already seized several American merchantmen believed to have been carrying cargoes consigned to the Spaniards. As insufficient time had elapsed for the proclamation to reach Europe and the United States, these seizures were clearly illegal. Moreover, Peruvian warships were rarely present on their blockading station, and the whole blockade was conducted in a very haphazard fashion. The new commander in chief at once questioned the legality of such a procedure, but with little success. His task was not eased by the fact that Great Britain, hoping to win favor with the government obviously winning the war in Peru, had acquiesced in the blockade. It must be added that the British could hardly protest with consistency against an illegal blockade when they had so recently been guilty of much more flagrant violations of internationally recognized principles of blockade.

Finally, Stewart addressed to General Antonio José de Sucré, civil and military commandant at Callao, a letter so forcefully setting forth the American position that the Peruvian government was moved to recognize the justice of the American argument and to free the detained ships. In this letter, which Chief Justice John Marshall called the best statement of the principles of blockade that he had ever seen,[2] Stewart also took the opportunity to warn the Patriots against too-eager acceptance of British friendship lest the newly established Latin American republics find themselves indebted to England to an undesirable extent. This dignified statement may not have won the affection of the Patriot government for Stewart, but it must have gained him Patriot respect, however unwilling.

Meanwhile, a ukase issued by the Tsarist government of Russia had caused some alarm in Washington. Foreign contraband trade with Russian America was increasing, and the St. Petersburg regime, in September 1821, forbade foreign merchantmen to approach the coast within 100 Italian miles north of 51° North latitude. Such an assertion of sovereignty over the high seas was quite indefensible, and in addition, the southern boundary of Russian America was thus moved southward into the Oregon Territory, an area claimed jointly by the United States and Great Britain.

American interests in the Pacific Northwest were not then suffi-ciently extensive for the ukase to cause widespread alarm in the United States, but the House of Representatives did inquire of the Secretary of the Navy the best means of obtaining information about our harbors on the Pacific Coast and of landing artillery at the mouth of the Columbia River. Secretary Smith Thompson referred the questions to the Board of Navy Commissioners, and Commodore Rodgers replied:

. . . these objects might be accomplished by engaging a suitable mer-chant vessel by the month and sending her with one of the Schooners now in service . . . If the *Dolphin* could be spared from Commo. Stewart's command, the transport might join her at Valparaiso. . . . it is probable that it might not be convenient for the *Dolphin* to be detached from the command of Commo. Stewart. . . .[3]

Rodgers' closing statement was correct; the *Dolphin* could not be spared from her normal duties, and many years were to elapse before American artillerymen landed their guns in Oregon. The Russian edict was not enforced, and the United States government limited its action to an official remonstrance.

As Stewart's cruise was coming to an end, he was ordered to be at

Valparaiso in January 1824 to turn over the command of the Pacific Station to Commodore Isaac Hull, who was coming out in the frigate *United States*. Repeated requests for additional force had met with success; the sloop-of-war *Peacock* was designated to accompany the "Old Waggon" (*United States* was so called because of her sluggish sailing), but her outfitting was delayed and she did not sail until later. The *United States* was also bringing out new officers for the *Dolphin* which was to remain in the Pacific.

Commodore Stewart returned to the United States to find that his conduct while in command of the Pacific Squadron had not met with universal approbation. He was informed that the Peruvian government had made official complaint against him, and that this complaint had been seconded by American consular officials. Under the circumstances, Secretary of the Navy Samuel L. Southard felt it necessary to order an official investigation into the matter.

As a result of the investigation, a general court-martial was ordered to convene in Washington on 18 August 1825 to try Captain Charles Stewart on charges of unofficerlike conduct, disobedience of orders, neglect of duty, and oppression and cruelty.

Undoubtedly the most important of the charges was the first. Specifically, Stewart was accused of building and operating vessels for his own account, carrying specie for American merchants for his own benefit, transporting horses to Lima where they were sold to the Spanish forces besieged there, and generally showing undue partiality to the Spaniards. The third charge, neglect of duty, was concerned with the infrequency of target practice on board the *Franklin;* and the last, oppression and cruelty, dealt with the alleged mistreatment of a lieutenant who had been confined in the flagship while awaiting trial by court-martial.

The delay in convening the Stewart court-martial was due to the time allowed him to gather evidence and witnesses for his defense. Finally, in the soggy heat of a Washington August, the most noted officer of the United States Navy faced the glittering ranks of nearly all of the senior officers not serving afloat. (The members of the court were Captains James Barron, William M. Crane, Robert T. Spence, John D. Henley, Jesse D. Elliott, Stephen Cassin, James Renshaw, Thomas Brown, Charles C. B. Thompson, Alexander S. Wadsworth, George W. Rodgers, and George C. Read, with Captain

Barron serving as president and Mr. Richard S. Coxe as judge advocate.)

Stewart's defense was dramatic. Certainly he had obtained and employed the *Peruvian* and *Waterwitch,* but only once had either been used for other than government business, and then merely to safeguard a cargo owned by American merchants until stowage space could be obtained in a merchant vessel. Consul Jeremy Robinson, who had taken great exception to the building of the schooners, had welcomed the opportunity to send his dispatches in them. Specie had been carried in the flagship for American merchants; this was the usual practice in the Royal Navy, and no direct orders against it had been issued in the American service. Indeed, this manner of guarding American interests in the Pacific was considered most valuable. The horses sold in Lima had pulled the commodore's carriage in the various cities visited, and had been sold only because they were unlikely to survive the Cape Horn passage on the way home. Perhaps the commodore had seemed partial to the Spaniards, but Captain James Biddle felt that Peruvian opinion on this point might be unreliable:

I believe it is impossible for any commanding officer to be in the Pacific without giving offence to the one side or the other. The royal party, knowing the general feelings of our countrymen, are jealous of them; the patriots, on the other hand, expecting too much, are dissatisfied.[4]

For the remaining charges, it was admitted that the *Franklin*'s great guns had not been fired as often as was desirable. Much of her time necessarily had been spent in ports where target practice was not practicable, but the ship's company had been drilled frequently in every evolution short of actual firing. The lieutenant in question had not been kept in close confinement, and a doctor had examined him periodically to make certain that his health was not deteriorating as a result of his arrest. No court-martial had been convened on the station because a sufficient number of officers of the required rank could not be mustered without immobilizing the *Dolphin* for an undesirable length of time.

Commodore Stewart's peers were not long in deciding the case. On 5 September 1825, Secretary Southard informed him that he had been honorably acquitted of all charges. Moreover, the members of the court unanimously stated their belief that Commodore Stewart had acted with the highest distinction during the whole period of his command in the Pacific.

Commodore Isaac Hull, meanwhile, was finding it necessary to keep his flagship at Callao most of the time. The fighting against the Spaniards was centered around Lima, and Hull wished to be close to the scene of likely trouble. No doubt this was pleasant for Mrs. Hull and her sister who accompanied the commodore. Furthermore, the American Minister at Lima, a cultured gentleman by the name of William Tudor, quickly became a good friend of Hull; and Simon Bolivar, commanding the Patriot forces in the region, was favorably impressed by the commodore's charming sister-in-law. Whether his interest was genuine or merely politic is not now apparent, nor can it be ascertained to what extent the lady returned his favor.

This is not to imply that command of the Pacific Station was a mere pleasure cruise. Under Bolivar's orders, Admiral Guise had resumed the blockade of the Peruvian coast, but no more effectually than before, so Hull was soon protesting against illegal detention of American vessels. Bolivar was assured that any legal blockade would be respected by the Americans, but sister-in-law or no, Hull intended to prevent any infringement of American rights.

The sloop-of-war *Peacock* finally left the United States some months after Hull had sailed. This little ship must have experienced one of the more unpleasant passages out:

A few days after our departure from the U.S. we experienced a very heavy Thunder Shower attended with frequent vivid flashes of Lightning, one of which struck the Ship, killed four Men instantly & wounded several others dangerously, however they recovered partially, yet the greater part of them will never perfectly be restored. . . . Adding to this [the low temperatures] the constant heavy gales prevalent off the Cape, however our time would have been rather more pleasant had the small Pox not paid us a long & exterminating visit. We lost 12 valuable men by this disease, and at a time when the ship appeared at the mercy of the waves, their loss was severely felt owing to the vessel being then already too short manned.[5]

Hull found it necessary to send the *Peacock*'s commanding officer home for trial soon after the sloop arrived at Callao. Lieutenant Beverly Kennon was detached from the flagship to take command,

and Hull, desiring to give Kennon a more experienced first lieutenant, ordered Lieutenant William Ramsay to the *United States.* The latter objected to the transfer, and the commodore sent him home with his late commanding officer. When the two reached Washington, Secretary Southard immediately ordered Master-Commandant Thomas ap Catesby Jones to the Pacific to assume command of the *Peacock,* and Ramsay was sent out as Jones's first lieutenant. He looked on this as a personal victory over the commodore and treated him with some condescension. Hull was too dignified to notice lapses from a respectful attitude in so junior an officer, but Ramsay was so unwise as to treat Master-Commandant Jones in the same manner. The fiery Virginian accepted the challenge, and Lieutenant Ramsay was soon on his way to the United States once more, this time under arrest. He had to be sent home for trial on the charges preferred by Jones because, once again, a competent court could not be convened on the station without detaining the smaller warships.

While Ramsay was setting a record of sorts for assignments to and detachments from the Pacific Squadron, Commodore Hull was presented with a more serious problem. Supposedly, the Spanish viceroy at Lima had licensed several vessels as privateers, and these were showing small respect for neutral flags. Later it appeared that the privateers were fitted out under orders from the governor of the province and without the knowledge of the viceroy. Since the latter alone had the authority to grant commissions to privateers, it was possible to regard these vessels as pirates. Hull had no definite instructions for this contingency; therefore, when the "Old Waggon" overhauled one after a chase in which the privateer lost her topmasts, the "pirate" was left to the tender mercies of Patriot Admiral Guise who quickly burned her. The problem was made more serious by the tendency of the privateer crews to seize their vessels and turn pirate in earnest. However, this annoyance was ended before the Navy Department could take any steps to cope with it. The Patriot triumph in Peru in 1826 relieved Commodore Hull from further troubles of that sort.

But in 1824 the Spaniards were still fighting and sent warships out to lift the Patriot blockade. On 12 September, their squadron arrived off Callao to bring Admiral Guise to account, and the latter got under way to meet the challenge although his force was clearly inferior. Apparently the *United States* would have been directly in the line of fire, so Hull also weighed anchor to shift his position. Almost at once the Spanish admiral appeared to change his mind, and stood out to sea again. Hull learned soon afterward that the Spaniard had explained his conduct by professing to believe that the American frigate was coming to the assistance of the Patriot ships. Clearly this incident could have led to another general court-martial; therefore, Commodore Hull took the precaution of getting a letter from the senior British officer present to support his report. This proved sufficient to counteract the Spanish allegation that he had been guilty of unneutral conduct.

In August 1825, Commodore Hull received orders to send one of the smaller vessels to the Mulgrave Islands (now Mili Atoll) in search of the American whaleship *Globe*. This vessel's company had mutinied, killed her officers, and set out for a cruise among the Pacific islands. The *Dolphin* could be spared at the time, so Lieutenant-Commandant John Percival (later the fabulous Captain "Mad Jack" Percival) was ordered to prepare for this duty. In order that the little schooner might embark the necessary stores, Percival reduced his crew to seventy men before sailing.

The *Dolphin* proceeded to the Mulgrave Islands by way of the Galápagos and Marquesas Islands. In the Mulgraves, Percival found that the natives had murdered all except two of the mutineers, these being kept as slaves. After some difficulty, their release was procured, and the *Dolphin* sailed for the Hawaiian Islands, leaving behind seeds, pigs, and strict instructions that visiting mariners be well treated.

The schooner arrived at Honolulu on 9 January 1826, the first American warship to visit the island group.[6] The *Dolphin* remained at Honolulu until 11 May. American merchants were overjoyed at the presence of one of their country's men-o'-war to protect their interests, but missionaries were less enthusiastic, particularly since the "Dolphins" expressed great dissatisfaction over the recently realized suppression of prostitution. Percival was accused of sympathizing with his men, and of having a hand in a riot in which American sailors were involved. Despite this he seems to have used his influence to keep order among the crews of the numerous whalers wintering there, and his men did good work in salvaging cargo and specie from the wrecked merchant ship *London*.

Before the *Dolphin* had returned from her pioneer cruise, Hull was ordered to take the *United States* on an island cruise in support of American trade. In return, he reported that the hostilities on the Pacific coast of South America were finally at an end, but that his presence was still required at Callao. It seemed likely that the Chilean and Peruvian navies would decommission their warships, and there was a real danger that the hardened seamen so discharged might seize vessels and become pirates. Therefore, he ordered the *Peacock* to prepare for the island cruise.

Commodore Hull had nothing of importance to add to the general Department orders under which the *Peacock* sailed, but he may have shown to Master-Commandant Jones the private letter in which Southard urged him to co-operate with missionaries whenever possible, "and [you] will receive the benedictions of the pious for the good you may perform."[7]

The sloop-of-war made sail in June 1826. She called at the Marquesas, informally regarded as American since Porter had used them as a base of operations in 1813, and then sailed to Tahiti, the first American man-o'-war to visit this alluring island. Jones drew up a treaty—between the government of the United States and the dusky Queen of the island—relating to the treatment of American vessels and citizens touching there.

The *Peacock* flew to the northward once more and anchored at Honolulu, where word of her coming had preceded her. American merchants were hopeful that her captain would intervene in their quarrel with King Kamehameha III over a sandalwood contract, but if they expected swift action, they were disappointed. The over-bearing Jones showed that he could be very diplomatic on occasion, and spent several weeks learning all he could about prevailing conditions, incidentally winning the good will of the King. His efforts to collect the sums owed to American merchants by the monarch were not entirely successful, but he did negotiate a treaty with Kame-hameha on behalf of the United States. Much like the previous agreement which Jones had drawn up at Tahiti, but more comprehensive, it covered the problems of desertion from American whalers, treatment of merchantmen visiting the Hawaiian Islands, and salvage of American ships wrecked in the vicinity; furthermore, it provided most-favored-nation status for the United States.

Probably because this treaty amounted to American recognition of Hawaiian independence, its ratification was never advised by the United States Senate. Nevertheless, it seems to have been a very able document and was regarded as binding by the Hawaiian rulers for some years afterward; thus, most of the objectives sought by Jones were realized.

Master-Commandant Jones further interested himself in the conditions prevailing among the crews of the large number of merchant vessels in Hawaiian waters, and submitted a very interesting report on the general situation in the Pacific Ocean area. Although he appears to have exaggerated the success of his negotiations with Kamehameha, Jones's cruise was very profitable.

The *Peacock* left Hawaiian waters early in January 1827 and sailed to the eastward, touching at Californian and Mexican ports to replenish her supplies. Arriving at Callao, Jones found that Hull had departed for the Atlantic in the *United States,* having been relieved by Commodore Jacob Jones with the *Brandywine* frigate and the sloop-of-war *Vincennes.* The *Peacock* also was to return to the United States, but the "roaring *Brandywine*" had brought out a new complement of officers and men for the little *Dolphin* and the schooner remained on Pacific Station.

The enlistments of the "Old Waggon's" crew expired some time before the frigate reached New York, and her men did not appreciate their detention in the service. Soon after she came to anchor, the entire ship's company gathered and demanded immediate discharge. Hull reported: ". . . I did not think proper to detain them by force for had I attempted it, I am confident the ship would have been in great confusion."[8] Nor was this rather unpleasant episode the end of Hull's troubles. In 1833 his command in the Pacific was investigated by Congress. Apparently Michael Hogan, United States consul and navy agent at Valparaiso, instigated the inquiry. All charges were dropped after the commodore's secretary testified. Fortunately, few succeeding commanders in chief were required publicly to justify their conduct on Pacific Station.

With the wars in South America virtually at an end, the situation in the Pacific was much less vexatious for American warships on that station. Commodore Jacob Jones took care to prevent the outbreak of piracy feared by his predecessor, nor did it develop to any extent. The Navy Department was apprehensive lest its successful campaign against the picaroons in the Gulf of Mexico and the Caribbean Sea should have driven those desperate men across Central America to continue their lawless careers on the western coast. As a precaution against this danger, the light vessels of the Pacific Squadron added the coast of Mexico and the Panama area to their more southerly cruising grounds, but there is no indication that the picaroons ever operated in the Pacific Ocean.

The most urgent problem which faced Commodore Jones upon his arrival at Callao was that caused by impressment of American citizens into the armed forces of Peru. Most of the men so impressed had deserted from American merchant vessels to sail in coasters flying the Peruvian flag and offering much higher pay than their original ships. The government of Peru, which obtained men for its army and navy principally by impressment, took the stand that sailing under the Peruvian flag made the men citizens of that country. Jones and the American chargé d'affaires both protested, but the situation was not finally relieved until March 1828 when most of the Peruvian warships were decommissioned and the seamen were discharged.

Early in 1829, Secretary Southard ordered that the *Vincennes* be sent to the Society and Hawaiian Islands to render aid and protection to American merchantmen and whaleships frequenting those waters. Master-Commandant William B. Finch was to exert himself especially to prevent desertion from these ships, and to repatriate those men who had already deserted.

The *Vincennes* followed much the same track as the *Peacock* had sailed. In the Marquesas Islands, the good will of the islanders toward Americans had deteriorated, due in large part to the irresponsible behavior of merchant and whaleship crews, but Finch was able to arrive at a satisfactory arrangement with the Marquesans. The sloop then stood on to Tahiti, and again amicable relations were maintained with the people of the area.

At Honolulu, Finch took up the perennial questions of debts and sandalwood contracts, but he seems to have been little more successful in settling them than was his predecessor, Master-Commandant Jones. However, he established a cordial relationship with the missionaries there and praised them highly in his report. On leaving Honolulu, the *Vincennes* sailed to the westward in accordance with her orders. She touched at Macao and various East Indian ports, and then returned to New York by way of the Cape of Good Hope, the first American warship to circumnavigate the globe.

Meanwhile, the time was approaching when Commodore Jacob Jones must leave the Pacific, and he was relieved in 1829 by Commodore Charles C. B. Thompson in the *Guerrière* frigate. As usual, the *Dolphin* received a fresh complement by the newcomer, while her erstwhile company was given passage home in the *Brandywine*. The squadron was completed by the sloop-of-war *St. Louis* which had come out a few weeks before Thompson.

Commodore Thompson's orders contained a paragraph instructing him to collect information relative to the different types of sugar cane and their cultivation—an indication that warships on this distant station might be able to further agricultural knowledge in the United States. Henceforth, this was a standard part of the sailing orders issued to prospective commanders in chief of the Pacific Squadron. Its political significance lay in the fact that the government could point to knowledge so gained as evidence that the Navy was helping interests other than those of shipowner and merchant. At all times, however, the orders made it very clear that efforts to gain and transmit this agricultural information should not be allowed to interfere with the primary mission of the Pacific Squadron, which remained unchanged.

For the most part, Thompson's cruise was uneventful; this was fortunate, as his flagship seems to have been very poorly prepared for this service. Reports of her decayed state reached the Navy Commissioners, and they recommended that her relief be prepared somewhat earlier than usual. Secretary of the Navy John Branch was not convinced that this was indeed necessary, so Commodore Rodgers replied with a quotation from Thompson's report of the *Guerrière*'s condition:

. . . the most important parts of the decks and upper works of this ship are in a state so defective, and so liable to increasing disability as to render her capability of returning extremely doubtful if the cruize should be protracted beyond 18 months or 2 years from the time of her departure from the United States.[9]

This was decisive, but Branch was still unwilling to incur the added expense of outfitting another frigate at once. Finally, work was begun to ready the *Potomac* frigate for sea; in the meantime, orders went out for Thompson to quit his station as soon as possible. Since the order was dated 10 February 1831, the *Guerrière* could hardly expect to be off the Horn before winter. Thompson's departure left Master-Commandant John D. Sloat of the *St. Louis* as senior American naval officer on Pacific Station until he was relieved by Master-Commandant Francis H. Gregory in the sloop-of-war *Falmouth* some five months later.

Thus, a little more than a decade after the Pacific Squadron had first been formed, it had come to consist of three vessels: a frigate, a sloop-of-war, and the veteran schooner *Dolphin*. Commanders in chief of this force had repeatedly asked for reinforcement, but the Navy Department did not believe it necessary. In all conscience, though, a good argument could be made for sending more warships to the Pacific Station. Its geographical area was expanding as American commercial and other interests continued to grow in the eastern Pacific. The island groups in that region had become a permanent responsibility of the Pacific Squadron, and the single sloop-of-war usually spent much of her cruise in a visit to their waters. The frigate-flagship remained in the vicinity of Callao and Valparaiso, still the most important ports of call for American merchant vessels bound out or home. The little *Dolphin* was employed in visits to the smaller South American harbors, with an occasional run to Panama to carry dispatches and passengers.

The Navy Department, however, did not question the policy of maintaining a squadron on Pacific Station. Secretary Southard had assured the President of the United States that "the squadron in the Pacific has continued to be useful to the interests of the nation."[10] And Secretary Branch, reluctant though he was to authorize a speedy relief for the *Guerrière,* obviously had no thought of changing the Navy's policy in the eastern Pacific.

4. *Aground on Her Own Beef Bones*

Although it was obviously undesirable that the important Pacific Station be left in the hands of so junior an officer as a master-commandant, the Navy Department was unable to resist the opportunity to assign a supplementary task to the outward-bound *Potomac.* Commodore John Downes, returning to familiar waters, was ordered first to give passage to Martin Van Buren, newly appointed minister to the Court of St. James. Before the frigate could get under way for England, however, the Navy Department received news of an outrage committed against an American merchantman. The Salem vessel *Friendship,* loading pepper in 1830 at the village of Quallah-Battoo (Kuala Batu), Sumatra, had been taken by people of the village, and several of her officers and men had been killed. As the East India Station had not yet been established, there was no naval force in those waters to take punitive action.

Secretary of the Navy Levi Woodbury, heeding the demands of merchants and shipowners that this crime be avenged, ordered Downes to proceed to Sumatra by way of the Cape of Good Hope. At Quallah-Battoo he was to make every effort to learn the true facts of the case and to punish the offenders. This mission accomplished, the *Potomac* would go on to the Pacific Station, touching at Macao, Canton, and such islands as might be on her track, for the dual purpose of replenishing her provisions and protecting American shipping.

Commodore Downes received information which led him to believe that virtually the entire populace of the village of Quallah-Battoo was involved in the *Friendship* incident and that they were ready to oppose a landing with force, despite the fact that the *Potomac* had been disguised as a Danish Indiaman. Thereupon, he sent ashore landing parties which captured all but one of the forts, and that was demolished by the frigate's guns. Ascertaining that

43

most of the culprits had been slain during these attacks, Downes had the village burned, and then entertained the request for peace. This was granted on assurances from the villagers that American merchant vessels would be treated well in the future, and the *Potomac* then proceeded on a leisurely passage to Callao.

This reprisal caused some repercussions in the United States. President Andrew Jackson, himself not above summary punishment of such offenders in the past, thought that Downes should have made a more thorough inquiry and proceeded more carefully so that innocent persons would not have suffered. Eventually, however, Downes's reports satisfied most of the critics, and the matter was allowed to rest.

The steps thus taken to protect American interests in East Indian waters were not completely effective, because only the continued presence of warships could ensure that such agreements as that made by Downes would be respected. With the establishment of the East India Station in 1835, this neglect was remedied, and the Pacific Squadron's responsibility for the region was ended.

During the *Potomac*'s passage among the islands, the centennial of the birth of George Washington was celebrated. This event was awaited eagerly by the ship's company since "scuttlebutt" rumors had circulated to the effect that an "extra-extra" ration of spirits would be issued in observance of the great occasion. Following the seventeen-gun salute, the men were mustered and Downes admonished them not to drink themselves into a state of intoxication. Then he announced that the "extra-extra" allowance of grog would consist of the usual amount of rum mixed with a double measure of water. The disappointment of the sailors may well be imagined; no one could get drunk on this grog. Downes's love of practical jokes was usually appreciated by the enlisted men, but doubtless he was thoroughly cursed in private by his crew on this occasion.

Commodore Downes must have found the Pacific Station very quiet by comparison with his earlier service in those waters. Again the flagship spent most of her cruise in the important harbors of South America, while the smaller vessels visited the more remote areas. Downes, like most of his predecessors, urged that more sloops or schooners be sent out, and his request met with the usual response—in comparison with the forces on other stations, the Pacific Squadron was large enough. He also desired that American citizens be appointed as consuls in some of the larger ports, with salaries sufficient to relieve them of the necessity of engaging in private business. The latter practice led to their involvement in the domestic affairs of the cities to which they were assigned, with consequent neglect of American interests in favor of their own. This recommendation also fell on deaf ears in Washington, so Downes's last cruise in the Pacific resulted in nothing which would alleviate some of the difficulties faced by commanders in chief of the Pacific Squadron.

While the *Potomac* was serving her time on the South American coast, Woodbury turned his mind to the problem of getting relief vessels to the distant stations before the ships on those stations were forced to depart for the United States by the expiration of enlistments. He asked the Navy Commissioners if it might not be practicable to rotate the vessels in commission among the stations. Thus the *Potomac* might be relieved by a frigate from the Brazil Squadron, and the vacancy so created be filled by a ship from the United States as soon as she could be readied. Commodore Rodgers, for the Board, answered with a categorical "no." Not only would the recommended practice make it impossible for the Navy Department to know exactly which ships were on each station, but the equipment required for one station might be entirely unsuited for service on another. The changes of climate involved might be deleterious to the health of the men. The difficulties of rendezvous with the commander in chief, already great, would be largely increased as the ships changed stations, and all of the squadrons would be weakened while vessels were passing from one to another.

Moreover, each of the officers commanding squadrons had his own code of signals and vague tactical and strategic plans, and Woodbury's proposal would require every commanding officer in the Navy to be familiar with all. In the face of this reasonable argument, the Secretary withdrew his suggestion, and the relief of ships on distant service proceeded as before, with the difference that the vessels were intended to go out at intervals rather than sailing at the same time. Thereby, invalids and men coming home on leave or for other purposes could be given passage in the homeward-bound warship at little extra expense to the government.

Notwithstanding Woodbury's concern, there was no large ship

46 . . . *Thence Round Cape Horn*

ready to carry Downes's successor out when the time came for the *Potomac* to be relieved, and she had already left the station when Commodore Alexander S. Wadsworth sailed in the sloop-of-war *Vincennes.* The latter's indignity at having to go out in so small a vessel was softened in part by the knowledge that he could shift his broad pennant to the *Brandywine* as soon as the frigate could be readied for sea and arrive in the Pacific Ocean.

National affairs were reflected in the Pacific in 1835 when Franco-American relations became tense over the failure of the French government to pay for the depredations of French privateers in the years immediately following the American Revolution. By a treaty of 1831, France had agreed to indemnify the Americans, but the French Chambers refused to vote the money. President Jackson's annual message to Congress in December 1834, proposed that a law be enacted authorizing the United States to seize French property if the money was not voted at the following session of the Chambers. The blunt wording of the message offended the French and stirred up anti-French feeling in the United States. Both nations made preparations for war and the situation seemed serious indeed. England, however, offered to mediate; Jackson included an explanation in his next message; and the French chose to regard this as an apology. The Chambers then voted the necessary money, and the whole episode ended amicably.

In view of the condition of the United States Navy, Jackson's proposal seems little less than foolhardy. The French naval forces in the Pacific Ocean were far superior to Wadsworth's squadron, and though her men might be sure that the "roaring *Brandywine*" was a match for anything afloat, it is likely that even the "Brandywines" would have been unable to prevent virtually a wholesale slaughter of American whalers and merchantmen in those waters. Closer to home, newly commissioned warships might have arrived on the various stations in time to be of use, but in the eastern Pacific hardly anything short of precipitous flight could have saved Wadsworth's force. American interests would, no doubt, have suffered cruel losses before the Pacific Squadron could have been reinforced.

Although 1836 saw Franco-American relations restored to a cordial plane, the awareness of the need for a stronger force in the Pacific had been established. Therefore, the line-of-battleship *North*

Carolina was chosen to carry the broad pennant of Commodore Henry E. Ballard, though she could not be readied for sea before expiring enlistments forced the *Brandywine* to sail for the United States. Ballard was informed that Wadsworth had already left the station, but that orders for direction of the squadron had doubtless been left at Valparaiso and no additional orders were given the new commander in chief. Ballard, however, asked for and received a copy of Wadsworth's original orders from Secretary of the Navy Mahlon Dickerson.

Early in January 1837, the *North Carolina* was ready for sea and stood out of New York Harbor on her way to the Pacific. One week out, a seaman fell from the fore topsail yard and was lost, a surprising similarity to the *Macedonian*'s experience, for she too had lost a man from aloft seven days after sailing. But here the resemblance ended. The *North Carolina* encountered some heavy weather, but nothing like the gale which dismasted the much smaller frigate. The passage to Rio de Janeiro was uneventful except for the fact that two men threw themselves overboard, only to be picked up by boats from the battleship. Apparently the *North Carolina* could not rival the *Macedonian* as a happy ship.

Ballard's flagship sailed from Rio de Janeiro on 25 March after a twenty-day visit. She was off Cape Horn on 20 April, and anchored at Valparaiso on 14 May after a routine passage. She seems to have been favored with relatively peaceful weather, although it must be remembered that a ship-of-the-line would not suffer so greatly as a smaller vessel in any but mountainous seas.

Commodore Ballard found that Chile and Peru were at war again; accordingly, he proceeded to Callao almost immediately in order to be as close to the scene of hostilities as possible. The *North Carolina* arrived in the Peruvian port on 27 May, after a passage of nine days. Those newcomers to the Pacific among her company must have looked around this harbor with some curiosity, but they need not have troubled themselves. It was to become very familiar to anyone on board the *North Carolina* during the next two years.

The flagship of the Pacific Squadron remained at Callao until 10 December 1837. Throughout this period of more than six months, her officers and men were not idle—the ship's company of a man-o'-war is never idle. While Commodore Ballard spent much of his time at Lima in the company of American diplomatic representatives and Peruvian officials, his subordinates were occupied with the never-ending duties necessary to keep the *North Carolina* efficient as a warship. Setting up rigging, painting, caulking, and work on the great guns and their appurtenances went on almost continuously, while Lieutenant Thomas O. Selfridge, acting commanding officer of the flagship, permitted no cessation of the drills without which no ship's company remains an effective fighting unit.

Nor was their concern with the big battleship alone. By this time, the squadron also included two sloops-of-war and two schooners, and whenever these appeared at Callao, they could depend on assistance by working parties from the flagship to effect necessary repairs. The *North Carolina*'s sailmakers would turn out new sails for one of the little schooners, while her carpenters were helping to recaulk the latter's hull and her gunners were lending a welcome hand to reeve new gun tackles to schooner carronades. Meanwhile, seamen from the larger ship would assist the crew of the little vessel in filling her water tanks. Ballard also used his flagship to some extent as a supply ship for the squadron, and her boats ferried loads of bread and other provisions from her capacious lockers to the schooner. Moreover, the battleship's large complement served as a reservoir of manpower from which vacancies in sloop and schooner complements were filled. This gave some members of the flagship's crew a chance for more active service than that afforded by duty in the *North Carolina*.

Occasionally the flagship did weigh anchor and stand out of the harbor, but she never got beyond the sight of land. The purpose seems to have been to give her men more realistic sail drill than was possible while she rode at anchor. During these extremely short cruises, the big ship never remained under way overnight.

Although the *North Carolina*'s inactivity must not be interpreted as idleness, many of her men must have repeated the old proverb to the effect that she would eventually ground on the beef bones thrown overboard every day by the cooks.

An uncertain peace had come to Peru when, on 10 December 1837, the flagship weighed anchor and stood out for Valparaiso. She was giving passage to the United States chargé d'affaires from Lima, but much of the three-week run was devoted to sail handling. At Valparaiso she fell into her old habits, and was not induced to leave the harbor until 5 April 1838, when hostilities again threatened to break out farther north.

The *North Carolina* sailed in company with the British frigate *Imogene,* a vessel boasting a reputation as an able sailer. The battleship found none of the strong winds which would have given her an advantage in the race, but neither did the light airs help her rival. The two vessels remained in sight of one another virtually the whole time at sea, and the *Imogene,* aided by an inshore wind, entered the harbor at Callao on 13 April several hours ahead of the *North Carolina,* which had been becalmed farther out. She seems to have sailed very well for a ship-of-the-line, a type of warship usually much slower than a frigate, except in winds strong enough to force the smaller vessel to shorten sail without endangering the strong rigging and massive spars of the larger.

Almost a month later, a Chilean squadron arrived to blockade Callao, but this was certain to be a legal blockade since all of the nations having considerable commercial intercourse with Peru maintained sizable squadrons at that port, and were prompt to intervene on behalf of merchantmen under their flags. This time, the *North Carolina* remained at Callao no less than nine months, and during a considerable part of that period, Commodore Ballard kept his entire squadron—*Lexington, Falmouth, Boxer,* and *Enterprise*—anchored there also.

It is not clear what motives governed Ballard in this course. Obviously, it was necessary that the activities of the blockaders be watched, but this should not have required the services of the whole squadron. The big *North Carolina* alone should have been a match for several of the Chileans, if necessary. To be sure, the presence of the commodore was desirable at the most troubled harbor on his station; the senior British and French officers were at Callao also, but occasionally departed to cruise elsewhere. Moreover, Ballard must have received the letter of 20 December 1837 wherein he was informed of potential difficulties with Mexico and was told it was the President's wish that:

. . . until you shall be otherwise instructed you cause as large a portion of your Squadron as may be convenient to visit the Harbors and cruise upon the Coast of that Govt. at such points as in your opinion may afford the best means of protecting our commerce. . . .[1]

But Ballard did not see fit to send more than one of his small ships at a time, and for much of his cruise it was not convenient to send any.

Whatever the commodore's reasons, his squadron remained at Callao and busied itself with the usual activities. An embarrassing moment came when, on 16 July, the schooner *Enterprise* was hove down for repairs. Her garboard strake was exposed and a sudden gust of wind heeled her even farther. Within a short time, she had filled and disappeared in twenty-one feet of water. Only the barge to which she had been secured kept her from capsizing, and made her ultimate recovery much easier. The *North Carolina* weighed anchor the next day and stood over to the disaster scene, where her great bulk and strong spars made her invaluable in raising the schooner. On 21 July the *Enterprise* was again afloat, and she was ready to go to sea on 10 August. The *North Carolina*'s crew performed most of the tasks necessary to make the schooner seaworthy after her brief immersion.

So time passed. Occasionally the flagship shifted her berth to be clear during the sporadic bombardments carried out by Chilean warships, and she weighed anchor a few times to stand out in succor of American merchantmen detained by the blockaders, although one of the sloops usually went out for this purpose. A few men deserted, but these frequently were recovered after a few days absence. Desertion was undoubtedly kept to a minimum by the policy of granting liberty fairly generously; most of the men got ashore three times during the cruise.

All things must come to an end, however, and even the *North Carolina*'s time at Callao did so. She put to sea on 15 January 1839, arrived at Valparaiso on 10 February, and got under way homeward bound on 23 March. The battleship made her ponderous way around the Horn without incident, and stopped at Rio de Janeiro for stores and dispatches. Here she lingered for only two weeks and then stood to the northward, carrying some mutineers from the whaler *Georgia* home for trial. Her Pacific cruise ended in New York Harbor late in June 1839, surely one of the most uneventful and least active in the early history of the Pacific Squadron.

During her cruise of some two years and six months, the *North Carolina* lost twenty-six men out of her complement of more than 800. Four of these were killed in shipboard accidents, while the remainder died of unspecified illnesses. This casualty rate compares favorably with that of the frigates, but it must be remembered that living conditions in those small and overcrowded vessels were much worse than in a comparatively spacious ship-of-the-line.

As stated above, the foregoing description of the *North Carolina*'s cruise was presented in order that it might be contrasted with the far more eventful voyage of the *Macedonian*. However, this is not intended to be either a criticism of Commodore Ballard or a glorification of Captain Downes. The conditions prevailing on the station dictated the way in which the senior officer used his ships, and the interests of the United States seem not to have suffered unduly during either cruise. If at times Ballard's policy is not easily understood and he appears to have ignored important Department orders, it must be remembered that he was present on the Pacific Station and so had much more current information as to its needs than could be available to his seniors many thousands of miles distant.

While Commodore Ballard was commanding in the Pacific, one of the most notable exploring expeditions ever sent out by the United States government sailed from Hampton Roads, Virginia. This project had been the darling of President John Quincy Adams, who saw in the unexplored reaches of the Pacific Ocean an opportunity for his nation to make a significant contribution to geographic knowledge. Adams had attempted to win Congressional support for such an expedition in 1826, but he was rarely successful in his relations with that body, and had failed to gain its consent. Thereafter, the great project was all but forgotten until revived by President Andrew Jackson almost ten years later.

The honor of commanding the exploring squadron first went to Captain Thomas ap Catesby Jones, earlier mentioned as commanding the *Peacock*. He was an officer of undoubted ability, but was possessed of somewhat uncertain temperamental qualities which made themselves known as preparation of the squadron dragged along. The especially designed and built exploring vessels turned out to be miserably slow, and even worse, they drew too much water for their intended duties. Jones had been promised the new frigate *Macedonian* (built to replace Downes's old ship) as flagship, but she too was not suited for exploration. He became enraged over the problem of choosing subordinates, the emotional tension disturbed a troublesome wound received in 1815, and the resulting illness led him to resign the command.

Several other captains were suggested for the vacant command, but none possessed the necessary scientific training and eventually the post went to Lieutenant Charles Wilkes. He had already served as director of the Depot of Charts and Instruments (forerunner of both the Hydrographic Office and the Naval Observatory), and had been mentioned earlier as a likely astronomer for the expedition. A better selection could not have been made, but Wilkes should have been promoted for squadron command. However, he remained a lieutenant, although adopting the style of commodore at sea.

When the United States Exploring Expedition finally left Hampton Roads on 18 August 1838, it consisted of the sloops-of-war *Vincennes* and *Peacock,* the brig-of-war *Porpoise,* the pilot schooners *Flying Fish* and *Sea Gull,* and the storeship *Relief.* The first was flagship with Wilkes himself in command, and the slightly senior Lieutenant William L. Hudson subordinated himself to Wilkes to command the *Peacock.* The other officers were junior to Wilkes in rank. In all, the vessels were manned by eighty-three officers and 342 men.

The squadron's track led to Cape Horn by way of Madeira and Rio de Janeiro. Some time was devoted to surveys of the inhospitable region around Cape Horn, and there the little *Sea Gull* went missing with all hands during a search for the storm-delayed *Relief.* This was a serious loss, for the handy pilot boats had been counted on for yeoman service in shallow and restricted waters.

The squadron entered the Pacific Ocean in 1839, worked its way through the Tuamotu and Society Islands, and stopped briefly at Samoa. Accurate surveys were made of many of the islands and reefs in the waters through which the vessels passed, and much hydrographic and anthropological information was recorded. The four ships remaining in the squadron (*Relief* had returned to the United States after depositing her supplies at ports to be visited by the other vessels) anchored at Sydney, Australia, in November and made preparations for a visit to Antarctica.

They set out on this venture in December 1839. Despite almost unbelievable hardships and the near loss of the *Peacock,* the two larger vessels succeeded in sighting land, thus indicating the possibility of an Antarctic continent, a possibility which became a certainty as the *Vincennes* and *Porpoise* fought through the ice along its coast for some hundreds of miles. To the surprise of experienced British mariners, the squadron made its way back to Sydney during the southern hemisphere autumn, and refitted once more. Next came a visit to New Zealand, and then the squadron resumed its work of surveying in the Fiji Islands. The period from May to August 1840 was spent in those waters, where Wilkes encountered the only trouble with islanders to mar the cruise. Two officers were killed, and the islanders were soundly defeated by punitive landing parties.

After touching at Honolulu in October, the vessels scattered to the southward, surveying islands as far south as the Tuamotu Archipelago. Early in 1841, the squadron sailed to the Puget Sound region on the coast of North America, and undertook the surveys which had so long been desired of the Pacific Squadron. Shore parties went east and south from Puget Sound, while the vessels coasted to the southward. Another disaster overtook the expedition when the *Peacock* was wrecked, fortunately without loss of life, while entering the Columbia River. The spit on which she grounded still bears her name.

Undismayed by this loss, Wilkes sent a third exploring party to the southward along the Willamette River, while the remaining ships, together with a merchant brig chartered to replace the *Peacock,* proceeded to San Francisco. More surveys were made in the vicinity of the Sacramento River, and the party coming south overland joined the squadron once more. In November, the four vessels stood out for Honolulu to replenish provisions, and then sailed to the westward through the Caroline Islands, surveying as they went. At Manila, Wilkes decided that the projected visit to Japan should be given up because the *Peacock*'s loss had so weakened his squadron; instead, he stopped at Sulu to conclude trade agreements with the ruler in February 1842.

Its work finally ended, the Exploring Expedition returned to the Atlantic by way of the Cape of Good Hope, and arrived at New York early in June 1842.

In all, the officers of the squadron had surveyed more than two hundred islands and hundreds of miles of North American and

Antarctic coastlines. The hydrographic information so gained was invaluable, and Wilkes's surveys have proven to be accurate almost without exception. His vessels were not well fitted for the duties they performed, and it is amazing that only two were lost in the course of a voyage of circumnavigation during which the Pacific Ocean was crossed three times and many uncharted regions were visited. The excellence of the work done by the Exploring Expedition may be indicated by the fact that American warships operating in the central Pacific during World War II frequently used charts which bore the notation "U.S. Ex. Ex."

Unfortunately, Lieutenant Wilkes's homecoming was marred by a series of charges and countercharges which culminated in a general court-martial. He was found guilty of punishing some of his men illegally, and was publicly reprimanded. No doubt he was something of a martinet, and his subsequent difficulties during the Civil War were in large part due to his own conceit, but these cannot lessen the value of the work he performed in the Pacific Ocean. The Exploring Expedition remains one of the greatest peacetime accomplishments of the United States Navy.

The naval vessels cruising on distant stations received the usual orders to render every assistance to Lieutenant Wilkes, but it cannot be stated that the Pacific Squadron was able to give him much aid. At no time did he fall in with the commander in chief on Pacific Station, and no help seems to have been desired. However, it must be admitted that the Pacific Squadron was one of the principal beneficiaries of Wilkes's work. Many of the islands and reefs charted by his squadron were within the limits of the Pacific Station.

Meanwhile, Commodore Alexander Claxton had been ordered to the Pacific in 1839 as Ballard's relief. He was allowed the privilege of naming a commanding officer for the flagship *Constitution,* and chose his good friend Captain Daniel Turner for the position. This led to complications, for Claxton himself was officially only a captain, and two officers of that rank, even when one is decidedly junior to the other, are apt to find one ship too small for their combined dignities.

At the outset all went well. Claxton and Turner converted the commodore's and captain's quarters into one large apartment, shared mess expenses, and generally existed as equals. However, it was not long before Claxton began to take an interest in the ship's organization as well. This was not surprising—he had no duties at all to perform on the long outward passage, and time passed slowly. The first sign of trouble came when Captain Turner found that the purser had issued certain articles of slop clothing to the *Constitution*'s crew without the knowledge or permission of his commanding officer. Claxton assumed the responsibility; he felt that the men needed this clothing and had not thought it necessary to trouble his good friend with so minor a matter. Further investigation disclosed that the commodore had taken more than a passing interest in the outfitting of the flagship, and Turner sought to impress upon his senior that he did not wish the latter to become involved in details which were the responsibility of the commanding officer.

All was forgiven after this little incident, and relations between the two captains remained cordial while "Old Ironsides" plowed southward through the Atlantic and then northward in the Pacific. But this harmony gradually ceased to prevail in the monotony of cruising along the western coast or swinging idly at anchor in a sleepy South American harbor. There was simply too little to keep the commodore occupied, and soon Turner began to be aware of minor infringements of his duties. Mild remonstrances led to sharper rejoinders, for each man felt the dignity of his position, and both shared the delicate sense of honor which characterized captains of the United States Navy. Claxton was surprised and hurt that the officer whom he regarded as a younger brother (or more nearly, as a son) should resent his efforts to be helpful. Turner, for his part, began to find the commodore's manner irritatingly condescending, and the rift widened rapidly. Once more the commodore's and captain's quarters resumed their separate identities, and the manner of each captain toward the other became increasingly cold.

Matters reached an impasse on 2 February 1840, when Turner asked to be allowed to return to the United States. This request brought the following exchange of letters on the next day:

[*Claxton to Turner*] A sense of public duty forbids that I should grant your request of this date. [The request is dated on the preceding day in Turner's letter book.] If I had the *will,* I have not the *power,* according to my view of Service.

[*Turner to Claxton*] I request you will grant me permission to leave this Ship, and remain on shore, until the pleasure of the Hon. the Secretary of the Navy may be known respecting my return to the United States.

[*Claxton to Turner*] By a rule of service the command of this Ship is entrusted to a *Captain*. No Captain being present whom I could with *propriety* order in your place, I am unable to grant your request to remain on shore.[2]

This decidedly unpleasant situation was not improved with the passage of time. Claxton persisted in being amazed at the ingratitude of the man for whom he had done so much, and continued his efforts to bring Turner to a more reasonable attitude. The latter became more sensitive to the wrongs done him, and the enmity grew. Neither seemed able to drop the formal correspondence which had become their only method of communication. From the veiled, and later, open threats which appeared in these letters, it is apparent that an official inquiry, and probably, one or more general courts-martial might have resulted when the *Constitution* returned to the United States.

However, the whole matter was decided suddenly by a higher authority even than the Secretary of the Navy. Commodore Alexander Claxton died on 7 March 1841 after being stricken by an especially virulent form of dysentery. His remains were respectfully interred at Lima, and his late antagonist assumed command of the Pacific Squadron. In accordance with Navy Regulations, he did not presume to hoist a broad pennant or take the title of commodore.

Reports of this and similar altercations between commodores and officers commanding flagships reached the Navy Department, and Secretary Abel P. Upshur issued a circular for the future guidance of those officers concerned. This pointed out that the flag officer's relationship to the captain of the flagship should be the same as that to every other officer commanding in the squadron. Further, the commodore would lessen his own dignity by taking part in the internal organization of a particular ship, and this practice would tend to undermine the authority of the vessel's rightful captain. Upshur closed with a strong intimation that too much familiarity between a flag officer and any one of his captains was very likely to cause trouble. But a mere circular was hardly enough. The commodore commanding on a distant station was nearly an absolute monarch, and his conduct could rarely receive official attention before the end of his cruise. A more effective solution to the problem lay in the creation of an official rank above that of captain, but Congress was not yet ready to authorize such a flag rank.

Captain Turner, on taking command of the Pacific Squadron, found that he had the *St. Louis* sloop and the schooner *Shark* under his orders. The storeship *Relief* was at Callao, and the third-class sloops *Dale* and *Yorktown* were on their way to join the squadron, the former as the *St. Louis*'s relief and the latter to cruise on the Pacific whaling grounds. His predecessor's orders advised him that the entire west coast of South America as far north as Panama was his responsibility and that he might be called on to send vessels to the Hawaiian and Society Islands if the need arose. It was also desirable that one of the smaller ships cruise on the California coast occasionally. As usual, the primary motives for keeping a squadron in the eastern Pacific were "protection of commerce and improvement of discipline by affording active service to a portion of the officers and crews of our vessels."[3]

Actually, the coastal waters of Mexico and California were more important at this time than Secretary of the Navy James K. Paulding had foreseen when he sent out Claxton's sailing orders. The end of hostilities between Chile and Peru permitted the Pacific Squadron to give its attention to events farther to the north. Already, in June 1840, Commander French Forrest of the *St. Louis* had touched at Monterey in response to reports that American and British citizens had been imprisoned on suspicion that they were planning to set up a government independent of Mexico.[4] Diplomacy backed by a threat of force won their release and Mexican recognition of their claims for reimbursement. The *St. Louis* did not remain to enforce payment, however, and the claims dragged on for years.

When the *Yorktown* arrived at Callao, Commander John H. Aulick set out to collect such information as would enable him to perform his whale fishery protection duty efficiently. He learned in conversations with whaler captains that:

. . . the present Fishing Ground of a large portion of the Whalers in this Sea, is on this coast between Longitudes 118° and 125° west, but some go as far as the Marquesas and Society Islands. What they call the Japan Fleet, fish between the Latitudes 28° and 32° North, and Longitudes 165 West, and 155 East, and rarely go within sight of the Coast, with which, they say, they would not be allowed by the Natives to have any communications.

The season for whaling ther[e], is from April to October, they never remain to the eastward of 180° Longitude after the 1st Sept. when the hurricane season commences. They then draw to the Westward and generally assemble in Nov. and Dec. at the Sandwich Islands for refreshment and repairs, after which some visit the Coast of California.[5]

In accordance with his orders, Aulick fitted out for a long transpacific cruise, no new experience for him since in 1835-1836 he had commanded the *Vincennes* on a cruise through south Pacific islands, thence northward to Guam and the Palau Islands, and returned to the United States by way of the Cape of Good Hope. This time, however, he was ordered to return to the Pacific Station at the termination of his voyage, since it was not expected to last for more than a year.

The Claxton-Turner cruise was marked by a definite increase in the size of the Pacific Station. The growing importance of areas in Central and North America has been noted, and in 1839 the Congress had become concerned about the defense of the Oregon Territory. Secretary Paulding referred the question to the Board of Navy Commissioners, and Commodore Isaac Chauncey answered that this area could be defended only by land forces and fortifications. However, the Pacific Squadron would co-operate with the military to the fullest extent.

Two years later, Commodore Lewis Warrington, president of the Board, recommended the first geographical limits for the Pacific Station: "All the west coast of America, and westward from the meridian of Cape Horn to the 180th degree of longitude; and southward between those meridians to the South Pole."[6] Perhaps the absence of a northern limit reflects uncertainty as to the probable importance of the waters north of Hawaii; more likely it was understood that the limit of navigation in the unknown seas to the north was also the northern boundary of the Pacific Station. If so, the Pacific Station had finally come to encompass the area which was to be included within its limits for more than eighty years.

5. The Flying Welshman

After resigning the command of the Exploring Expedition in 1838, Captain Thomas ap Catesby Jones remained on half pay for three years. Early in 1841, his health restored, he applied for active service and stated his preference for the Pacific Station. His wish was granted, and he was named to succeed Commodore Claxton in command of the Pacific Squadron.[1] The old frigate *United States* was refitted to relieve her equally aged sister as flagship, and early in 1842 Commodore Jones sailed to take up his command.

The outward passage was uneventful, except for the fact that the run to Rio de Janeiro revealed that the *"States* frigate" could not face Cape Horn seas until she had been recaulked. This evidence of incompetence at the navy yards was nothing unusual, but Commodore Jones, enraged at a delay that might cause him to face a winter passage around the Horn, wrote one of those letters which help to explain his unpopularity with senior officers:

> The history of repairs put upon this ship at Boston, New York and Norfolk within three years past, not only proves great incompetency somewhere, but readily accounts for the enormous, and I might say, criminal waste of public treasure appropriated for the Navy.[2]

This direct affront to the senior officers commanding those yards, and to the Board of Navy Commissioners, under whose jurisdiction such affairs came, could hardly have led these men to feel favorably toward its author.

The Welshman from Virginia took drastic action to end another practice which was against the public interest. Even as they had in Captain Ridgely's time, midshipmen were becoming involved in arguments which had to be settled on the field of honor. The commodore was responsible for the training of the "young gentlemen" and so felt constrained to curb dueling immediately. His remedy was that

59

which Ridgely had tried earlier—a pledge that they would abstain before allowing them to go ashore—and the result was the same. Midshipman Thomas B. Shubrick, of the South Carolina naval family, was the first to submit his warrant on the ground that no gentleman could accept such tyrannical treatment. Secretary Upshur, himself a Southern gentleman, agreed; Commodore Jones's action was strongly disapproved by the Navy Department. As before, no better solution to the problem was suggested.

The arrival of the *United States* in the Pacific was not an entirely happy one. Captain Turner had sailed for home, leaving Captain Aulick of the *Yorktown* as senior officer. The latter had expected orders to remain in command of the Pacific Squadron—in spite of the fact that he had only recently been promoted to captain—and was mortified to learn that the command had been given to Jones. He was so unwise as to show his disappointment in his relations with the commodore, who showed a tolerance and understanding unusual for him before relieving Aulick of his command. Even then, he took pains to point out that his action was due entirely to the fact that Aulick was too senior in rank to continue in command of a third-class sloop-of-war, and there was no command suitable for him in the squadron.

Jones's sailing orders reflected the uncertainty felt with regard to Pacific area affairs in December 1841. The Oregon question was unsettled, American relations with Mexico were tense, Great Britain had just taken possession of New Zealand to keep France from occupying it, and it seemed quite likely that the powers would attempt to acquire additional territory in the region. As a result:

You will therefore omit no opportunity of affording them [Jones's officers and men] occupation and excitement by keeping your ships in motion as much as possible without losing sight of other objects, frequently exercising your guns, clearing the ships for action, exemplifying the arrangements necessary in the alarms of fire, and as often as they shall be together, passing them through such manouvers [sic] as their limited number will permit, so that should it ever be their fortune to be called upon to act in concert, the officers and men will not be taken altogether by surprise.[3]

Here was something new; for the first time the Pacific Squadron was to be what its name implied.

Gathering the ships of his command, Commodore Jones proceeded to carry out that part of his orders referring to squadron maneuvers. An unusually long passage from Callao to Valparaiso was explained by the constant exercises. Most of the officers had never seen warships sailed in this fashion, and the "excitement" desired by Upshur was not lacking. Tacking, wearing, making and shortening sail together, all required a degree of precision undreamt of in handling a single ship. Moreover, this force was hardly homogeneous, either in size or in sailing qualities. The flagship had won for herself the reputation of being the fastest frigate in the world since, some years earlier, it had been found that trimming by the head had remedied her previously poor sailing.[4] The sloops *Cyane* and *Dale* nearly equaled the *States* frigate on most points of sailing, while the *Yorktown* and *Shark* lagged far astern.

These maneuvers revealed clearly the limitations of the visual signal code then in use in the United States Navy. Most commodores had either substituted their own codes, or had dispensed with visual signals almost entirely—a lieutenant of the *United States* told Jones that he had served in the Pacific earlier with a commodore who made signals only twice during his entire cruise. Commodore Jones had devised a code which he hoped might become the standard for the Navy, but this seems never to have been adopted.

Before Commodore Jones receives full credit for transforming a group of individual ships into an efficient squadron, it is well to consider his plans for the number and employment of vessels on Pacific Station:

. . . My plan for the employment of a naval force on this station, if I had the requisite number of vessels, would be to keep one constantly cruizing between Conception and Callao, one at Callao, one between Callao and Panama, one on the coast of Mexico, and Gulph of Calafornia [sic], one on the coast of Calafornia, and N.W. coast, and two among the Islands, one entering and the other leaving at the same time. . . .[5]

He went on to point out that this would require seven vessels, exclusive of the flagship and her tender, a Baltimore schooner of superior sailing qualities. The ships would change stations every four months, so that each would visit every station twice during a three-year cruise. No doubt this would have kept the ships employed under way, but what about squadron maneuvers similar to those then being

practiced, to the enthusiasm of the junior officers? This plan made
no allowance for periodic rendezvous for that purpose at all, and
one is forced reluctantly to conclude that Commodore Jones was no
more advanced than his naval brethren as regards the value of the
squadron maneuvering as a whole.

In one respect, however, he proved that he was not averse to
change. The earlier quoted plan for employment of the Pacific
Squadron ended with this statement:

> Two 2^d class steamers would well perform the work of three or more
> sail vessels and there is no station where they could be employed to more
> advantage or with less expense than this. Coal at Talcahuano [Chile] is
> cheaper than anywhere in the U.S., and it is also said to abound on the
> Mexican coast.[6]

Alas, coal did not abound on the Mexican coast, and that at Talcahuano proved very unsatisfactory as steaming coal, but there
could be little doubt that steamers would be very useful on Pacific
Station. In time they would come, but Thomas ap Catesby Jones was
never to direct the movements of a squadron of war-steamers.

As August 1842 drew toward its close, Commodore Jones was at
Callao with his flagship, and the *Cyane, Dale,* and *Shark.* There was
a feeling of tension in the air—rumors of war between Mexico and
the United States flew about; France had just taken the Marquesas
and Washington Islands and was casting a covetous glance at Tahiti,
a glance soon to be supplemented by the thunder of French guns as
the empire of Louis Philippe was again enlarged. No one could foresee the final outcome of the situation in Oregon where the joint
Anglo-American possession seemed likely to be short-lived. It would
not have been surprising had an occasional twinge of excitement
joined the usual twinges of pain caused by the British musketball
still lodged in Commodore Jones's shoulder.

On 27 August, HMS *Dublin,* the flagship of British Rear Admiral
Richard Thomas, arrived at Callao, and the American commodore
was invited on board to dinner. In return, the latter issued an invita-
tion for Thomas to dine on board the *United States.* Meanwhile, the
British consul at Callao died, and the senior officers of foreign war-
ships present attended the funeral as a matter of course. There, a
Peruvian diplomat told Jones of a secret mission upon which the
British squadron was soon to sail. On 5 September, the mail steamer

from Panama arrived at Callao, and soon afterward, HMS *Dublin* weighed anchor and stood out; Jones's dinner for the British admiral would never be served.

The same steamer had brought Commodore Jones disturbing news. Not only was there information leading observers to believe that Mexico was already at war with the United States, but a letter from the American consul at Mazatlán furthered this belief. Moreover, Boston newspapers contained the news that Mexico had ceded Upper California to Great Britain for seven millions of dollars and a British guarantee of Mexico's possession of Lower California. Her Majesty's Pacific Squadron, the report continued, was to call at Panama to embark troops sent from the British West Indies for the occupation of Upper California.

Commodore Jones knew of his country's interest in California; he himself considered it the most important area in the eastern Pacific, after the Hawaiian Islands. Some years earlier Secretary of State John Forsyth had been directed to offer $500,000 for San Francisco Bay and the region to the north, but Mexico had refused. Prevented by adverse winds from hurrying after the British, Jones conferred with the American chargé d'affaires at Lima. The diplomat agreed that everything tended to confirm the newspaper report, and that the country's interests demanded that the commodore act to prevent British occupation of California. He could only recommend action, however; the responsibility was Jones's alone.

At Callao, the wind veered fair on 7 September, and Jones got his ships under way, leaving a letter explaining his intentions for Lieutenant-Commandant John S. Nicholas of the *Yorktown,* then absent on a cruise to the southward. One day out, the ships backed main topsails long enough for their commanding officers to board the flagship. Captain James Armstrong of the *United States,* the *Cyane*'s Commander Cornelius K. Stribling, and Commander Thomas A. Dornin of the *Dale* gathered in the frigate's flag-cabin where their commodore laid before each a letter summarizing briefly the evidence which had caused him to order them to sea. Each concurred in his decision to occupy Monterey.

With this support for his intended action, Jones ordered the squadron to keep on to the northward. The three square-riggers were able to maintain an approximately equal pace, but the little *Shark,* feeling all of her twenty-one years, lagged behind and was ordered back to Callao. Off Panama, the *Dale* was detached to carry the commodore's dispatches for transmission to Washington, while the flagship and the *Cyane* kept on for Monterey. Off that port, they spoke the merchantman *Fama* who confirmed the news of war with Mexico, and on 19 October their anchors splashed to the bottom of Monterey Harbor.

Neither British warship nor British soldier was to be seen, so it was apparent that Jones had won his race. No preparations for defense had been made ashore, and the governor acceded to Captain Armstrong's demand that he surrender. On the next day, the American flag was hoisted over the capital of Upper California, and the American occupation had begun.

But it did not continue for long. Commodore Jones's eloquent proclamation had hardly been completed when it became apparent that someone was acting on erroneous information. The townspeople knew of no war, and an American whaler in the harbor was equally mystified. Jones wrote the United States Minister at Mexico City:

The day after the capitulation, I ascertained satisfactorily that as late as Aug. 25, 1842, no act of hostility had been committed against the U.S. by Mexico, from which I infered [*sic*] that the crisis in the dispute with that Country had terminated amicably;—whereupon I immediately restored the Mexican flag and authority over Monterey, *in all due form and ceremony,* and interchanged friendly salutations and visits.[7]

Jones understandably omitted a detail of the lowering of the American flag. His son, the *Cyane*'s Midshipman Meriwether Patterson Jones, was sent ashore for this purpose, but he dramatically proclaimed that he would never strike the American flag; then he drank too much whiskey and rolled down a cliff. Young Jones, in a pleasantly relaxed state, was not badly hurt by his fall, but another had to haul down the flag.

The local authorities were inclined to view the whole mistaken occupation lightly, and a round of entertainment for the American officers preceded their departure. The merchants of the community were gratified to receive full payment for all commodities supplied the warships, especially since Mexican forces rarely paid for anything.

Unfortunately, the Mexican government could not share the attitude of its representative at Monterey. The United States disavowed the act of the too-zealous commodore, and Commodore Alexander J. Dallas was ordered to the Pacific by way of Panama to relieve Jones of his command. Upshur made it clear to the Welshman that this course was necessary to appease the Mexican demands and was in no sense an official judgment of his proceeding. But this letter did not reach Jones for some months because it was entrusted to Commodore Dallas.

It is very difficult to judge Jones harshly for acting indiscreetly. In a very real sense, he was a victim of the communications difficulty earlier pointed out. Everything led him to believe that his information was correct, and those with whom he conferred, concurred in his decision. He had received no orders from the Navy Department since his departure from the United States. As soon as his error became apparent, he restored Monterey to its rightful government, and it is obvious that his conduct was correct for the local authorities took no offense, nor were there any serious claims for indemnification of damage. Perhaps he should have taken more pains to learn the true state of affairs upon his arrival at Monterey. But this would have given the Mexicans time to prepare their defenses, and his force, a frigate and a sloop-of-war, was small enough in all conscience. Moreover, he expected British warships and soldiers to arrive at any time. Of one thing we may be sure—had the rumors been true, and had Jones failed to act, he would have faced official inquiry on much more serious charges.

It is less easy to understand the commodore's attitude toward his recall. He must have realized that Mexico would accept nothing less as evidence of American good faith; yet he continued to act as though he expected the Navy Department to overlook his excusable error. After his eventual return to the United States, he persisted in his demands that he be returned to command the Pacific Squadron and refused all other posts offered by the Secretary. His querulous letters accusing his superiors of treating him unjustly must have made him enemies he could ill afford, and even his strongest supporters must have found his conduct trying.

After leaving Monterey, Jones had cruised leisurely along the California coast, touching at many ports and giving evidence of his friendship for Mexico. He had transferred his flag to the *Cyane* and sent the *United States* to Honolulu to load provisions for the squadron. The "Old Waggon" belied her nickname and early reputation by returning to Monterey thirty-one days after she had cleared that port. Four days of that period had been spent at Oahu. Jones considered this to be the "most extraordinary voyage ever made under canvas."[8] At Los Angeles, Jones conferred with Mexican General Micheltorena who had led a military force toward Monterey when its seizure was reported. The meeting was quite amicable, although Jones refused to entertain seriously the Mexican's demand that he be reimbursed for damage to uniforms during his forced march.

Having completed the round of friendly visits, the ships stood southward to Valparaiso. Here, there is reason to believe that Commodore Jones heard that his relief was on the way to the Pacific Station. At any rate, the *United States* sailed for the Hawaiian Islands soon after she had arrived at Valparaiso, supposedly because the Pacific islands had been largely neglected during Jones's cruise. However, it was believed in Valparaiso that the commodore did not wish to be relieved until his normal tenure of command had expired, and so sought to avoid Commodore Dallas in the more remote waters of the Pacific Station. In support of this view, there is the incident recorded years afterward by a distinguished officer who had been a midshipman in the *United States*. During this island cruise, a sudden squall carried away the frigate's main topgallant mast and the commodore's broad pennant at the main truck also fell "by the run." This being mentioned to the officer of the deck, he remarked that it did not matter since the pennant had been kept aloft "by the run" for some time. Moreover, the *United States* went first to Oahu and then stood to the southward through the other island groups, whereas the normal track for island cruising was just the reverse of this because of prevailing winds. Whether or not Jones had definite word of his impending relief, all events made it seem that he was trying to avoid anyone desirous of meeting him.

Arriving at Honolulu, Commodore Jones found that he was not the only naval officer who had taken possession of a foreign territory without authorization from his government. At the request of the British consul, Admiral Thomas had sent the sloop-of-war HMS *Carysfort* to Honolulu to protect British interests. The sloop's Captain Lord George Paulet presented a series of demands to the King of the Hawaiian Islands, and that monarch agreed to cede his kingdom to Great Britain on 25 February 1843. Not long afterward, the American sloop-of-war *Boston* came in with dispatches from Commodore Lawrence Kearny of the East India Station, and remained at Honolulu to ensure that American interests did not suffer under British rule. Early in July, Commodore Kearny arrived in the *Constellation,* and immediately registered a strong protest against the cession. A few weeks later, Rear Admiral Thomas himself arrived on the scene and promptly disavowed Paulet's action. The Hawaiian Islands were thereupon returned to their monarch, and the British rule was ended after five months. Thus, the situation had already been resolved when the flagship of the Pacific Squadron stood into the harbor at Honolulu.

At least one officer had no doubt as to the true reason for Jones's island cruise. Commodore Alexander J. Dallas was surprised to find that no vessel of the Pacific Squadron awaited him at Panama. He made his way to Callao, and there found only the schooner *Shark,* although he might reasonably have expected to find several American warships at that port. But the *Shark* was a man-o'-war, so he broke his broad pennant in her and assumed command of the Pacific Squadron on 12 July 1843. A letter was left for Jones, and the new flagship set out in pursuit of the old. It was a long chase, and for the next few months the few people who were aware of the situation could laugh at the comic spectacle of one commodore chasing another through the eastern Pacific.

Dallas met the storeship *Erie* in the course of his pursuit, and shifted his flag to her—she was faster and more comfortable than the little *Shark,* but was no more successful in catching the flying Welshman. Dallas continued to dispatch letters after his predecessor even while continuing the pursuit. Jones finally received official word of his relief from French Rear Admiral Dupetit-Thouars at Nukahiva. In accordance with the implied desires of the Navy Department, the commodore headed toward Callao, where, for all he knew, Dallas was awaiting his arrival. On the way, he touched at Tahiti and there received a letter from Dallas which stated that his presence was desired in the United States as soon as possible. Commodore Kearny in the *Constellation* was likely to be at Valparaiso, and to that port Jones sailed in hope of getting passage.

The retiring commander in chief did not find the *Constellation* at Valparaiso, but he did find more letters from Dallas. These contained conflicting instructions, and Jones was left to ponder whether he should await Dallas at Callao or return home immediately. Probably he had no desire to meet his irate successor, but it did seem more important that he return to the United States, and so to Callao he went to join Kearny in the latter's flagship.

Dallas had accused Jones of deliberately avoiding him and this accusation could not go unanswered. The Welshman was quite blunt in his rejoinder:

> That the activity of the Squadron under my command, and the punctual movements of my Flag Ship, should strike you with surprise is not very unnatural, when compared with the indolence of my Predecessors on this, and I may add, on most other stations, where a Broad Pendant has flown since you and I entered the Navy.[9]

This aspersion on the activities of such revered naval officers as Charles Stewart, Isaac Hull, Jacob Jones, and their fellows, would have been most unwise under any circumstances, and its effect on Dallas was immediate. He wrote the Secretary of the Navy:

> Commodore Jones' entire conduct since his knowledge of the intention of the Govt. to relieve him from the command of the Pacific Station, and also his disobedience of my orders, render it necessary that I should particularly call the attention of the Dept. to the same and request that he be placed on his trial before a Court Martial.[10]

However, Jones arrived in the United States to find that his fellow Virginian, John Y. Mason, was Secretary of the Navy. After reviewing the evidence, the latter decided that Dallas had been correct in assuming command of the squadron when he did, but that Jones also had acted properly in continuing to exercise his command until he received official notice of his relief. No action on Dallas's charges was taken, and Jones was not censured for the Monterey episode.

Commodore Dallas did not have long to enjoy his command in the Pacific. The *Savannah* frigate came out to carry his broad pennant, and in her he resumed the normal round of visits to Callao and Valparaiso. He complained that his health had been impaired by the discomforts suffered in small vessels during the pursuit of Commodore Jones (Dr. Maxwell thought it in large part attributable to overindulgence in strong drink). Dallas finally decided to return home as his illness was growing worse. Accordingly, orders were drawn up for Captain James Armstrong of the *United States* to assume command of the squadron pending the arrival of Dallas's relief.

The *States* frigate stood into the anchorage at Callao on 5 June 1844, and her officers observed that the flags of all ships present were at half-mast, while the American warships were firing minute guns. Commodore Alexander J. Dallas had died on board the *Savannah* on the preceding day. Armstrong immediately assumed command of the flagship and of the Pacific Squadron, the *Cyane*'s Commander Stribling took charge of the *United States* which was to return home, and Commander George N. Hollins shifted from the *Savannah* to the *Cyane*. Arrangements were made for Dallas's interment at Lima, notwithstanding the late commodore's request that he be buried at sea.

The Dallas-Jones episode had an ironic sequel. When the latter again assumed command of the Pacific Squadron in 1848, his first duty upon arriving at Callao was to supervise the disinterment of Dallas's remains for return to the United States. As chief mourner, Commodore Jones occupied a place in the boat immediately astern of that bearing the coffin to the storeship *Erie;* finally Commodore Dallas had caught up with Commodore Jones.

Captain Armstrong's interim command was not so eventful as the cruises of his immediate predecessors. He engaged in a controversy with the Peruvian government and with the American chargé at Lima over the practice of sending carpenters from the ships of his squadron to repair American merchantmen in Peruvian harbors. Local shipwrights not unnaturally felt that this business should go to them, and complained bitterly. The chargé thought their arguments reasonable, but Armstrong did not believe that he should depart from the established practice. Repeated remonstrances by the chargé were finally effective, but Armstrong retained the right to assist merchant vessels whenever it seemed that local prices were unduly high. Since naval personnel so employed were not supposed to receive any compensation in addition to their normal pay, American shipowners were eager to avail themselves of the services of experienced naval carpenters, rather than pay often exorbitant sums for the doubtful repairs made by local laborers.

Meanwhile, in San Francisco Bay General Micheltorena was showing his resentment against Americans by ordering their whaleships to anchor in an area inconvenient for taking on wood and water, and by imposing irksome restrictions on their barter with the Californians. The whalers appealed to Captain Armstrong, and he took the flagship to Monterey for a conference with Micheltorena. Perhaps the *Savannah*'s 32-pounders were the convincing argument; at any rate, the general promptly removed the restrictions. Once more the whalers could anchor off Sausalito and trade for produce with only nominal regulations to observe.

When news of Dallas's death had reached Washington, Commodore John D. Sloat had been ordered to assume command of the Pacific Squadron. He arrived at Callao to find only the *Shark* present. Armstrong had left no indication of his intended movements; indeed, he had left no information at all to guide his successor. Sloat was critical of the officer who had left the vast American commerce in the southeastern Pacific virtually without protection, and for a time it seemed that Dallas's chase of Jones all over the eastern Pacific might be re-enacted. However, Armstrong was not seeking to avoid his relief, and Sloat was able to break his broad pennant in the *Savannah* at Callao on 20 March 1845.

Strong apprehension still existed that Mexico might cede California to Great Britain in exchange for sizable loans, and Sloat was cautioned to guard against this contingency. His squadron was to be concentrated on the Mexican coast to assure American merchant shipping of protection, but the commodore was to do everything possible to maintain harmonious relations with Mexican officials. Somewhat later, Secretary of the Navy George Bancroft sent out orders for Commodore Foxhall A. Parker, returning with the East India Squadron, to remain on the Mexican coast with Sloat. If Parker himself desired to return home, he could do so in a merchantman or across the Isthmus of Panama. Or, if he wished, he could assume command on the Pacific Station (he was senior to Sloat), but in any event, his ships were to remain with the Pacific Squadron. However, Parker did not receive the order in time and took most of his squadron back to the United States. Only the *Constitution* was retained by Sloat for some months.

Meanwhile, Anglo-American relations were strained over the Oregon Country, and Commodore Sloat soon felt the superiority of British sea power. The Pacific Squadron went to Callao for supplies during the summer, there finding Rear Admiral Sir George Seymour in the British battleship *Collingwood* in company with a frigate, two sloops, and a steamer. The British squadron was about to sail for Tahiti, but a mail steamer brought news of the passage of the Oregon Bill by Congress and of the annexation of Texas by the United States. For nearly a month this formidable force watched the much smaller American squadron, and the latter could not put to sea for want of supplies. Relations between the two squadrons were friendly, Sloat reported, but:

> . . . I had not the least doubt that if his dispatches from his govt. would have justified him, he would have immediately attacked me, without the least regard to the neutrality of the port, and I was fully prepared for such an event, being entirely confident that the Peruvian govt. would not fire a gun for my protection or to sustain the neutrality of their port.[11]

The commodore's letter went on to advise Bancroft of the inferiority of his force and of the lack of any safe port on his entire station in event of war with Great Britain or France.

However, the next steamer brought dispatches that led Seymour to depart for Tahiti with his squadron, and Sloat could relax once more.

Then came news of trouble between American diplomatic representatives and the government of the Hawaiian Islands, so Sloat got under way for Honolulu where he arrived in September. Seemingly the difficulty had begun when American Commissioner George Brown claimed that an American citizen charged with rape of an Hawaiian girl was entitled to trial by a foreign jury. The local government refused to concede this point, and claimed that Brown was the author of anonymous letters containing "offensive attacks on the characters of some of H. M. ministers." The commissioner had been interdicted from further correspondence with the Hawaiian government, and all American affairs were in the care of the consul. Brown asked Sloat not to render the usual salutes, but the naval officer felt such a course would be unwise and refused to comply. After a month of meetings with Brown and the government, Sloat decided that both were wrong. The King and his advisers were favorably impressed by the commodore, but refused to settle the affair and conclude a treaty with the United States. Sloat could not well prolong his absence from the coast; accordingly, he left the consul to exercise the duties of the commissioner until a relief for Brown could be sent out. Pending settlement of the controversy, American citizens were to be accorded the privileges given Englishmen and Frenchmen under the existing treaties between their governments and the Hawaiian Islands.

While the commodore was at Honolulu, the *Constitution* arrived on her way to the United States from Asiatic waters. Captain "Mad Jack" Percival was informed that Sloat felt it necessary to detain his frigate for service with the Pacific Squadron. Before "Old Ironsides" stood out for Mexico, Dr. G. P. Judd, Hawaiian Minister of Foreign Affairs, who well remembered the Paulet incident, asked the frigate's lieutenant of Marines to survey the Honolulu region with a view toward planning fortifications against foreign aggression. Lieutenant I. W. Curtis made the desired survey secretly, and recommended that Pearl Harbor be developed as a fortified base. Nothing came of this, but Curtis was among the first to realize the potential importance of Pearl Harbor.

Back on the Mexican coast, conditions seemed unchanged, and Sloat settled down to await information definite enough to justify action under the "secret and confidential" orders sent out by Bancroft:

. . . Should Mexico, however, be resolutely bent on hostilities, you will be mindful to protect the persons and interests of citizens of the United States near your station, and should you ascertain beyond a doubt, that the Mexican Government has declared war against us, you will at once employ the force under your command to the best advantage. The Mexican ports on the Pacific are said to be open and defenseless. If you ascertain with certainty that Mexico has declared war against the United States, you will at once possess yourself of the port of San Francisco, and blockade or occupy such other ports as your force may permit. . . .

The great distance of your squadron, and the difficulty of communicating with you, are the causes for issuing this order. The President hopes, most earnestly, that the peace of the two Countries may not be disturbed. The object of these instructions is to possess you of the views of the Government, in the event of a declaration of war on the part of Mexico against the United States; an event which you are enjoined to do everything, consistent with the national honor, on your part to avoid.[12]

But if peace should continue, there were other important duties to be performed by the Pacific Squadron. Sloat was directed to send an exploring party to show the flag in the Columbia and Willamette valleys in order to gain information about those regions and to convince American citizens that they were not being neglected. Afterward, the party might proceed overland to Puget Sound to gain information as to the strength of British posts in that area and to survey Vancouver Island.

However, this was a mission to be undertaken "should peace continue," and as yet the threat of war was undiminished. Therefore, November 1845 found the Pacific Squadron concentrated at the Mexican port of Mazatlán, chosen because messages sent overland across Mexico could reach Sloat there at the earliest moment. However, this display of force was alarming to the inhabitants of Mazatlán, so the commodore separated his vessels. The *Shark* was absent to the southward, the flagship *Savannah* remained at Mazatlán, and the other ships were sent to make surveys and to inquire into conditions at various California ports.

At least one of these visits resulted in a humorous incident which helped to confirm Sloat's belief that most of the Mexican harbors were virtually unprotected. The sloop-of-war *Levant* touched at La Paz, capital of Lower California, and Commander Hugh N. Page was amazed when several magistrates boarded his ship to surrender the town. The governor, without means to protect the place and sure that the *Levant*'s appearance confirmed the rumors of war, decided that he could only yield immediately. Instead, Page graciously accepted the hospitality of the townspeople. Some of his officers even visited silver mines forty miles inland, and reported that the populace was most friendly. The *Levant* was the first American man-o'-war to touch at La Paz, but she would be followed by others, not on friendly visits.

As spring came on, Commodore Sloat continued the dispersal of his forces. The *Cyane,* newly arrived from the United States, was sent to Oahu for supplies and thence to Monterey; the sloop-of-war *Warren* and the storeship *Erie* were ordered to follow the same route soon afterward; and the *Portsmouth* sloop was designated for the Columbia River mission. On second thought, Sloat diverted the *Portsmouth* to Monterey and thence to San Francisco, while the *Shark* carried out the sloop's original orders. It was the last mission for the veteran schooner. The *Shark* joined the *Peacock* as a victim of the Columbia River bar on 10 September 1846, but Lieutenant Neil M. Howison and his ship's company reached the shore safely.

In the meantime, Sloat had other problems as well. Captain Percival reported that the *Constitution* was no longer fit for service, and the *Levant* and *Warren* were in little better condition. The *Savannah*'s crew was also becoming troublesome; enlistments would soon expire for most of her men, and while they could be held with a twenty-five per cent increase in pay, this was not a sufficient enticement. Appeals to their patriotism were meaningless for many were foreigners. Moreover, there was danger that officers ordering punishment to men so held might have to face civil lawsuits upon their return to the United States. However, there could be no thought of detaching the *Savannah* at that time; the *Constitution* had already weighed anchor homeward bound, so the flagship remained the only large ship in the squadron.

Information had reached Sloat by the *Cyane* that Commodore Robert F. Stockton was on his way to the Pacific in the *Congress* frigate with orders to transfer her to Sloat, while he shifted his broad pennant to the *Savannah* and sailed for the United States in company with the *Levant* and *Warren*. If Sloat was in ill health, he might order Stockton to relieve him as commander in chief of the Pacific Squadron, but not otherwise. When one considers the strain under which Commodore Sloat had served during his cruise in the Pacific, it is not surprising that his health should have suffered. In March, he reported that he was "suffering severely with a diseased liver, Rheumatism, and neuralgia," while early in May, his health was "declining rapidly & becoming very precarious."[13] But Stockton had been ordered to take a new commissioner to the Hawaiian Islands before joining the Pacific Squadron, and there could be no thought of Sloat's leaving the station for some time yet.

Sloat remained at Mazatlán in the *Savannah* during the month of May. The *Cyane* joined him and, on 18 May, was ordered to Monterey with a letter for Consul Thomas O. Larkin. Sloat knew of the attack by Mexican troops on American forces north of the Rio Grande, but was not certain that this would lead to war; accordingly, he cautioned the sloop's Captain William Mervine to make no mention of the occurrence. If, however, Mervine learned that a state of war existed, he was to take any measures necessary to prevent Mexican cruisers from putting to sea. Finally:

> Should you fall in with a fast sailing vessel under Mexican colours that would answer for a small cruiser or dispatch vessel you will capture her and take her with you, but you will be careful not to let it be known that she is a prize, you will take out every person belonging to her and be careful on your arrival at Monterrey [*sic*] or San Francisco that these persons have no communication with anyone, until my arrival. . . .[14]

Sloat wanted to be sure that no action of the ships under his command was responsible for the outbreak of war, but he need not have worried; on 13 May, Bancroft had sent official notice of the beginning of hostilities. Commodore David Conner, commanding the Home Squadron in the Gulf of Mexico, was also ordered to relay the news to Sloat, but the messengers so sent could not reach Mazatlán for some weeks.

Hence the *Savannah* remained at Mazatlán, closely watched by vessels of Sir George Seymour's British squadron. The American commodore believed that the British had no designs on California, and were merely interested in his movements because of the Oregon situation. At any rate, it was useless to ask for reinforcements: ". . . it is immaterial what force we have here, they will always send double."[15]

On 31 May, Sloat received news of the battles of Palo Alto and Resaca de la Palma. Surely this meant war, so the *Savannah* weighed anchor and put to sea. But on 5 June, she returned to her usual anchorage.

The meaning of this false start has received some attention from historians, and there is a persistent story that Sloat meant it to throw the British off their guard. According to this story, the *Savannah* stood out for the purpose of hanging a man condemned by court-martial; the sentence (reduced to 100 lashes) having been carried out, she returned to harbor. In a few days, the ship would signal once more that she was getting under way for that reason, but this time she would head for Monterey.

However, no official document supports this story. It is almost inconceivable that Sloat would have omitted it in his reports to Bancroft, but no mention of it is made. Instead, the commodore's coded letter on the subject reads in part:

. . . I have upon more mature reflection come to the decision that your instructions of twenty fourth June last and every subsequent order will not justify my taking possession of any part of California or any hostile measure against Mexico (notwithstanding their attack on our troops) as neither party have declared war. . . .[16]

With this in mind, it is not difficult to understand the *Savannah*'s return to Mazatlán. Sloat did indeed intend to proceed to Monterey when he sailed on 31 May, but once at sea, he had time to think over the situation. Battles did not necessarily lead to a declaration of war, but if the issue was not yet decided, a repetition of Commodore Jones's occupation of Monterey would almost certainly bring on a war. On the other hand, the *Levant* and *Cyane* were at Monterey, the *Portsmouth* was at San Francisco, and there was no Mexican force to oppose them. Admiral Seymour was at Panama, and so was in no position to intervene in Upper California. Under these circumstances, it is probable that Commodore Sloat required no other motive for his return to Mazatlán than to await more definite information of war.

It was not long in coming. The *Savannah*'s anchor was weighed once more and she made sail on 8 June. She rounded Cape San Lucas, and Commodore Sloat ordered her put on a course for Monterey.

6. *Too Many Commodores*

The strong American interest in California which has been noted was increased by reports that the people of that region were apathetic, or even disloyal, to the Mexican government. Thomas O. Larkin, a prominent merchant of New England origin serving as American consul at Monterey, had been appointed a confidential agent in 1845 by Secretary of State James Buchanan, with instructions to encourage a pro-American feeling among the Californians and to minimize the influence of foreign agents, especially those of the British government. Buchanan hoped that it might be possible to win California without engaging in a war with Mexico, much as had been done in the case of Texas.

In June 1845, an expedition of U.S. Army Topographical Engineers, commanded by Captain John C. Frémont, had set out from the United States, and arrived at Sutter's Fort in northern California early in 1846. Ostensibly its mission was the improvement of communications between the United States and Oregon, so its presence was tolerated by the Mexican authorities. Actually, Frémont seems to have worked all along to further the disaffection of the Californians from Mexican control. He and his men assisted in the formation of the Bear Flag Republic which declared its independence from Mexico on 14 June 1846, an action which alienated many prominent Californians and brought Larkin's efforts largely to naught.

The USS *Savannah* joined the *Cyane* and the *Levant* at Monterey on 2 July, but Commodore Sloat did not take possession of the town at once. He obtained permission from the civil authorities to grant liberty to the flagship's company, and he conferred with Larkin at some length. We do not know what transpired during these conversations, but it seems likely that Sloat was remembering the caution enjoined by Bancroft's orders. Larkin wanted him to act on

4 July, and it may be that his urgings finally nerved the "wavering Commodore" to take the crucial step. At any rate, on 6 July Sloat sent word of his intended action to the *Portsmouth*'s Commander John B. Montgomery at San Francisco, together with orders to take possession there if his force were strong enough, or to await the arrival of the irregular troops raised and led by Frémont if necessary. On the next day, 7 July, Captain Mervine led a landing party which hoisted the American flag at Monterey. Larkin wrote Commander Montgomery:

> 10 o clock [*sic*]
> The Step is taken
> The Deed is done
> The Flag is flying[1]

Officers from the warships were appointed to act as temporary civil officials, and arms were furnished to equip small bodies of cavalry recruited and commanded by naval officers. A leading part in the latter work was taken by Lieutenant Archibald H. Gillespie, U.S. Marine Corps, a secret envoy of President James K. Polk and bearer of dispatches for Sloat and Frémont.

Montgomery received his orders on 8 July and sent a party of sailors and Marines to take possession of Yerba Buena on the following morning. Again, no opposition was encountered, and the *Portsmouth*'s officers assumed civil duties temporarily. The commander had to summon his subordinates on board hastily on 11 July when an unidentified warship was reported standing into the bay. She proved to be HMS *Juno* of twenty-eight guns, and the Americans feared that the expected British intervention was at hand. The Briton, however, accepted the situation calmly, supposing that Sloat had given his orders in accordance with instructions from the United States. Nevertheless, Montgomery soon consolidated his position by building a shore battery mounting a number of old cannon brought from former Mexican posts in the vicinity. Its construction was directed by Lieutenant John S. Missroon, and although the work was called Fort Montgomery, the sweating sailors quickly dubbed it "Missroon's Folly."

Meanwhile Sloat continued to employ his ships at Monterey in support of the comparatively weak landing parties. This would seem to have been an obvious precaution, but when Frémont arrived at

Monterey with his irregulars, he protested against the commodore's inactivity. Sloat, however, was unwilling to enter into close co-operation with Frémont on the ground that the legal status of the latter's force was uncertain. Gillespie joined Frémont in urging a more active policy, but to no avail since the naval officer distrusted the Marine's political maneuverings also.

At this point, the USS *Congress* arrived at Monterey, flying the broad pennant of Commodore Robert F. Stockton. And on the next day, 16 July, HM line-of-battleship *Collingwood,* flagship of Rear Admiral Seymour, stood in and anchored. Sloat immediately sent an officer "to tender him the usual courtesies and facilities of the Port." Seymour received the American civilly enough, and accepted a set of topgallant masts and other spars for his ship. He sailed for the Hawaiian Islands a week later. Sloat reported:

> The visit of the Admiral was very serviceable to our cause in California, as the inhabitants fully believed he would take part with them and that we would be obliged to abandon our conquest, but when they saw the friendly intercourse subsisting between us, and found that he could not interfere in their behalf, they abandoned all hope of ever seeing the Mexican Flag fly in California again.[2]

No official news of the declaration of war had yet been received when Stockton arrived at Monterey, and his letters implied disapproval of Sloat's actions on the ground that the United States would probably return Monterey and San Francisco to Mexico. This attitude likely was intended to clear Stockton of any responsibility in case there was no war; at any rate, the new arrival promptly undertook to convince Commodore Sloat that he should avail himself of the opportunity to return home on account of ill health. After conferring with kindred spirits Frémont and Gillespie, Stockton ordered them to "volunteer" to serve under his command. Sloat remained obdurate, so Stockton addressed him:

> It is very important to take General Castro or to drive him out of the country—until one or the other is done I can see no hope of restoring peace and good order to this territory.
>
> I wish to send the *Cyane* with Captain Frémont's men, to the Southward to head him off, and drive him back here.
>
> Had you not better send me an order to take command at once, and make my own arrangements.

It will facilitate operations and relieve you from a great deal of trouble.[3]

This urging was effective; Stockton assumed command on the same day, 23 July, and Sloat sailed for Panama in the *Levant* six days later. He carried a full report of his proceedings, but Bancroft did not wait for the commodore's explanations. On 13 August, the Secretary sent the erstwhile commander in chief a strongly worded letter of reprimand for his unwillingness to initiate offensive action, and followed this five days later by an order for Stockton to relieve Sloat if he had not already done so. But even Bancroft could vacillate; he reinstated Sloat on 3 September.

Needless to say, Bancroft's whims had no effect on the Pacific Squadron. However, it may be well to consider the Secretary's actions. Sloat had been notified of the earnest hope of President Polk that peace might be preserved, and was particularly cautioned against any act which might precipitate hostilities.[4] Yet little over a year later, the same Secretary of the Navy was extremely critical of Sloat for his circumspection. In retrospect, it does not seem that American interests were endangered by Sloat's reluctance to act until he had received definite information. His squadron, except the flagship, was stationed ready for immediate action, and the *Cyane*'s orders of 18 May 1846 contained one section that implied a definite willingness on Sloat's part to take a risk.[5]

Frémont's biographer has characterized Commodore Sloat as "wavering, indecisive and timid."[6] Cautious the naval officer was, but there seems to be no reason to believe that he should be condemned for desiring to be sure of hostilities before acting. He knew the situation in California quite well, and no time was lost in implementing his conquests once they had been made. Stockton has escaped criticism on the same point, but the junior commodore implied that Sloat's occupation of Monterey and San Francisco was wrong some eight days after it had occurred. The Frémont biographer further states that Sloat "took himself off the scene at the earliest possible pretext."[7] This statement needs no refutation other than that contained in Stockton's Letter Book. Sloat was more cautious than Commodore Jones, with the latter's experience to guide him, but no one can fairly criticize the result of his actions.

When Commodore Sloat's broad pennant was broken in the

Levant, several officers changed commands. Stockton continued in the *Congress,* Commander Samuel F. DuPont left that vessel to relieve Captain Mervine in the *Cyane,* and the last-named took command of the *Savannah.* Gillespie was ordered to serve as Frémont's second-in-command, and the latter's riflemen were afforded every assistance from the squadron.

This military force, numbering 150 rifles, was embarked in the *Cyane,* and the sloop sailed for San Diego on 26 July. The attempt to cut General José Castro's Mexican army off from Lower California was unsuccessful, but Lieutenant Stephen C. Rowan of the *Cyane* hoisted the American flag at San Diego on 29 July. Stockton himself departed for San Pedro in the *Congress* a few days later, leaving the *Savannah* at Monterey with Mervine in charge of matters in northern California.

San Pedro and Santa Barbara were taken without trouble, and Stockton's landing party of sailors, Marines, and riflemen experienced no difficulty in occupying the *Ciudad de los Angeles.* The commodore wrote Bancroft:

Thus in less than a month after I assumed the command of the U.S. Forces in Calif., we have chased the Mexican Army more than 300 miles along the coast—pursued them 30 miles in the interior of their own country, routed and dispersed them, and secured the Territory to the U.S.— ended the war, restored peace and harmony among the people, and put a Civil govt. into successful operation. . . .[8]

He expanded on this report in a private letter to President Polk:

My word is at present the law of the land—my power is more than regal. The haughty Mexican Cavalier shakes hands with me with pleasure, and the beautiful women look to me with joy and gladness as their friend and benefactor. In short all of power and luxury is spread before me, through the mysterious workings of a beneficent Providence.

No man could or ought to desire more of power and respect, but my work is almost done here, and my duty calls me again upon the ocean, to protect as well as I may, the lives and property of our fellow citizens engaged in commerce. I will go without the least hesitation, and will transfer my power to other hands without [resisting].[9]

Frémont, promoted to the rank of lieutenant colonel by Stockton, was appointed Governor of Upper California, and the commodore returned to Monterey in the *Congress.* Gillespie was left at Los Angeles with an occupation force of forty-eight riflemen. On 19 August, Stockton proclaimed a blockade of "all ports, harbors, bays, inlets, outlets, . . . on the west coast of Mexico south of San Diego."[10] The *Cyane* and the *Warren* were sent to enforce this blockade a few days later. The two sloops-of-war found good hunting and virtually wiped out all commerce under the Mexican flag. One of the prizes was the fast New York-built brig *Malek Adhel* which was captured by a cutting-out expedition from the *Warren* at Mazatlán. She mounted ten guns and was utilized as a dispatch vessel for the Pacific Squadron. A *Cyane* prize, the schooner *Liberdad*, was also taken into the service as a tender. In spite of their success, however, it was obviously impossible for two ships to blockade some twenty-five hundred miles of coastline, and this was to cause the United States government some annoyance.

Before leaving Los Angeles, Commodore Stockton had imposed duties on all foreign ships and cargoes entering ports controlled by his forces: fifty cents per ton on shipping and fifteen per cent ad valorem on imports. These duties were extended to harbors on the Gulf of California and the Pacific coast of Mexico, as they were occupied by the Pacific Squadron, and furnished a respectable source of revenue for the United States until the end of the war.

At Monterey, the commodore found that the men of the *Savannah*, whose enlistments had all expired, were in a very disaffected state, and for this he blamed Captain Mervine. That officer seems to have been unpopular with most of his contemporaries, but it will be remembered that Sloat also had experienced difficulty with the frigate's crew before he departed.

With conditions seemingly quiet in Upper California, Frémont was sent to raise more irregular troops and to obtain additional horses. Commodore Stockton had formulated an extremely ambitious plan for his squadron and Frémont's force, nothing less than a landing at Acapulco or Mazatlán. From the debarkation port, the troops were to fight their way inland toward Mexico City. "I would that we might shake hands with General [Zachary] Taylor at the gates of Mexico."[11]

It is hardly necessary to comment on this grandiose project. Upper California was held by ridiculously small forces, two ships were blockading 2,500 miles of enemy coast, the crew of one of his two major vessels was nearly mutinous, and still Stockton could plan such a campaign. Moreover, the bulk of the invading army would have to be Frémont's poorly equipped and undisciplined riflemen. It is probably very fortunate that news reached Monterey which caused the ambitious commodore to abandon his great plan. A large party of Walla Walla Indians was said to be approaching San Francisco from the north, bent on avenging the murder of a tribesman by a white man, so Stockton sailed for that port in the *Congress* to meet the threat.

Hardly had the frigate reached San Francisco, when more serious trouble was reported. Gillespie sent word that all of southern California was in a state of rebellion. His small force had been besieged by some six hundred armed Californians, and after holding out for a week, was allowed to withdraw to a refuge on board a merchant vessel at San Pedro. It is not easy to explain this uprising, but some American officers thought it was caused by Gillespie's arrogant manner toward the proud Californians. Certainly the weakness of the occupation force must have tempted many to break their paroles.

Notwithstanding the serious nature of this crisis and the fact that his orders placed the greatest importance on American possession of Upper California, Stockton continued to await the Walla Wallas, sending only the *Savannah* to San Pedro. There, Captain Mervine carried out his orders to land a force for the purpose of recapturing Los Angeles.

The landing party, sailors and Marines together with Gillespie's riflemen, was ready to march on 7 October, but the lack of horses compelled the Americans to proceed without artillery, and Mervine's preparations in general seem to have been quite haphazard. The force encountered mounted Mexicans almost at once, and unable to match their mobility, could only beat off their harassing attacks and continue on the road to Los Angeles. A horse-drawn fieldpiece was particularly irksome, although its gunners proved less adept at hitting their targets than at removing it quickly whenever an American detachment approached. His inability to overtake this gun seems to have been an important factor in Mervine's decision to retire after his men had proceeded some thirteen miles inland. Naturally, the retreat was more difficult than the advance, for the encouraged Mexicans pressed their attacks; the landing force, correspondingly dispirited, had sustained some casualties, for whose transportation no provision had been made. The exhausted men re-embarked in the *Savannah* on 8 October, having lost four of their number killed and several wounded.

Meanwhile, Stockton had found the force of the Indians greatly exaggerated—instead of 1,000 braves seeking vengeance, Chief Yellow Serpent was followed by some forty Indians whose main interest was in trade—and news of Mervine's defeat brought the commodore south under a press of canvas.

Before he left San Francisco, Stockton had arranged with Commander Montgomery that the worn-out *Warren* should relieve the *Portsmouth* as guardship there. The latter had to await the arrival of a storeship and so was still at San Francisco when the *Warren*'s launch was sent to Sacramento with currency and $846 in gold to pay the garrison. Passed Midshipman William H. Montgomery of the *Warren* commanded the launch, and was accompanied by his brother Elliott, captain's clerk in the *Portsmouth,* and Midshipman Daniel C. Hugunin, also of the *Portsmouth*. The boat departed on 13 November and was never heard from again. The *Portsmouth* was ordered to get under way for San Diego a few days afterward, and Commander Montgomery was forced to depart before search parties could bring any news of his sons. At first it was thought that the boat had foundered in a gale one day after her departure, but almost two years later, it was reported on fairly good evidence that the boat's crew had mutinied, murdered the three young officers, and escaped to the interior. Actual proof remained lacking, although the latter account was widely believed, and no subsequent information has solved the tragic mystery.

When Commodore Stockton arrived at San Pedro, he learned that an attack on San Diego was imminent, so he ordered the *Savannah* to return to Monterey and hastened southward himself, leaving word for Montgomery to follow with the *Portsmouth*. The flagship's entry into San Diego was nearly disastrous, for she grounded on the bar, and only extreme exertions prevented her from rolling over on her beam ends. But Stockton was in time to prevent the Mexican occupation of San Diego, and began to prepare for the recapture of Los Angeles.

Meanwhile, 100 dragoons led by Brigadier General Stephen W. Kearny were coming overland from Santa Fé. As this force approached, the commodore sent a small party under Gillespie to inform the general of the existing situation. They met on 5 December and planned an attack on a smaller group of Californians in the San Pascual Valley. It was launched on the next morning and turned out badly, for the enemy withdrew with little loss after his lances had killed eighteen Americans and wounded as many more. Both Kearny and Gillespie were among the wounded, and their force, short of both food and water, encamped to await assistance from Stockton. The relief expedition, 215 strong, reached Kearny's battered command on 11 December, and escorted the dragoons into San Diego the next day.

The arrival of General Kearny led to more difficulty. By a direct order of President Polk, designed to eliminate friction between senior officers of Army and Navy, the former was in charge of all land operations, while the Navy conducted affairs in its own sphere. Thus, Kearny should have assumed command of the military forces in California, although most of the men in their ranks came from the Pacific Squadron or from Frémont's improvised regiments. But Stockton could not allow his protege, Frémont, to be ousted from the position of military governor, to which the commodore had appointed him. After some unpleasantness, Stockton did offer the command of the expedition against Los Angeles to Kearny, but the general refused to accept it as a gift at the disposal of the commodore, and chose to serve as the latter's chief of staff instead. Nevertheless, Kearny may be said to have triumphed finally. After his return to the United States, he preferred charges of insubordination against Frémont which led to that officer's trial by court-martial. He was sentenced to be dismissed from the Army, but Polk remitted the sentence, and Frémont resigned his commission.

Command difficulties having been settled for the time, Stockton turned his attention to the organization of an "army" composed of 600 sailors, Marines, and dragoons, which he led northward overland at the end of December. This time his force was adequate for its purpose, fighting and winning the battles of the San Gabriel River and La Mesa on 8 and 9 January 1847, sustaining only slight losses. Soon thereafter Frémont arrived at San Fernando with some four hundred mounted men from northern California, and faced with encirclement, the Californians capitulated at Cahuenga on

13 January. All of Upper California was again held by the Americans.

With the end of hostilities north of San Diego, the Pacific Squadron turned its attention once more to the coastline of Lower California and Mexico. Stockton's blockade had been discontinued when it became necessary to concentrate the squadron to cope with the rebellion. The *Portsmouth* went south to re-establish the blockade of Mazatlán, and there Commander Montgomery found HMS *Fisgard.* The Briton's Captain John A. Duntze took issue with the American's notice that he was renewing the blockade. Duntze was willing to acknowledge the existence of any legal blockade which might be enforced by the *Portsmouth,* but he held that the original blockade proclaimed by Commodore Stockton had, in fact, never existed because it had never been enforced by a sufficient number of warships. Therefore, Montgomery was renewing an illegal blockade, and the Royal Navy could not recognize it.

An exchange of letters between the two commanding officers followed, each citing historical precedent and quoting international law to uphold his opinion. One suspects that this correspondence was carried on with tongue in cheek, since the two men became close personal friends and dined together on occasion. In time, the *Fisgard* was relieved by HMS *Constance,* and Captain Sir Baldwin Walker took the same stand as had his predecessor. He also became a friend of the personable American commander.

The British officers were joined in their protest by the consular representatives of Prussia, Spain, and France. All requested relaxation of the blockade in favor of their ships on the ground that the merchant shipping of other nations had not been prevented from entering Mexican ports by the nonexistent cruisers.

The general language used in Stockton's blockade proclamation had already been brought to the attention of the United States government. Secretary of the Navy John Y. Mason advised the commander in chief on Pacific Station that Polk wished to avoid any inconvenience to neutral commerce, and that Stockton's proclamation had caused alarm in neutral commercial circles. He directed that the blockade be revised so as to allow trade in articles not considered contraband.

Mason did not address the commander in chief by name because no one in Washington was sure who was commanding the Pacific Squadron. Before George Bancroft left the Navy Department, he had ordered Commodore W. Branford Shubrick to the Pacific in the razee frigate *Independence*. Earlier, he had sent orders to Commodore James Biddle, commanding the East India Squadron in the line-of-battleship *Columbus,* to proceed to the Puget Sound area on an exploring mission much like that on which the *Shark* had been lost. Biddle's orders were changed when the war began, and he was directed to go to California instead.

It seems probable that Bancroft's orders to Shubrick were prompted by the news that Stockton had assumed command of the Pacific Squadron. Stockton was relatively junior and inexperienced; thus, the Navy Department likely considered him only as an interim commander.

Shubrick met Commodore Biddle at Valparaiso and was told that the latter had been ordered to look in on affairs in California, but would remain there only if the presence of the *Columbus* was necessary to ensure success in that theater. The *Independence* sailed on toward Monterey, and there Commodore Shubrick assumed command of the Pacific Squadron on 22 January 1847. On 2 March, Commodore Biddle arrived at Monterey to reveal that he had received orders to become commander in chief of the Pacific Squadron. The sensitive Shubrick thereupon asked that he be ordered home since Bancroft had showed so little confidence in his ability. Biddle carefully pointed out that this move would probably end Shubrick's naval career and would not be in the best interest of the United States. He promised to forward Shubrick's letter of protest to the Navy Department, and to give him every opportunity to serve on more or less independent missions in the meantime. Furthermore, as soon as the aged Biddle felt that he could, he would relinquish the command and sail for the United States. Shubrick accepted this generous offer, and departed to direct operations in Lower California.

Commodore Stockton's "paper" blockade had been revoked by Biddle, and its place was taken by a number of proclamations referring to specific ports which were in fact blockaded by American warships. However, it was obvious that the blockaders would be unable to keep their stations during the summer months because of the frequent storms in those waters. A blockade was not considered to have been broken if the cruisers had merely been driven off station by foul weather, but the small number of ships available, the lack of protected anchorages, and the fact that the nearest base was at Monterey, combined to make the blockade a difficult operation. Occupation of the blockaded ports by American forces would have eliminated much of the difficulty, and the United States could have imposed customs dues on all commerce using the ports. Unfortunately, there was insufficient military force to hold these ports unless some of the men-o'-war were present.

Commodore Shubrick was given the frigates *Independence* and *Congress* and the sloops *Portsmouth, Cyane,* and *Dale* to carry on operations in his area. Biddle in the *Columbus* remained on the northern coast with the *Warren* sloop, and the storeship *Erie* was armed with a light battery so that she could cruise for the protection of American commerce. The *Warren*'s condition was deemed too poor to allow her use as an active cruiser, so she combined the functions of guardship and storeship in San Francisco Bay.[12] The *Savannah* was sent home to discharge her discontented company.

The ships cruising off the coast of Lower California lost no time in occupying its principal ports—La Paz, San José del Cabo, and San Lucas—because Secretary Mason had informed Commodore Stockton that both Californias were to be retained by the United States. The actual occupation was easy in each instance, but the Mexican forces withdrew only a few miles inland and were reinforced from the mainland. Shubrick's vessels could not furnish large garrisons for these ports, nor could the ships themselves remain to keep the Mexicans at a distance. As a result, the garrisons at San José del Cabo and La Paz were subjected to bitter attacks in the succeeding autumn and winter months. Naval Lieutenant Charles Heywood and his twenty-five men at San José del Cabo were besieged for three weeks and suffered some losses before the *Cyane* arrived to relieve them in February 1848. La Paz, occupied by a small force of New York Volunteers under Lieutenant Colonel Henry S. Burton, was also beleaguered by greatly superior numbers, and only the timely assistance of a warship enabled Burton to hold his position.

Somewhat earlier, Bancroft had informed the naval commander in the Pacific that the ports farther south were thought to be disaffected from the Mexican government; accordingly, naval officers were authorized to enter into agreements with local officials who wished to remain neutral. That these agreements might leave the local inhabitants liable to punitive action by the Mexican government after the war does not seem to have occurred to Bancroft. However, the naval officers serving on Pacific Station realized their responsibility to the peoples who responded to their overtures of friendship. Some of the inhabitants of the regions occupied were won over, although there was never a wholesale secession of states from the central Mexican government. This reluctance on the part of the populace to respond to American gestures of friendship may be ascribed in part to the memory of Commodore Jones's brief occupation of Monterey. Many of the Mexicans feared that the Americans would again surrender their conquests, and in fact this did occur in part.

As operations were proceeding satisfactorily under the direction of Shubrick, Commodore Biddle decided that his presence was no longer required on Pacific Station. Therefore, he sailed for the United States in the *Columbus* after turning the station over to the junior officer in July 1847. Shubrick's assumption of the command was not accompanied by any radical change in strategy since he had had virtually a free hand before Biddle's departure. However, he did request that the *Congress* be replaced by one or more sloops, much better suited for his purposes than frigates. The third-class sloop *Preble* was already on her way out, but Shubrick would receive no other reinforcement before he was relieved.

Before Commodore Biddle sailed, he had rendered the cruising units of his squadron good service by establishing a prize court at Monterey. Thus, captured ships could be judged and sold or released, according to their guilt, without being sent around Cape Horn. Otherwise it would have been necessary for prize crews to sail the ships to the United States for adjudication—a practice which the squadron was too shorthanded to follow.

Commodore Shubrick decided to supplement the blockade by occupying as many ports as he could garrison, and to this end his vessels were employed as soon as the summer hurricane season was past. Captain Elie A. F. LaVallette took Guaymas on 20 October after an hour's bombardment by the *Congress* and *Portsmouth*. Shubrick arrived off Mazatlán on 11 November with the *Independence, Congress, Cyane,* and *Erie.* Light winds delayed the attack, but it was carried out as planned in spite of darkness. Both Shubrick's tactical planning and the manner in which it was executed won the praise of British officers who observed the attack. San Blas and Manzanillo were blockaded and then occupied in January 1848, but the few ports remaining in Mexican hands could not be occupied because of the lack of men. However, Commodore Shubrick held the commercially important towns on the Pacific coast, and to have spread his inadequate forces over a greater area would have been unwise.

Commodore Shubrick's indignant letter regarding his supersession by Biddle reached the Navy Department in the autumn of 1847, and Secretary Mason grasped the opportunity to satisfy the demand of Thomas ap Catesby Jones that he be reappointed to command the Pacific Squadron. The one obstacle standing in the way of the assignment had disappeared as soon as Mexican sensibilities had no longer to be considered, so Jones was ordered out in the line-of-battleship *Ohio.* Commodore David Geisinger accompanied him as a passenger; he was to transfer to the *Congress* and proceed to the East India Station as commander in chief.

Arriving on his station, Jones found that the *Congress* was in no condition to undertake another long cruise and that her crew's enlistments were due to expire soon; consequently, Geisinger was given the *Preble* for the East India Station. The necessity of detaching a sloop for this duty made Jones extremely critical of Commodore Shubrick for allowing the *Portsmouth* to sail for the United States because of expiring enlistments, although Mason had approved of Shubrick's action. Able Commander Montgomery had won his crew's respect and affection to a degree seldom seen, and on his recommendation Shubrick had decided that the fine sloop should be allowed to return home.

Jones relieved Commodore Shubrick on 6 May 1848, and the latter asked to be allowed to serve under his successor until the cessation of hostilities. Actually little remained to be done. It took some time for news of the Treaty of Guadalupe Hidalgo to reach the Pacific coast, but Commodore Jones had no opportunity to distinguish himself in the Mexican War. Soon after he assumed the squadron command, the *Cyane* was sent to San José del Cabo to quell a mutiny of the New York Volunteers, and this marked the end of warlike activities on the part of the Pacific Squadron.

Of the roles played by the successive commanders in chief on Pacific Station during the Mexican War, Commodore Sloat's part has already received some attention. It may be noted, however, that he prepared the way quite well for his successor's more ambitious plans. Commodore Stockton must be given due credit for his vigorous conduct of the campaign which won Upper California. It cannot be denied, however, that his conquest was endangered by the wide dispersal of his forces, and his ill-considered proclamation of blockade was an embarrassment to his government. His co-operation with Frémont and Gillespie helped to further the success of his plans, but his treatment of Kearny was neither just nor in accordance with his orders. Stockton's ambition seems never to have been curbed fully by good judgment.

Commodore Biddle took no direct part in the operations of the squadron, but his tact in dealing with the angry Shubrick probably saved a valuable officer for the United States Navy. Commodore Shubrick deserves commendation for his conduct of operations against Lower California and Mexico—one is tempted to believe that he showed more real ability than any of the other officers here considered. Commodore Jones arrived on the scene too late to affect the turn of events materially.

That the frequent changes in over-all command did not hamper the operations of the Pacific Squadron must be ascribed to the fact that the basic strategy was so obvious as to be readily acceptable to all of the senior officers concerned. This fact should not be allowed to vitiate the very undesirable aspects of no less than five changes of command in less than two years. George Bancroft, mainly responsible for this policy, can receive here no praise for his unwillingness to maintain one officer in command of the Pacific Station during that short period.

As stated, the strategy governing the Pacific Squadron during the Mexican War was sound. Upper California was secured first, and then all of the ports through which the Mexicans could receive supplies were blockaded or occupied. Virtually all of the Mexican merchant vessels in the Pacific Ocean were taken or destroyed, and the revenues resulting from opening the occupied ports to trade paid a large part of the expenses of the Pacific Squadron.

Events might have developed much differently had Admiral Seymour's British squadron become involved, but Great Britain did not desire trouble with the United States over California, and Commodore Sloat helped to ensure British friendship by his courteous reception of Seymour at Monterey in July 1846.

American possession of California was guaranteed by the success of the Army and the Navy in another theater of operations, but the Pacific coast area was seized and held by the Pacific Squadron. The activities of Kearny and Frémont were of minor importance, despite the credit given them by some historians. California might not have been won, except for the successful performance by United States Naval Forces on Pacific Station.

7. *The Gold Mania*

The acquisition of California and the concurrent settlement of the Oregon controversy afforded an extensive Pacific coastline for the United States. American claims to a vague region centered around the Columbia River mouth had given way to definite possession of the Pacific coast between the parallels of 49° and 33° North latitude. The entire area was very sparsely populated—there was not a single settlement worthy of the name of city—and of this small population, by no means a majority was American by origin. Manufacturing facilities did not exist, and the true natural wealth of the region was unknown. Nor was the addition of this vast territory to the United States accompanied by any facilitation of communications. To the extent that its activities were extended to the northward by the acquisition of California and the Oregon Territory, the Pacific Squadron was more remote from the Navy Department in Washington than it had been before the Mexican War.

The extension of American sovereignty to the west coast made it possible for the warships of the Pacific Squadron to be based on seaports of their own country. But only provisions could be supplied the vessels, and even these were not always available in sufficient quantity to satisfy the needs of the squadron. Thus, immediate benefits from the success of American arms and diplomacy were few for the United States Navy.

On the other hand, the Pacific Squadron now had a grave responsibility in addition to its usual duties. The whole burden of the defense of the newly acquired territory rested on the few American warships present. The small standing army would be unable to send more than several garrisons, and these could not be reinforced quickly until the projected transcontinental railroad became a reality. In addition, no stable civil governments yet existed, and the handful of men in authority possessed no adequate means to enforce their enactments.

These facts did not escape the notice of the government at Washington. Navy Secretary Mason made an argument for an additional naval force, but much of its value was lost by his statement that the force would be needed only in the event of war. He made no mention of the time which would be required for the additional ships to reach the Pacific Station.

To one man, however, the need was plain, and he did not hesitate to bring it to official attention. Commodore Thomas ap Catesby Jones had no doubt of the value of California, and he concentrated his ships in that area to the exclusion of the affairs of the southern waters of his station. Meanwhile, his reports to the Navy Department were full of ideas for the protection of California and requests for more ships.

Immediately after the cessation of hostilities, Jones employed his vessels to ferry soldiers from Mexico and Lower California to American territory. He offered passage to any of the Mexican families who might fear reprisal for the assistance and friendship they had afforded the occupation forces; some three hundred and fifty Mexicans accepted and were settled in California. There was some delay about returning the customhouses in the occupied towns to the Mexican government, as Colonel Burton refused to surrender those held by his men until ordered to do so by proper authority. Commodore Jones was powerless by reason of Polk's order referring to Army jurisdiction over military forces. Not until 31 August 1848 did the Mexican government regain control of La Paz, the last post evacuated by the Americans.

Commodore Shubrick sailed for the east coast of the United States by way of the Hawaiian Islands in August. The islanders had reason to remember this visit by the *Independence*. A large portion of the razee's company had suffered from a mild form of measles, and a much more virulent type quickly became epidemic among the susceptible Kanakas soon after the arrival of Shubrick's flagship. It has been estimated that approximately a tenth of the population of the islands died from this disease before the epidemic spent its force. Few warships can have wrought more havoc in wartime than did the *Independence* during this friendly visit.

Commodore Jones and the remaining vessels of the Pacific Squadron went on to San Francisco Bay, already recognized as the natural center of the Pacific coast of the United States. Here the doughty commodore encountered another problem, more ominous than any faced thus far, and one upon which he himself was to wreck his naval career. While the warships were yet involved in the Mexican War, gold had been discovered at Sutter's Fort, and the news spread rapidly. Soon anyone who could find any means at all to get to the gold fields was on his way, and San Francisco became a thriving settlement almost overnight. Merchant vessels entered the harbor with eager passengers, but these had to be swift indeed to win the mad race for gold over the ship's crew. The need for strong government was now more apparent than ever, but it could be met only by a few hastily elected or appointed officials who had little real authority. Under these circumstances, the presence of Jones's warships was of great value. The commodore directed that his officers and men were to give every assistance to the civil authorities, but ensured that naval personnel would not arbitrarily usurp civil powers. It is impossible to evaluate the exact importance of this naval assistance in a territory where American authority was new, but it was unquestionably beneficial.

It might have been much more beneficial but for the fact that the ships' companies of the Pacific Squadron were only human. Their lust for gold was just as avid as that of their civilian brethren, and they did not hesitate to depart the naval service in favor of the gold fields. Desertion had always been a problem on Pacific Station, especially because it was virtually impossible to find replacements anywhere west of Cape Horn. However, nothing had been seen to compare with the exodus of enlisted men, and some warrant officers, from the warships at anchor in San Francisco Bay. An unwatched boat was certain to be stolen, and little trust could be placed in anyone but an officer—on some occasions the boats were stolen by the very men ordered to prevent such an occurrence. The officer sent ashore in charge of a boat could confidently expect to lose at least a part of his men, for not even the threat of the pistols habitually carried by all officers on leaving the ship could discourage the gold-crazed seamen. Jones offered a reward of $200 for every deserter returned to the squadron, but not a single man was regained.

In desperation, the commodore ordered that all line officers remain on board their ships at all times. This order caused much dissatisfaction among the gentlemen thus restrained, and was of doubtful value, since boats continued to ply between ship and shore, frequently losing a few men. Finally the desertion rate decreased, and Jones ascribed this to his exertions, but had to admit that lack of activity in the gold fields during winter months was one of the major factors.

Yet another danger showed itself during the summer of 1849. Many of the enlisted men had not been ashore for over a year, and began to show the effects of their confinement. All foodstuffs were in short supply in the San Francisco region so the warships were unable to procure enough fresh provisions. Even as late as 1849, seamen could get scurvy, and the dreaded disease made its appearance in the flagship *Ohio*. Prompt medical attention and renewed efforts to obtain fresh vegetables prevented fatalities, but when the *Ohio* was relieved by the *Savannah* frigate in September, Commander Stribling was ordered to give his men a run ashore at Valparaiso and to steer for any port where fresh food might be obtained if scurvy broke out again.

The food problem was intensified in still another manner. Normally, the supplies for the squadron were stored ashore at selected ports; in 1849, these were Valparaiso, Callao, Panama, Mazatlán, Monterey, San Francisco, and Honolulu. But in the two California ports it was nearly impossible to protect the stores. Everything had to be imported, for almost every able man had departed for the gold fields, and any stores not closely guarded were soon stolen. Jones did not dare to station armed guards around his storehouses because they would be too likely to desert. So he asked that the next store-ship be sent to the Hawaiian Islands; he would send his men-o'-war in turn to Honolulu to replenish their stores.

Obviously, the solution to Commodore Jones's difficulties was to order the ships of the Pacific Squadron to weigh anchor, make sail, and stand out through the Golden Gate. Desertion would be a comparatively minor problem elsewhere on the station, and he bore the responsibility of protecting American interests elsewhere in the eastern Pacific. Nor could officers and men remain proficient in their duties if their ships continued to swing idly at anchor in San Francisco

Bay. So thought the Navy Department; Secretary William B. Preston sent orders for the Pacific Squadron to get under way, and Commodore Jones was instructed to cruise actively in his flagship.

These orders, however, came from a man far distant from the scene. Jones felt himself able to decide in what manner the interests of the United States could be served best, and had already justified his continued presence at San Francisco:

Nothing, Sir, can exceed the deplorable state of things in all of Upper California at this time, growing out of the madning [*sic*] effects of the Gold mania. . . . To withdraw the Squadron from this coast altogether in the present state of affairs, would be to abandon the inhabitants and commerce of the coast to their fate, and remove the only real impediment to rapine, murder, and *piracy,* for which there is the strongest temptation in the large quantity of uncoined gold now finding its way to the seaboard for exportation.[1]

This was followed by a statement of the commodore's intention to stay at San Francisco and to employ the other ships of the squadron between that port, the Gulf of California, and the Hawaiian Islands.

Truly the situation seemed to require Jones's presence at San Francisco, but it is not unlikely that he was motivated, at least in part, by the fact that he was involved in land speculation in the Benicia area, and was turning a tidy profit in the purchase of gold dust on his own account. The dangers of such practices should have been apparent to an officer of Jones's experience, but he was not wealthy and so seized the opportunity to enrich himself. However deplorable his motives, the fact remains that Commodore Jones's course in staying at San Francisco was the correct one.

Slowly the desertion rate declined, aided by the commodore's policy of discharging time-expired men on the Pacific coast. This course was not approved by the Navy Department, but the commander in chief was allowed to grant discharges at San Francisco to men whose service had been of an honorable character. He used this discretionary power to release a large number of men, and the sailors were much more content to serve out their enlistments as long as there was some ground for hope that they would not be returned to the Atlantic coast for discharge. Jones also filled the complements of the smaller vessels from the crew of the flagship. This allowed more of the ships to be employed on protracted cruises, and also meant

that the *Savannah* was forced to remain in San Francisco Bay because she did not have enough men to take her to sea.

It must not be assumed that desertion ceased to be a problem in
the Pacific Squadron, however. San Francisco remained the worst
port in this respect, but other harbors on the station were better only
by comparison. For nearly a decade after 1850, all ships' boats
plying to the shore carried armed officers, and no officer got much
rest while his ship was at anchor, for there was never any lack of men
willing to chance the marksmanship of the watch officer in a break
for freedom.

Reports of imminent Indian outbreaks in the Oregon region led
the Navy Department to order dispatch of a warship and some Marines to the Pacific Northwest soon after the end of the Mexican
War, but the orders received by Commodore Jones made it clear that
the Navy did not intend to assume lasting responsibility for the
safety of that area from Indian attacks. Upon the arrival of a military force from the east, the vessel was withdrawn, and while an occasional cruise in northern waters was made by units of the Pacific
Squadron, the United States Navy did not take an active part in the
development of the future states of Oregon and Washington. One of
the main reasons for the Navy's reluctance to cruise in that region was
the lack of adequate harbors. The Columbia River mouth had already claimed two warships, and Puget Sound, for all its seeming
advantages, was not devoid of hazards for sailing vessels. Its mountainous shores tended to rob the ships of the wind they required, its
currents were strong and little known, and the depth of its waters
made it impractical for the ships to seek safety by anchoring.[2]

Commodore Jones finally had the satisfaction of seeing naval
steamers in the Pacific Ocean before he was relieved of his command. In August 1849, the Army transports *Edith* and *Massachusetts,* both requisitioned merchant vessels, were transferred to the
Navy. The latter was detailed to transport a joint board of Army and
Navy officers which was making surveys for future military posts
along the northwest coast, and this ship was not considered a part of
the Pacific Squadron. The smaller *Edith,* however, was placed under
Jones's orders.

The Pacific Squadron did not have its steamer long. She was sent
to southern California to give passage to that region's delegates to

the constitutional convention held at Monterey. During the run to the southward, continued overcast weather and fog forced her commanding officer to rely on dead reckoning, and this was seriously in error. On the night of 24 August 1849, the *Edith*'s lookouts reported breakers close aboard, and soon afterward the ship grounded on Point Conception (or more likely, on Point Argüello a few miles to the northward). All hands reached the shore safely, and much material was salvaged on the following day, but the steamer was a wreck. This was hardly an auspicious beginning for steam in the Pacific Squadron.

One more unusual event occurred during Commodore Jones's last cruise. On the night of 13 September 1849, a small boat from the Coast Survey schooner *Ewing* (officered and manned by naval personnel, but operating under the direction of the Superintendent of the Coast Survey) ferried some visitors from the vessel to the shore. The boat crew mutinied on the return passage, threw Passed Midshipman William Gibson over the side, and deserted in the boat. Civilians ashore heard Gibson's cries barely in time to rescue him.

Upon hearing of the mutiny, Lieutenant William P. McArthur, commanding the *Ewing,* offered a reward of $500 for the return of each of the mutineers; all were delivered to the schooner in Suisun Bay three days later. McArthur turned them over to Commodore Jones, senior naval officer present, and they were confined in the flagship *Savannah* to await trial.

A general court-martial was convened on board the guardship *Warren,* and after ten days of deliberation, it sentenced all five of the seamen to death. Later evidence made it seem that John and Peter Black alone were responsible for the attempt on Gibson's life, and they were hanged, the first on board the *Ewing* and the other from the *Savannah*'s yardarm. Jones commuted the sentences of Jonathan Biddy, William Hall, and Henry Commesford to 100 lashes and ordered that they serve out their enlistments at hard labor or in solitary confinement without pay.

Commodore Jones's command of the Pacific Squadron came to an abrupt end on 1 July 1850. Ten days earlier, Commodore Charles S. McCauley had arrived to relieve him, and Jones was ordered to return to the Atlantic coast. His hot temper flared at this peremptory relief, but he submitted with such grace as he could muster and sailed for Panama in the USS *Falmouth* the day after he was relieved.

Soon after he arrived in Washington, Jones was informed that serious charges had been brought against him, and a general court-martial was convened in the capital on 16 December 1850. Commodore Charles Stewart, the only other commander in chief of the Pacific Squadron to defend his conduct of affairs on that station before a general court-martial, was named as presiding officer. (The court included the following officers: Commodores Charles Stewart, Lewis Warrington, John Downes, Henry E. Ballard, W. Branford Shubrick, Lawrence Kearny, John D. Sloat, and M. Calbraith Perry, with Mr. J. M. Carlisle serving as judge advocate.)

The charges against Jones were five in number: fraud against the United States, attempting a fraud against the United States, scandalous conduct tending to the destruction of good morals, neglect of duty, and oppression. These referred to his activities in purchasing gold dust with government funds, engaging in land speculation, dubious accounting of government moneys placed in his care, his long period of inactivity at San Francisco despite orders to the contrary, and his treatment of junior officers who had protested against some of the measures taken to curb desertion.

The court found Captain Thomas ap Catesby Jones guilty of the third, fourth, and fifth charges, and sentenced him "to be suspended for five years, and that his pay and emoluments be suspended for the first two years and six months of the said time of his suspension." Further:

The Court thinks it proper to remark that it has been induced to add to the suspension of the accused, the suspension of his pay and emoluments for a portion of the time, from a consideration of the facts proven before it touching the profits made by him from the improper and unauthorized use of the public money.[3]

In vain, Jones sought to have the findings reversed on the grounds that the court included personal enemies, that he had not been given sufficient time to muster his witnesses, and that the Department did not understand conditions in California. Secretary of the Navy William A. Graham ordered that the sentence be carried out.

The "contentious Commodore," undone as much by the many powerful enemies he had made as by his misconduct, retired to his Virginia home to spend his last years composing irate letters to the Navy Department. He was returned to the active list in 1855, but his health had so much declined as to preclude any employment before his death in 1858.

Meanwhile, Commodore McCauley was doing his best to comply with Department directives that all vessels of the Pacific Squadron, not excepting the flagship, be employed as active cruisers. Certainly most of the ships logged more nautical miles under sail than they had during Jones's second cruise, but:

> *Savannah,* from the number of discharges made by my predecessor in command and being obliged to furnish, in connection with *Falmouth,* a crew for *Preble,* is already crippled and rendered powerless as a ship of war, having barely a sufficient number of men on board to take care of her at anchor, and unless men can be sent to her from home, or they can be procured here, which is not likely from the high wages given out of the port, her efficiency as a cruising ship must be entirely destroyed.[4]

Secretary Graham seemingly was not satisfied that McCauley would not be seduced by the attractions of California, for he sent orders that the *Raritan* frigate, coming out from the Atlantic coast, and one or more of the squadron's lighter vessels were to be kept cruising in the southern waters of the station.

This attempt to dictate employment of a large part of the force on Pacific Station from Washington seems to have been very ill-advised. Even in a day of rapid communications, the senior officer on the scene is often better able to comprehend the needs of each situation than the man thousands of miles away. This was even more true in 1850 when letters still spent weeks or months in transit between the Pacific coast and Washington. Graham would have been wiser to have limited himself to general orders to be carried out by the commander in chief according to the other requirements of his station. If the Secretary felt that McCauley could not be trusted to this extent, he should have sent a more trustworthy officer to assume the command. Fortunately, neither Graham nor his successors habitually followed this policy.

Commodore McCauley was ordered home in 1853, leaving the Pacific Squadron under the command of Captain Bladen Dulany of the *St. Lawrence* frigate, already in the Pacific. No change in the primary missions assigned to the squadron had occurred since McCauley had advised Commander George A. Magruder of the sloop-of-war *St. Mary*'s that:

. . . the objects of our government in keeping a Naval force in these Seas [are] to afford aid and protection to our commerce and to look after the interests of our Citizens generally, where engaged in their lawful pursuits, more especially our whaling interest, which is by far the most extensive and important we have in the Pacific. Another object is increasing the efficiency of our Navy by affording active service to the officers and crews of our vessels.[5]

Dulany quickly made known his desire that steamers be sent out to join his squadron. He wanted two, and intended to use them for cruising along the full length of the coastlines of North and South America. They would meet at Panama, and each would thus have alternate tours of duty in the North and South Pacific. This would release the sailing vessels for cruising among the islands where they would not be troubled by the calms which occurred frequently just off the coast. Neither the commodore nor the Navy Department seems to have considered the possibility of using steam warships as a reserve to be kept cruising in company with the flagship ready to be dispatched to any point where naval force might be needed. Nor does there appear to have been any thought that the squadron might be concentrated occasionally for such maneuvers and tactical evolutions as those carried out in 1842. The Pacific Squadron continued to be a police force with no apparent pretensions of becoming an efficient naval assemblage.

The terms of the Treaty of Guadalupe Hidalgo had not satisfied a number of the more ardent American expansionists. Some of these felt that the United States should have annexed all of Mexico; many of the Southerners who shared this view thought annexation had been prevented by the foes of slavery in order to curb the spread of that institution in areas under the American flag. In addition, there were persistent advocates in favor of wresting Lower California or other remote provinces from Mexico, while others turned their eyes farther south, to the undeveloped and extremely weak states of Central America. Included in all categories were the unprincipled adventurers ready to join any expedition sent out to seize these areas, and the inevitable idealists who looked upon such undertakings almost as semi-divine missions.

Either type of filibuster would be very embarrassing to the government of the United States, whose protection they were sure to invoke when they got into trouble. Secretary of the Navy James C. Dobbin therefore warned Dulany in 1854:

It is important that Officers in the Pacific Squadron should be prompt and vigilant in arresting and suppressing all such unlawful expeditions as may take place within the jurisdiction of the United States. You will exercise all lawful means of preventing the violation of law and the infraction of Treaty stipulations.[6]

This was easy enough for Dobbin to order, but difficult indeed for Commodore Dulany to put into effect. There were many ports on his station whence filibusters might sail, and he did not have enough warships to watch all closely even had he concentrated the whole Pacific Squadron for that purpose, and this his orders precluded.

The commander in chief ordered Commander Thomas A. Dornin of the *Portsmouth* to cruise along the California coast to disband such illegal expeditions as might be fitting out, and authorized him to charter a suitable steam merchant vessel to assist in the performance of the assignment. Dornin conferred with several merchants of San Francisco before finally procuring the Pacific Mail Steamship Company's propeller-driven *Columbus* for $1,500 per diem. The owners agreed to furnish everything necessary for operation of the vessel except coal, and this they sold to the Navy for $35.00 a ton. Dornin sent three officers on board and mounted two 12-pounder guns in the *Columbus*. The owners were not enthusiastic about this last development; they did not wish to risk any injury to their ship.

With his chartered steamer towing the *Portsmouth* when calms or adverse winds baffled the sailing vessel, Dornin succeeded in stopping more than one planned expedition in 1854. But that led by William J. Walker, a filibuster rejoicing in the appellation of "the grey-eyed man of destiny," set forth on its mission to deliver Lower California and Sonora from the rule of Mexico. The plan was too ambitious for the means, and Walker led the bedraggled remnant of his "army" back to the safety of California, there to make new plans for filibustering activity. Several of his sick and wounded men were rescued by the *Portsmouth,* and Commander Dornin also interceded successfully on behalf of American citizens imprisoned at Mazatlán.

The year 1854 also witnessed the fruition of plans for the establishment of an American naval base on the Pacific coast. For years it had been realized that San Francisco Bay was the logical site for this base. The Mexican War had hardly ended when Commodore Jones began to recommend that a base be established, and he reiterated the recommendation several times. For obvious reasons, he favored Benicia as its site, but when the gold mania was at its height, even Jones despaired of ever keeping an adequate force of civilian and naval personnel there. Notwithstanding his pessimism, Congress voted funds for a sectional or floating dock and a basin and a marine railway at a selected harbor on the Pacific coast. A contract for construction of the dock was let to eastern builders, and in 1852, Commodore John D. Sloat was appointed to head a board of naval officers to select a site for "a Navy Yard and Depot, including a Naval Hospital and Marine Barracks."[7]

Commodore Sloat and his companions agreed that Mare Island (*Isla de la Yegua*) was the most suitable location, and Congress had already appropriated $100,000 for purchase of land. Mare Island was bought for a little less than that sum early in 1853, but difficulties respecting its title kept the transaction in doubt until June 1854. In that year, Commander David G. Farragut was ordered to the Pacific to take command of the Mare Island Navy Yard. Commodore Dulany was ordered to turn the *Warren* over to the new commandant, and Farragut had the old sloop-of-war towed to Mare Island to become the first naval establishment at the site.

Development of a barren island into an efficient and well-equipped naval base took time, especially since the funds allotted for the purpose were not overgenerous. However, the floating dock was already there, and ships of the Pacific Squadron soon began to use the facilities of the Mare Island Navy Yard. So too did merchant vessels, for no other docking facility was available on the Pacific coast.[8]

Another advantage of the new base was that henceforth a senior officer of the United States Navy would be present in the vicinity of San Francisco. This was of some importance, for it freed the commander in chief on Pacific Station from any necessity to remain in that area. San Francisco might be the most important harbor on the Pacific coast of the United States, but it was undesirably distant from the more remote parts of the Pacific Station. Moreover, most of the mail from the east coast was now passing across Central America. To keep in close contact with the Navy Department and to guarantee the uninterrupted transit of the mails, it was necessary that the commander in chief spend much of his time in adjacent waters, usually at Panama. This he could do, secure in the knowledge that affairs to the northward would be dealt with by the commandant of the Mare Island Navy Yard. One or more warships were usually present in San Francisco Bay to act as the latter might direct in case of emergency. To be sure, this lent the undesirable aspect of divided command, but only on a few occasions did this cause difficulty, and in any case the post of commander in chief was senior to that of commandant.

The plan for a mail route across the Isthmus of Tehuantepec had given way to the much shorter routes across Nicaragua and the Isthmus of Panama, and of these the latter was the more important. The United States had agreed to maintain the neutrality of the Panamanian area in return for transit rights by a treaty of 1846 with New Granada, present-day Colombia. A somewhat suspicious United States Senate failed to advise ratification of the treaty until 1848, but the future importance of the Isthmian route was assured. The American Panama Railroad Company completed a railroad across the Isthmus from Aspinwall (Colón) to Panama in 1855, and the Pacific Mail Steamship Company had established a regular service between Panama and San Francisco in 1849, while a year earlier the United States Mail Steamship Company began scheduled sailings between New York and Chagres (in 1855 Aspinwall became the southern terminus). Both lines were subsidized by the United States government.

In the knowledge that Great Britain and France regarded development of American influence in the Isthmian area with misgivings, and that the government of New Granada might not be able effectually to force the Panamanians to respect the treaty stipulations, the commander in chief of the Pacific Squadron was ordered to arrange occasional visits to Panama by his warships, and later a station ship at Panama was placed directly under Department orders. Thus the practice noticed above received official sanction from the Navy Department.

However, Panama did not monopolize the attention of the Pacific Squadron. Its vessels continued to range as far afield as ever. Fears that the whaling fleet might suffer heavy losses from the hostility of the Samoans and the Fiji Islanders, whose ports provided replenishment for whalers in southern waters, kept some of the sloops actively cruising in their vicinity. Many merchant vessels were loading from the rich guano deposits of Peru's Chincha Islands, and the presence of a warship was necessary to maintain order among the unruly merchant seamen, as well as to make sure that American interests did not suffer unduly from the whims of the Peruvian government. The demand for guano forced the Navy Department to send orders that warships in the Pacific Ocean should be alert to discover new deposits on lesser known islands, and both Dulany and Commodore William Mervine, who relieved him in 1855, sent ships out for this purpose, but without success.

The great advantage of steamships over sailing vessels was dramatically shown when the sloop-of-war *Decatur* and the steamer *Massachusetts* were sent out to join the Pacific Squadron. After leaving Rio de Janeiro, the *Massachusetts* was dismasted in a storm and had to return for repairs, while the *Decatur* kept on for the Strait of Magellan. After refitting for a month, the steamer stood to the southward once more and found her sailing consort still trying to beat through the strait against adverse winds. The *Massachusetts* passed a hawser to the *Decatur,* and the two fought onward, forced to anchor by violent squalls and detained by the parting of hawsers. Commodore Dulany was beginning to worry about their failure to arrive when the *Massachusetts* anchored at Valparaiso on 18 January 1855, more than six months out of Norfolk. The *Decatur* had spent eighty-three days passing through the Strait of Magellan and would certainly have been much longer but for the assistance of the steamer.

Other arrivals on the Pacific Station in 1855 were the sloop *Vincennes,* the steamer *John Hancock,* and the schooner *Fenimore Cooper*. These vessels belonged to the United States Surveying Expedition to the North Pacific Ocean which had departed from Hampton Roads under the command of Cadwallader Ringgold in 1853. After rounding the Cape of Good Hope, the ships separated and surveyed their way through islands of the western Pacific toward a rendezvous at Hong Kong. There they refitted, and ill health forced Commander Ringgold to relinquish his command. Lieutenant John Rodgers directed the survey of Japanese waters, where the brig *Porpoise* was lost with all hands, probably in a typhoon. Rodgers continued the survey work in the Kurile and Aleutian Islands, and the three vessels arrived at San Francisco with the funds allotted for their work exhausted.

The veteran explorer *Vincennes* was ordered back to the Atlantic coast, thus completing her fourth voyage of circumnavigation, and the two other ships were laid up at Mare Island. Three years later, Lieutenant John M. Brooke, the expedition's astronomer, was sent out to continue the North Pacific survey in the *Fenimore Cooper.* While so engaged, the schooner was wrecked in Japanese waters, Brooke and all of his men escaping.

The feared Indian outbreak in the Pacific Northwest occurred in 1855, and military commanders joined territorial legislatures in asking that warships be dispatched to quell the uprising. Before Commodore Mervine could reply to these requests, Captain Farragut ordered the Coast Survey steamer *Active* and the *John Hancock,* left over from the Ringgold-Rodgers North Pacific expedition, to join the sloop-of-war *Decatur* in northern waters. The *Active* sailed in accordance with her orders, but the *Hancock*'s boilers required extensive repairs, and before these could be effected, Secretary Dobbin ordered that the steamer be detained because no naval officer of suitable rank was available to command her. Meanwhile, Mervine would have sent the *Vincennes* to Puget Sound, but the sloop's pending departure for the Atlantic coast forced him to send the *Massachusetts* northward in her place.

In spite of this apparent confusion, the Pacific Squadron did help to pacify the Indians. Their attack on Seattle disintegrated under the fire of the *Decatur*'s 32-pounders, to which the Indians could make no effective reply, and the whole situation was cleared up soon afterward. Complaints that the sloop's Commander Guert Gansevoort refused to co-operate properly with military forces caused Commodore Mervine to withdraw the *Decatur,* but the steamers *Massachusetts* and *Active* remained in Puget Sound to guard against further Indian trouble.

Hardly had the Navy's role in pacification of the Oregon and Washington Territories terminated when another disturbance flared up. In 1856, the activities of the Vigilance Committee in the San Francisco region threatened to destroy the civil government. After some vacillation, the governor asked the area's commanding general to intervene, but that officer did not wish to become involved. Captain Farragut was approached and refused on the ground that this was not a federal matter. However, another naval officer had different ideas. Commander Edward B. Boutwell took his sloop *John Adams* from Mare Island to San Francisco, anchored just off the city, and obtained the release of certain prisoners under the threat of his guns. Boutwell seems to have been quite ready to open fire, but was dissuaded by Farragut. The sloop-of-war remained at her anchorage and probably had a calming effect on the situation.

The Secretary of the Navy did not view these proceedings in a favorable light. Commodore Mervine (or the senior officer present) was instructed:

> . . . Before interfering with the domestic troubles in California, you will await the orders of your government. But duties of a somewhat different character may devolve upon you and events may possibly occur requiring your interposition. The laws of the Federal Govt. must be sustained and its property be protected from violence . . . you will . . . have either at Mare Island or San Francisco two or three National vessels, and retain them until the insurrectionary movements at San Francisco shall cease . . . The present object is the protection of public property and the officers of the Federal govt.—nothing more. . . .[9]

With San Francisco in a state of tranquillity, the attention of the Pacific Squadron was drawn to Panama. The government of New Granada had decided to levy a heavy duty on all goods passing across the Isthmus. Mervine, acting with unwonted determination, replied with a strong note pointing out that this duty was illegal under the treaty, and implying that his warships would use force to support the treaty provisions if necessary. Privately, the commodore doubted that his action would receive official approval, but he need not have worried. His apparent readiness to carry out the implied threat caused the Panamanian authorities to think better of the proposed taxation, and the Navy Department gave him unqualified support.

As Commodore Mervine's cruise neared its end, he was forced to consider the fitness of his flagship to make the long passage to the Atlantic coast. The poor work done by the New York Navy Yard in fitting out the old *Independence* for her Pacific cruise had become apparent long since, and Mervine concluded that the razee was neither able to face Cape Horn seas, nor worth the expense of a major overhaul. Secretary of the Navy Isaac Toucey concurred, and Mervine was ordered to turn the *Independence* over to the commandant at Mare Island for use as a receiving ship. He and his ship's company were transported to Panama, crossed the Isthmus by rail, and returned to the Atlantic coast of the United States from Aspinwall in a naval vessel. Some months earlier, the officers and men of the *St. Mary's* had returned home in the same manner, after having been relieved by a new crew sent across the Isthmus. However, neither Mervine nor his subordinates had originated this practice, which was to become the usual method of relieving time-expired men of the Pacific Squadron. Commodore Thomas ap Catesby Jones had advocated it some eight years earlier.

Flag Officer John C. Long—this rank having replaced that of commodore—came out in the new steam frigate *Merrimack* to assume command on Pacific Station. This famous vessel is not remembered for her service in the Pacific Ocean, and in truth Long's was a comparatively uneventful cruise. The smaller vessels of the squadron made the usual weary round of coastal and island cruises for the most part, while the flag officer spent much of his time in the vicinity of Panama.

One of the warships was kept in Nicaraguan waters for the purpose of offering assistance to the survivors of William Walker's unsuccessful regime in Nicaragua. This filibustering enterprise had endured from 1855 to 1857, and for a time it seemed that Walker, supported by New York shipping men, might be able to establish a permanent government. But the New Yorkers had lent their aid in order to gain the transit rights through Nicaragua which formed an essential link in one of the steamer routes between New York and San Francisco. Through Walker's influence, their rival and former partner, Cornelius Vanderbilt, lost his charter and so was forced to terminate his steamship service by that route. Vanderbilt, however, retaliated by assisting a Costa Rican force which invaded Nicaragua and defeated the filibuster in the spring of 1857. Commander Charles H. Davis of the *St. Mary's* intervened to stop the fighting. He arranged for the surrender and removal of most of the filibuster force, including its leader. Some of the sick and wounded were left behind, and Long was ordered to succor these if possible. Walker was not yet discouraged, however, and led another expedition against Honduras in 1860. British influence secured his downfall, and this time there was no American man-o'-war present to obtain his release. He fell before a firing squad on 12 September 1860.

The continuing importance of Central American waters caused Flag Officer Long to suggest that the _Massachusetts,_ unfit for duty as a cruiser, be stationed at Panama as a storeship. Supplies arriving from the United States could be transferred directly to the vessel, obviating the necessity of maintaining a shore depot there, and she could use her steam power to deliver stores to the sailing vessels cruising off the Central American and Mexican coasts. The Navy Department, however, disapproved this suggestion, and eventually directed that the _Warren_ be fitted as a storeship and moored permanently at Panama. Long's idea seems to have had considerable merit, but the Department felt that the cost of employing a steamer on this duty would be prohibitive.

Long's cruise was cut short by his poor health, and Flag Officer John B. Montgomery was ordered to proceed across the Isthmus to relieve him at Panama. His flagship, the screw-sloop _Lancaster,_ came out around the Horn, and the _Merrimack,_ hampered by the poor condition of her engines, returned to the Atlantic coast.

Montgomery's orders emphasized the necessity that filibustering expeditions be intercepted, but expressed the hope that operations in Central American waters would not cause the rest of the station to be neglected. At the same time, the flag officer was informed that his presence was required in the vicinity of Panama.

In the autumn of 1860, disturbances in Panama caused the landing of British, French, and American naval forces ostensibly to guard their respective consulates. Montgomery was absent to the southward, so Commander William D. Porter of the _St. Mary's_ assumed responsibility for the American action, apparently taken to prevent domination of local authorities by landing parties from foreign warships. The affair proceeded quietly, and the sailors were re-embarked in accordance with an agreement among the senior naval officers. But the British insisted on leaving sentries at their consulate, and these arrested some American citizens who refused to answer when challenged. Montgomery had returned to Panama by this time, and entered into an acrimonious exchange of letters with Captain Thomas Miller of HMS _Clio_ over this outrage. The contretemps was ended by the _Clio_'s departure, but American officers believed that the Britons were trying to gain some idea as to American reaction if Great Britain took over Panama. While this seems very unlikely, Flag Officer Montgomery's firm stand helped to guarantee respect for the rights of American citizens.

During the later days of the Panama incident, the flag officer had another reason for worry. He had been ordered to send one of his ships to the Hawaiian Islands to inquire into excessive expenditures of funds appropriated for the aid and protection of destitute American seamen in that area. The sloop-of-war *Levant* was assigned to make the investigation, and departed Panama on 11 May 1860. Her Commander William Hunt instituted a thorough inquiry as directed, and informed Montgomery on 3 September that his business would be concluded soon. He hoped to depart Hilo for Panama within two weeks. But weeks and months passed, and there was no sign of the *Levant*. The flag officer's reports make tragic reading as hope for the ship dwindled. Montgomery, for whom the Pacific Station had already been the scene of a great personal tragedy in the loss of two sons, refused to despair as long as there was any ground for optimism. Early in January 1861, he sent the steamers *Saranac* and *Wyoming* to search for the *Levant* along the usual routes. They found no trace of the sloop, and the flag officer sadly informed the Navy Department that the *Levant* must be presumed to have been lost with all hands, but that he still hoped to receive some news of the vessel.

. . . We have intelligence of a violent hurricane in September last in the region of Ocean through which the "Levant" would have had to pass in which an American clipper ship (since arrived at Valparaiso) was dismasted, and H. B. M. Line of Battle Ship "Ganges" had her sails blown from the yards. . . .[10]

Fifty years later men were still coming up with new theories to account for the *Levant*'s disappearance, but it has never been explained. There was some apprehension lest the ship have been seized by her crew for piratical cruising in the Pacific Ocean. However, Commander Hunt's last letter referred specifically to the admirable discipline and morale of the ship's company, so this possibility was very remote. Some time after the storm reported by Montgomery, a large spar washed ashore near Hilo, and local maritime men identified it as the *Levant*'s foremast. A description was sent to Montgomery, and he had little doubt that such it actually was. In a man-

ner that will never be known, the USS *Levant,* together with her officers and men, had met her fate in the broad reaches of the Pacific
Ocean.

However, Flag Officer Montgomery already had an intimation of
a tragedy that would cause the mysterious disappearance of the little
Levant almost to be forgotten. Before the search for the missing ship
had begun, the *Wyoming*'s Lieutenant John R. Hamilton, a native of
South Carolina, had sent his commission, together with a letter of
resignation from the United States Navy, to Flag Officer Montgomery
—his resignation was effective 15 December 1860, five days before
his state seceded from the Union.

8. Guarding the Gold Steamers

The importance of the California gold which the mail steamers carried to Panama is evident from the order under which Flag Officer John B. Montgomery took the Pacific Squadron to war:

> The difficulties that have developed themselves in certain States which have assumed an attitude of hostility to the Federal Government may extend to the Pacific and call for vigilant and energetic action on your part and that of your Command. Apprehensions having been expressed that attempts may be made by privateers or lawless persons to seize one of the Calif. steamers, your particular attention will be directed to that subject. The ports of San Francisco, Acapulco, and Panama, are points of special danger, and you will, in this crisis, concentrate your force on the route from Panama to San Francisco, unless there should be a demand for you in other quarters, of which the Department is not advised. You must exercise your judgment in discharging the responsible duties that devolve upon you.[1]

The gold bullion was not only badly needed by the Union, but there was an even more pressing necessity that it be kept out of Confederate hands. The foreign credit of the Confederacy would have been strengthened greatly by the capture of a single gold steamer, and to the Pacific Squadron was assigned the task of assuring the safe arrival of the treasure at Aspinwall.

The force with which Montgomery undertook these duties included the screw-sloops *Lancaster, Narragansett,* and *Wyoming,* the side-wheel sloop *Saranac,* and the sailing sloops *St. Mary's* and *Cyane.*[2] The system of commerce protection adopted in the Pacific required that the warships cruise along the steamer route between San Francisco and Panama, with particular attention being given to the points where privateers would be most likely to intercept the gold steamers.

113

Lower California also was watched, because it was feared that Confederate sympathizers might try to seize that area for the South. Vessels carrying gold from Aspinwall were escorted by gunboats on occasion, but no convoy system was adopted in the Pacific, probably because the merchant steamers were much faster than the warships. The *Cyane* and *St. Mary's,* entirely dependent on the winds, would have been useless as escorts for steamers.

The question of the loyalty of officers and men was of some concern, for approximately fifty per cent of the commissioned officers serving on Pacific Station in 1861 were natives of southern or border states. The danger of disloyalty was demonstrated in the case of Commander John K. Mitchell, commanding the *Wyoming.* He was about to sail from San Francisco when he received orders to cruise off the Golden Gate to protect the mail steamers. However, the *Wyoming* stood out through the Golden Gate and then steered a southerly course until she arrived at Panama. For this flagrant disregard of orders, Commander Mitchell was dismissed from the Navy, and next appeared leading Confederate gunboats at New Orleans as a flag officer of the Confederate States Navy. Most of the officers and men willingly took the oath of loyalty required by Secretary of the Navy Gideon Welles, but there was some doubt about whether or not Commander William D. Porter of the *St. Mary's* had caused it to be administered to his men. When Montgomery reported him for neglect of duty, Welles immediately relieved Porter of his command.

Montgomery's squadron was temporarily reduced by half during the summer of 1861. The *St. Mary's* was refitting at Mare Island; the *Saranac* was severely damaged by striking the bottom while anchored at Panama and had to be sent north for repairs late in July; and less than a week later, the *Wyoming,* leaving La Paz with a Mexican pilot on board, ran on a reef and also headed for Mare Island and dry-docking.

Under the circumstances, it is not surprising that Montgomery asked for reinforcements, but neither is it surprising that he did not get them. Indeed, Montgomery was fortunate that none of his ships was withdrawn. By July 1861, the Pacific Station was the only one of five distant stations which still possessed a squadron. All of the American warships had been recalled from the East India and Mediterranean Stations, while the Brazil and Africa Stations were left with one vessel each. The requirements of blockading the Atlantic and Gulf coasts of the Confederacy were too rigorous; the Pacific Squadron could expect no additional ships.

The situation would have been much more serious had it not been for the Mare Island Navy Yard. Thanks to this establishment, the damaged and weary ships could be thoroughly overhauled without leaving the station. Engine and boiler repairs could be made by San Francisco's Union Iron Works, but the cost was so prohibitive that its facilities were seldom used by the Pacific Squadron. Mare Island's magazine was stocked well enough so that none of the warships was forced to borrow gunpowder from a foreign government, as the *Decatur* had done only three years earlier. Nor was there any need for a repetition of target practice wherein the great guns were fired against a prominent cliff in order that the shot might be recovered for future use.

The effects of the temporary disability of half of the Pacific Squadron were not as serious as they might have been. Montgomery himself pointed out that the areas of calm off the coasts of North and Central America would make it difficult for privateers to operate effectually under sail, and steamers would find it almost impossible to obtain fuel, for the only coal supplies were the property of governments or steamship companies, neither likely to supply a rebel vessel. Nor was there any news of hostile ships cruising anywhere in the eastern Pacific.

Secretary Welles ordered that one ship be kept at Panama at all times, both to ensure uninterrupted transit of the Isthmus and to keep in close communication with the Navy Department. Because of the unhealthy climate, he desired Montgomery to arrange for periodic relief of the vessel at that port. However, the flagship *Lancaster* was partially immobilized by a cracked crankshaft so the flag officer found it convenient to remain there in her.

When it would have been possible to send the flagship to Mare Island for repairs which would have enabled her to cruise under steam, Montgomery had advised Welles that she could not possibly leave Panama until a court-martial then considering charges against the commanding officer of the storeship *Warren* had reached a decision. The presiding officer was the *Lancaster*'s Captain Henry K. Hoff. Thus, the most powerful ship of Montgomery's force did not receive essential repairs. This indicates the type of war being fought by the Pacific Squadron.

Montgomery was relieved by Flag Officer Charles H. Bell on 2 January 1862. The new commander in chief introduced a more active policy than that of his predecessor, and since conditions in Panama were tranquil, soon took the *Lancaster* north to have her defective crankshaft replaced.

At Mare Island, the flagship's detachment of Marines replaced the army personnel lent to guard the navy yard, and Bell interested himself in the defenses of San Francisco. News of the losses caused to the blockading squadron at Hampton Roads by the CSS *Virginia* (ex-USS *Merrimack*) reached the Pacific coast via the new Atlantic and Pacific telegraph line, and on 4 April, Bell advised the Department that "a single steam ram mounted with a few heavy guns would be sufficient to deter any wooden vessels of a hostile power from entering the Port."[3] Since it would take so long for such a ship to come out from the Atlantic coast, Bell made another suggestion:

> There is now lying at this Navy Yard the hulk of the old line-of-battleship "Independence." She was built in the strongest manner of seasoned oak and is reported to be perfectly sound below the waterline. Her planking appears sound, in all respects, up to the wales and she is, at present, with her gun deck battery and the crew of the "Lancaster" on board, as tight as any ship afloat. Her bow, above the waterline, is very full. With a false bow extending from the keel to a few feet above the water and rising from thence at an acute angle to the top of the bulwarks, or where the ports of two or three heavy guns would be placed, all this cased in iron and the ship propelled by steam power would produce a more formidable vessel than any ship which could be brought across the ocean.
>
> I would also suggest that the steam power could be applied to two shafts, placed, one on each side of the ship, under the counter, with two propellers. This arrangement, besides rendering the vessel more manageable, would prevent the necessity of removing the sternpost. . . .[4]

However, the Navy Department did not believe such an expenditure justified, and the old *Independence* was denied this transformation.

Flag Officer Bell was not thinking of the danger from Confederate warships when he made this suggestion. Two strong foreign squadrons were present in the eastern Pacific, and it seemed probable that at least one might become hostile to the United States. In November 1861, Captain Charles Wilkes, who was commanding the *San Jacinto* in Atlantic waters, had compelled the British mail-packet *Trent* to heave to and had taken off two emissaries of the Confederate States bound for Europe to seek assistance in the cause of the South. The tension resulting from the *Trent* affair caused Great Britain to concentrate a strong naval force for possible use against the American Pacific coast. Furthermore, a French squadron had gathered to assist in the conquest of Mexico which resulted in the enthronement of Maximilian as emperor in 1864. Both squadrons contained ships much heavier than the *Lancaster,* and there could be no doubt as to the outcome of any encounter between either and Bell's small force. The Navy Department placed its reliance on the inadequate fortifications guarding San Francisco, and instructed Bell to keep a warship at Mare Island whenever possible. It is fortunate that diplomacy averted any need for these precautions; almost certainly San Francisco and the entire American Pacific coast would have been lost had Great Britain entered the war.

When the *Lancaster* was ready for sea, Bell sailed for southern waters once more. He touched at the important ports on the way, and continued on down the South American coast, carrying out the recommendation he had made to the Navy Department earlier:

. . . In the present state of our affairs I think it desirable to send each of the Squadron in succession to cruise down the coast as far as Valparaiso, touching at the principal places, not only to give security to our countrymen engaged in business but to let these South American Governments see that notwithstanding our difficulties at home, we still have the power to punish any infraction of our Treaties, and to afford ample protection to any commerce along their coasts. . . .[5]

Just before the flagship departed San Francisco in June 1862, the Navy Department telegraphed that Confederate privateers were operating in the Far East, and ordered Bell to dispatch the *Wyoming* to the Orient to protect American commerce. Commander David McDougal was so informed, and the *Wyoming* weighed anchor on 21 June with orders from Secretary Welles to proceed with utmost speed, and from Bell to realize the greatest economy in coal, cruising under sail whenever possible. McDougal made what he could of these conflicting orders and sailed to the Orient.

A year later, the *Wyoming* was called to Japan by reports that rebellious feudal lords had fired on the American merchant steamer *Pembroke*. In spite of obvious navigational hazards, much more dangerous because he had no chart, McDougal steamed the sloop into the Strait of Shimonoseki and caused considerable damage to the offending forts in an hour's brisk fighting. Americans took little part in the later attacks which finally opened the strait, for the *Wyoming* went on to the Indian Ocean in fruitless search for the CSS *Alabama*. McDougal rejoined the Pacific Squadron with his ship in 1864.

Meanwhile, Bell continued Montgomery's requests for more warships, but had to be satisfied with promotion instead. After Flag Officer Farragut's brilliant victory at New Orleans, Congress had established the rank of rear admiral, and at the same time, the rank of commodore was revived to replace the awkward designation of flag officer. Bell was directed to assume the rank of acting rear admiral for the remainder of his command of the Pacific Squadron; doubtless, he would have preferred more vessels. His squadron was ridiculously small, and all of the ships, particularly the steamers, were showing the effects of long service. However, Rear Admiral Bell did convince Welles that he had to have a shallow-draft steamer to visit small Central American ports. The little side-wheeler *Saginaw,* the first warship built at Mare Island, had been refitting in her home yard after a cruise in the Far East, and she was assigned to the Pacific Squadron.

Personnel shortages also annoyed the commander in chief. He felt that the bad state of engines and boilers which held his steamers to a six-knot top speed was intensified by the lack of skilled mechanics and engineers. Benjamin F. Isherwood, Chief of the Bureau of Steam Engineering, replied from Washington that the vessels built and purchased for the blockade required more engineering personnel than he could provide; Bell would have to be content with what he had. Somewhat later, Bell reported numerous desertions, and recommended that Negroes be enlisted for the Pacific Squadron. Their ability to withstand heat would make them valuable in tropical waters. Permission was granted, but there is no evidence to show that many Negroes served in warships on Pacific Station.

In response to another of Bell's requests, Welles ordered some one hundred and forty Marines sent to the Mare Island Navy Yard for guard duty. The steamer *Ariel,* in which they sailed, was intercepted by the CSS *Alabama* in the Caribbean Sea on 7 December 1862.

It was an unfortunate capture for Confederate Captain Raphael Semmes. Had the *Ariel* been bound in the opposite direction, she would have carried a fortune in California gold; as it was, he had captured only some five hundred civilian and military passengers. Making the best of the situation, Semmes released the ship after obtaining paroles from all the military personnel.

The *Ariel* proceeded on to Aspinwall, and soon Bell had his Marines, but they were pledged not to fight against the Confederacy until exchanged. Wily Welles thought that they might still guard Mare Island, since the "so-called Confederacy" had neither military nor naval force in the Pacific. What might have been an interesting case for experts in international law failed to develop, however, as the Marines were exchanged soon after they arrived at Mare Island.

Eighteen sixty-three passed with no great change in policy and little excitement save that in San Francisco on 15 March when the *Cyane*'s Commander Paul Shirley sent a boarding party of Marines to seize the schooner *J. M. Chapman* which was thought to be fitting out as a Confederate privateer. The warships cruised as before for the protection of the gold steamers, one vessel remained at Panama, and an occasional cruise along the South American coast served to remind the governments in that area that United States interests must be respected. French activities received close scrutiny; the Pacific Squadron was too small to interfere effectively, but the *Saranac* was present at Acapulco in January when Admiral E. C. Bouet's squadron bombarded the town. After the departure of the French warships, the *Saranac* remained to assist in maintenance of order while the inhabitants were returning from the interior whither they had fled to escape the French fire.

Early in 1864, Bell's force was strengthened by the arrival of the iron side-wheel double-ender gunboat *Wateree*. Few stranger ships ever served in the Pacific Squadron. She was one of the vessels built especially for service on the sounds and rivers of the southern states, and had no pretensions to seaworthiness or to efficiency as a cruiser. Sail power had been virtually forgotten in her design, and her lack of endurance under steam made this an unfortunate omission. She burned the last of her coal soon after leaving the Strait of Magellan; consequently, her crew cut and dried wood on a Chilean island while the sailmaker worked feverishly to convert awnings into sails for the jury spars contrived by the carpenter and his mates. Sail and wood fuel together just sufficed to get her to the nearest Chilean port where coal could be obtained. Rear Admiral Bell cannot have been reassured by the addition of a river gunboat to his squadron. The *Wateree* was armed with heavy guns, but she possessed no other qualities which would fit her for duty on Pacific Station.

Even so poor a vessel, however, was welcome in light of French activities on the west coast of Mexico. Admiral Bouet proclaimed a blockade of Acapulco early in 1864, but this was eased to permit Pacific Mail steamers to touch there for coal and supplies. Bell thought the situation was serious enough to require his presence, so the *Lancaster* observed the blockade for a time and then was relieved by another American man-o'-war. The *Saginaw* was present at Acapulco when the French occupied the town on 2 June 1864. Mexican forces evacuated the area before the French landed, and shore parties from the *Saginaw* prevented looting during the interval when neither combatant controlled the town. In November, Mazatlán was occupied, but soon afterward the French evacuated Acapulco. Inhabitants feared that the town might be subjected to Indian attacks before an effective local government could be re-established, and the USS *Saranac* helped to prevent such an occurrence by her presence during the month following the French evacuation.

Rear Admiral Bell was relieved by Acting Rear Admiral George F. Pearson in October 1864. The squadron which Bell turned over to his successor was not markedly different from that of which he had assumed command nearly two years earlier. The addition of the *Saginaw* and *Wateree* has been noted, and the sailing bark *Farallones* (formerly the Pacific Squadron's steamer *Massachusetts,* with engines and boilers removed) had been obtained for use as a storeship. The *Warren,* completely worn-out, was sold at Panama in 1863, and the *Narragansett* went to the Atlantic coast in 1864 for extensive machinery repairs.

Rear Admiral Pearson's orders were short and direct:

Your aim and object will be, in a few words, to protect as far as the means in your command will permit, our countrymen residing abroad, to preserve our commerce in the Pacific from the depredations of piratical cruisers, to maintain the honor and discipline of the Navy, and to advance, by all proper means, the interests of your government.[6]

Like his predecessors, Pearson was also impressed with the importance of guaranteeing the Panama route against interruption.

Reports that a party of Confederates intended to board the Pacific Mail steamer *Salvador* at Panama as passengers and then seize her at sea, led Pearson to order the *Lancaster*'s Commander Henry K. Davenport to take preventive action. The steamer was scheduled to sail on 10 November 1864, and after all her passengers had been embarked, the *Salvador* received a boarding party from the flagship. She then weighed anchor and stood out, followed by the *Lancaster*. All of the passengers were mustered on the upper deck while naval officers examined their baggage, and found ample evidence that the plot did exist. The next morning, when the *Salvador* was beyond the territorial waters of New Granada, the American flag was hoisted, and naval officers arrested seven passengers whose leader was Acting Master Thomas E. Hogg, CSN. The prisoners were transferred to the *Lancaster,* and the *Salvador* continued her passage to the northward.

Hogg and his men were tried by general court-martial at Headquarters, Army of the Pacific, at San Francisco, on a charge of "Violation of the laws and usages of civilized war," and were found guilty. All were sentenced to death by hanging, but the sentences were commuted to life imprisonment for the leader and ten years imprisonment for each of his men. All were released, however, soon after the end of the Civil War.

So ended the one serious attempt by Confederates to seize a steamer for use as a commerce raider in the Pacific Ocean. The situation was handled admirably, with a minimum of confusion and a proper regard for the rights of neutrals, but it would not have been possible without the warning furnished Pearson by loyal American citizens residing in Panama. Other plots of the same sort were dealt with before they could become serious, again due to the information supplied by private citizens. After the *Salvador* incident, masters of merchant steamers became much more vigilant in the matter of baggage inspection, and the danger was lessened accordingly.

For the remainder of the Civil War, the Pacific Squadron continued its usual cruising duties. The gunboats *Mohongo* and *Suwanee,* near-sisters of the *Wateree,* arrived from the Atlantic coast to join Pearson's flag, but neither attracted the attention given to a warship launched by the Union Iron Works at San Francisco late in 1864.

This vessel, the monitor *Camanche,* had the distinction of sinking before she was launched. She was constructed on the Atlantic coast and disassembled for shipment to the Pacific in the merchant ship *Aquila.* The latter sank alongside a wharf in San Francisco Bay before the monitor sections could be landed. Thus *Camanche* had to be delivered from *Aquila*'s hold by a sort of maritime Caesarian operation before being assembled and launched.[7] The monitor's two 15-inch guns, iron armor, and seven-knot speed fitted her for the defense of San Francisco, but for no other duty on Pacific Station.

News of the Confederate surrender at Appomattox had hardly reached the Pacific coast before Captain McDougal at Mare Island received a telegram from Secretary Welles which plunged the whole region into mourning:

President assassinated yesterday and died today. Fire a gun each half hour from yard and vessels from sunrise to sunset. Put flags at half-mast —direct officers to wear crape.[8]

But the Civil War was not yet ended in the Pacific Ocean. Months after affairs had slowed to a leisurely peacetime gait, officials at San Francisco received news of a mysterious raider which was burning American merchant vessels in the Pacific. She was readily identified as the CSS *Shenandoah.* Admiral Pearson was watching the French at Acapulco when he heard of the raider's depredations early in August 1865. He promptly dispatched the *Saranac* and *Suwanee* in search of the *Shenandoah,* and ordered the *Saginaw* from San Francisco to relieve him at Acapulco.

San Franciscans feared that the *Shenandoah* might be lurking just off the Golden Gate to intercept the mail steamer *Colorado* which was about to sail with a gold shipment. McDougal ordered the little *Saginaw* out as an escort, a measure of dubious value since the side-wheeler was much slower than the *Colorado* and was hardly heavy enough to stand up to the larger *Shenandoah.* But the escort was not needed, and the hunters *Saranac* and *Suwanee* returned empty-handed for the very good reason that the Confederate raider had left the Pacific by the time the hunt started. After ruining the American whaling industry by burning some thirty-seven whaleships taken in the North Pacific and Arctic Oceans, her commander learned in August that the Confederacy had in fact surrendered in April, so the

Shenandoah returned to Liverpool under British colors. She was surrendered to British authorities, and they turned her over to the United States government.

With this unsuccessful hunt for the last of the Confederate raiders, the Pacific Squadron's part in the Civil War ended. In retrospect, it was not an exciting role, but the few ships assigned to the Pacific Station carried out successfully the major task ordered by the Navy Department. This was the duty of ensuring the passage of the steamers from San Francisco to Panama and the transit of the Isthmus. To be sure, there were few attempts at interference, but the constant presence of a warship at Panama was essential in preventing the organization of an anti-Union movement by Confederate sympathizers.

It is true that the Pacific Squadron did not keep the *Shenandoah* from destroying a major American interest in the North Pacific. However, Admiral Pearson's orders made no specific mention of the whaling fleet, and he could spare no warships for commerce protection in the remote waters of his station. Communication difficulties were responsible for Pearson's failure to intercept the *Shenandoah;* when he did learn of her presence, it was too late for any measures he might take.

In waters far removed from the war zone, the Pacific Squadron had performed its duties as satisfactorily as had all of the United States Navy in the Civil War—however unspectacular and routine these duties might have been.

9. *Economy and Decline*

The months succeeding the close of the Civil War were the beginning of a new era in the history of the United States. It was an era marked by great national growth by land and decline by sea. It is unnecessary here to review the familiar events. We need only remember that the Confederate commerce raiders and the fear they inspired, acted as a tremendously effective catalyst in hastening the decline of the American merchant marine. That decline had already begun some years before the guns at Charleston awoke Fort Sumter and the Union with their belated announcement of the birth of the Confederacy. Various reasons have been given: the unwillingness of American shipowners and builders to turn to iron ships, their failure to see that the dazzling speed of the clippers was comparable only to the rapidity with which those wonderful ships sailed across that horizon which separates reality from memory, and probably most important, the United States was "turning its back on the sea" in order to develop the vast and little-known territory included within its borders. A loss of interest in the sea was almost certain to be reflected in the nation's naval policy. It resulted badly for the United States Navy, and also for the Pacific Squadron.

But before the new outlook toward the Navy had time to develop, the Pacific Squadron received its first important reinforcement since before the Civil War. Preoccupation with that conflict had been largely responsible for American failure to invoke the Monroe Doctrine against European ambitions in Mexico. As soon as peace was restored, official interest in the Mexican situation became apparent. However, there is no conclusive evidence that the inferiority of the Pacific Squadron to the French naval forces on the Pacific coast caused the dispatch of the Special Service Squadron commanded by Commodore John Rodgers.[1]

At any rate, the squadron was formed around the double-turret monitor *Monadnock,* generally considered to be one of the most powerful fighting ships in the world, but one whose ability to make a long ocean voyage was seriously questioned. To accompany the iron-clad, Secretary Welles chose the wooden side-wheelers *Vanderbilt* and *Powhatan* and the wooden screw-sloop *Tuscarora.* Commodore Rodgers, a firm believer in the monitors, but no stranger to their discomforts, broke his broad pennant in the *Vanderbilt.*

The Special Service Squadron left Hampton Roads early in November 1865, and plodded to the southward at a leisurely pace, its speed limited to that of the sluggish *Monadnock.* The monitor came up to Rodgers' expectations as to seaworthiness and exceeded them with regard to the heat of her fireroom as she entered tropical waters. The sails set on a jury mast stepped forward of her fore turret helped to give her hard-pressed stokers, collapsing from the heat, some slight surcease. The squadron passed on through the Strait of Magellan and thence to Valparaiso.

At the Chilean port, Rodgers' squadron met the Spanish force of Admiral Méndez Núñez. Some four years earlier, Spain had launched one final attempt to regain her lost colonies on the west coast of South America. The immediate cause of the war was Peruvian failure to pay debts supposedly owed to the Spanish government. A Spanish expedition had seized the guano-rich Chincha Islands in 1864 and engaged in sporadic blockading operations without fear of American intervention. Chile had allied herself with Peru, so the Spanish fleet stood to the southward, threatening to bombard the undefended port of Valparaiso.

At this point, Major General Judson Kilpatrick, American minister to Chile, expressed his desire that the newly arrived Special Service Squadron intervene. For a time it seemed that Rodgers would do so, and seamen looked forward eagerly to a duel between the *Monadnock* and the Spanish broadside ironclad *Numancia.* But Rodgers made British co-operation a condition of his action, and Rear Admiral the Honorable Joseph Denman, RN, refused to intervene after verbal efforts to dissuade the Spaniard had failed. Rodgers also stood aside, with Kilpatrick's grudging approval, and the bombardment took place. Few lives were lost, as the negotiations had given time for removal of most of the civilians. A similar attack on Callao was repulsed, and Núñez returned to Spain with his squadron not long thereafter.

The Special Service Squadron made its way on to San Francisco and was incorporated into the Pacific Squadron. The *Monadnock,* having proved her ability to reach the west coast, joined the *Camanche* in ignominious reserve to rust away in peace. The threat of trouble with France, already lessening, faded even more rapidly before the diplomacy of Secretary of State William H. Seward, backed by the potential of the victorious Union armies.

Hostilities ended and difficulties with foreign powers no longer threatening, Secretary Welles was able to turn his attention to the peacetime disposition of the Navy. He seemed to have grasped the principle that a navy had to be concentrated to act effectively, but this was not carried out by his orders after the war. Once again the old distant-station policy was revived, this time with much less justification than before. Not only was the American merchant marine much smaller, but its relative importance to American prosperity was greatly diminished. The once-valuable whaling fleet had virtually disappeared in the fires lighted by boarding parties from the CSS *Shenandoah,* and years were to pass before the industry was revived on a much smaller scale. American interests abroad still remained, to be sure, and Welles could find some support for his belief that "one or more of our naval vessels ought annually to display the flag . . . in every port where our ships may trade."[2] But with diminished American shipping and greatly improved means of communication, the soundest arguments for the traditional policy had disappeared.

Without further ado, the following stations were re-established: European (former Mediterranean and African), North Atlantic (former Home), South Atlantic (former Brazil), and Asiatic (former East India). The Pacific Station had remained in existence throughout the Civil War, but now it came up for consideration also.

In a sense, the Pacific Station was not a distant station at all. The squadron in the area was based principally on Mare Island, and the whole region from Cape Flattery to San Diego was as much a part of the United States as was the Atlantic coast. The telegraph had ended much of the isolation of the Pacific coast, and the soon-to-be-completed transcontinental railroad would provide an even closer tie. However, the waters south and west of California were still remote, and the problems likely to be encountered in the southeastern Pacific differed widely from those in waters contiguous to the continental coastline of the United States. As early as 1856, Secretary of the Navy James C. Dobbin had recommended that the eastern Pacific be divided into two distinct stations, and Welles took advantage of the general reorganization to put the recommendation into effect.

Accordingly, on 6 August 1866, Rear Admiral Henry K. Thatcher broke his flag in the USS *Vanderbilt* at San Francisco and assumed command of the North Pacific Squadron. His force consisted of the screw-sloops *Pensacola, Lackawanna,* and *Mohican;* the side-wheelers *Vanderbilt* and *Saranac;* the screw gunboat *Resaca;* the side-wheel gunboats *Suwanee, Mohongo,* and *Saginaw;* and the sailing sloop *Jamestown.* The North Pacific Station encompassed the area from the west coasts of North and Central America westward to the 180th meridian of longitude and southward to the latitude of Panama.

Rear Admiral Pearson, formerly commanding the Pacific Station, took command of the South Pacific Squadron which included the side-wheel sloop *Powhatan* (flagship), the screw-sloop *Tuscarora,* the side-wheel gunboat *Wateree,* the screw gunboats *Nyack* and *Dacotah,* and the sailing storeships *Farallones* and *Fredonia.* These vessels cruised on a station south of the latitude of Panama, bounded on the east by the western coast of South America, and extending far enough to the westward to include Australia.

It will be noted that the South Pacific Station was much larger than its northern counterpart, but that the latter received a more powerful squadron. This seeming discrepancy may be explained by the fact that the North Pacific Station contained the important Hawaiian Islands in addition to the west coast of the United States. With the exception of the Callao-Valparaiso area, the South Pacific Station had no regions of particular importance. Panama, in many ways still the focal point of American interest in the eastern Pacific, was the joint responsibility of both squadrons, although the Commander in Chief, North Pacific, was primarily charged with maintaining its tranquillity. Naturally enough, the Mare Island Navy Yard was home base for both squadrons. One of the storeships was moored at Callao or Valparaiso, but shore depots came into more frequent use as time passed.

The separation of North and South Pacific Stations lasted for only two years. On 13 March 1869, the Navy Department directed that the two be combined to form the Pacific Station. A rear admiral would serve as commander in chief, while the warships were to be divided into North and South Pacific Squadrons, each commanded by a commodore. It took some time for this order to be put into full effect. Nearly two years later, the commodore commanding the South Pacific Squadron still had his flag flying in the storeship *Onward,* a former sailing merchantman, and the commander in chief of the Pacific Station had no vessel suitable to carry his flag on the visits to his squadrons, although he had been ordered to make such visits every three months. This shortage was remedied as ships completed refits at Mare Island, but again the combined station proved too large for one officer to oversee.

Accordingly, the eastern Pacific Ocean was again divided in 1872, the two stations having the same geographical limits as before. A few months later, the North Pacific Station was extended southward to the Equator, while its western limit was moved eastward to 170° West longitude. The Pacific Station was re-established once more in 1878, and was not divided again during the period considered by this study. Its limits were those customary in years past.

The reasons for this confusing policy cannot be ascertained. It is obvious that the Pacific Station was divided because it was too large for one command, but it did not grow smaller on those occasions when it was reunited, nor had any new developments occurred which might have facilitated communications over long distances at sea. One is tempted to attribute the re-establishment of a single command to a desire for economy—one station would require only a single flag officer and his staff—but this is only conjecture. Two squadrons usually did not receive a corresponding increase in force over one, nor did a change in the number of squadrons have any discernible effect as regards the types of warships comprising the forces in the eastern Pacific Ocean.

Nor did the classes of vessels assigned to the Pacific Station, or Stations, differ from those serving on other stations. Ships sent to the Pacific were apt to stay there, occasionally crossing the 180th meridian for duty with the Asiatic Squadron, until they were stricken from the *Navy Register,* usually after rotting in reserve at Mare

The USS *Macedonian* was the first ship assigned to the Pacific Station. With Captain John Downes as her commanding officer, the frigate sailed from Boston in September 1818. Running into a full gale, she almost foundered, and Captain Downes took her into Norfolk under a jury rig. One month later, with repairs completed, the *Macedonian* sailed again to the southward, rounded the Horn, and began her mission in the Pacific Ocean.

1 *USS* Macedonian *under a jury rig, September 1818.*
2 *Captain John Downes.*

3 *USS* United States.
4 *Commodore Isaac Hull.*
5 *USS* Peacock *in the Antarctic, 1839-40.*
6 *Lieutenant Charles Wilkes.*
7 *USS* North Carolina.
8 *American flag being raised at Monterey, California, 7 July 1846.* (Left to right) *USS* Cyane, *USS* Savannah, *and USS* Levant.
9 *USS* Vincennes *and USS* Columbus (left to right) *departing from Tokyo Bay, July 1846.*

6

7

8

9

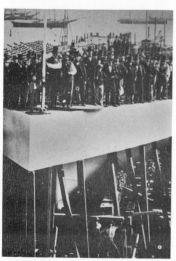

10 *USS* Camanche, *launched at Union Iron Works,*
San Francisco, 1864.
11 *USS* Ohio.
12 *Commodore Thomas ap Catesby Jones.*
13 *Commodore Robert F. Stockton.*
14 *Commander Robley D. Evans.*
15 *USS* Yorktown.

11

12

13

14

15

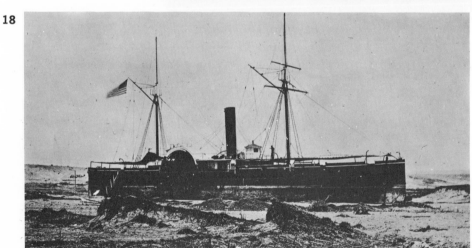

16 *Figurehead of USS* Trenton.
17 *Apia Harbor, 17 March 1889, following the hurricane.* (Left to right) *USS* Trenton, *USS* Vandalia, *SMS* Olga, *and USS* Nipsic.
18 *USS* Wateree *deposited above the high-water mark by a tidal wave at Arica, Chile, in August 1868.*

20

19 USS Pinta *in Juneau Harbor, 1889.*
20 *Pago Pago, Samoa, 1908. Destroyers and armored cruisers at anchor.*

21

22

21 *USS* Monadnock, *Mare Island Navy Yard.*
22 *USS* South Dakota *in her 1916 rig.*

Island for some years. Most of them were not well fitted for service anywhere, but this describes most of the warships of the United States Navy after the Civil War. The prewar ships were excellent representatives of their kind, but they had seen hard service during the war; furthermore, repairs had been hastily and, too often, poorly done. The war-built ships had been rushed to completion, and the green timbers used in their construction shortened their effective lives considerably. Economy-minded Congresses and Navy Department postponed overhauls as long as possible, and sometimes there was a very real danger that a vessel might not weather storms encountered on the passage to Mare Island when her commanding officer's oft-repeated request was finally granted.

The bad condition of the warships was not improved by the post-war Navy Department's attitude toward the use of steam. This attitude has been described in many places; it will suffice to remark here that the foolish economy of forcing the ships to cruise under sail worked a particular hardship in the eastern Pacific with its large expanses of calms or baffling winds. These had been annoying enough during the era of sail. With the advent of steam, it became peculiarly frustrating to possess the means to circumvent natural conditions, only to have its use forbidden. The circumstances were aggravated by the fact that the sail power of most of the ships in commission had been reduced during the Civil War to enable them to operate more efficiently under steam.

The Department met these objections by ordering that all vessels on Pacific Station be sent to Mare Island to receive full sail rig as soon as possible. The four-bladed screws were replaced by two-bladed propellers, less efficient for steaming, but causing less drag when the ships were under sail. In response to repeated complaints by succeeding commanders in chief, permission was granted in 1871 for ships of the Pacific Squadrons to use half steam power to cross areas of calm when "ordered on urgent duty."[3]

That the Navy Department's aversion to the use of steam was not based on an appreciation of the technical points of seamanship was demonstrated by Secretary George M. Robeson's comments on a minor collision. The USS *Mohican* was standing out under steam when she touched the merchant vessel *Ocean Express,* causing some slight damage to the latter's spars. Robeson thought that the *Mohican* could have avoided the collision had she been under sail, and pointed out that if the use of steam was necessary, it would have been preferable to hire a tug. The *Mohican* should have been much more manageable under her own steam than under sail, but Robeson was thinking only of the expense incurred by raising steam and thereby consuming coal.

If the warships were poor, the personnel often were no better. Most of the officers were those who had made fine reputations during the Civil War, but slow promotion and the political manipulations of their seniors often turned them into mere time-servers. Even those who did wish to keep abreast of new naval developments could hardly do so because the United States Navy contained virtually nothing that was new.

The enlisted men were of a different type. Native Americans had declined to serve in the merchant marine even before the war, and conditions in the postwar Navy were not calculated to make the service attractive to young men of ability and ambition. As a result, foreigners made their way into the forecastles of American warships in ever larger numbers. Officers found it necessary to give orders in several languages if they were to be understood by all. While there is no record that any of the warships serving on Pacific Station ever surpassed the Asiatic Squadron's *Monocacy* with her crew from nineteen nations, the same general condition existed throughout the United States Navy.

Such men could not be expected to feel a strong attachment for the flag under which they served, and must have been a very uncertain factor in time of emergency. They were even more suspectible to desertion than were their predecessors, and rare indeed was the small boat which returned its full crew to a ship. Desertion became so prevalent in the Pacific Squadron that the Department ordered all warships to stay away from San Francisco unless it became absolutely necessary to touch there. This did not cure the evil, and desertion plagued the Pacific Squadron throughout the period of naval decline. When the conditions of service and the pay and food are considered, it is very difficult to condemn the enlisted men for seeking to better themselves by flight.

In addition to the perennial task of protecting American commerce and interests in the eastern Pacific, the North and South Pacific

Squadrons were assigned the duty of increasing knowledge of the waters wherein they cruised. All vessels were equipped to make hydrographic surveys in 1866 and received orders to confirm or correct their charts at every opportunity. The value of this function cannot be denied, but the order made it apparent once again that the vessels comprising each squadron were to be dispersed within the limits of their stations. No mention of tactical maneuvers was made; the Pacific Squadrons were still police forces.

Mindful of Department orders, the warships cruised actively during the immediate postwar period. At least one vessel was almost always present in the Hawaiian waters where American interests clearly were supreme. Friendly relations there were strained in 1867, when the Hawaiian government became suspicious of an unusually long visit by the USS *Lackawanna*. An intemperate letter inquiring as to her intentions received no answer from the American chargé or from Captain William Reynolds. More letters failed to elicit a satisfactory explanation and the attorney general of the kingdom was asked for an opinion on the legality of closing Hawaiian ports to American vessels. Reynolds informed the United States government of the proceedings and asked that all American warships refrain from rendering the customary salutes in Hawaiian harbors. However, Admiral Thatcher disapproved this request, and the tense situation was resolved amicably when the *Lackawanna* conspicuously rendered passing honors to the King on the occasion of his visit to a foreign man-o'-war anchored nearby.

American purchase of Alaska in 1867 added to the responsibilities of the Pacific Squadron briefly. The USS *Ossipee* was detailed to convey Russian and American dignitaries to Sitka for ceremonies transferring the territory in the summer of 1867. She was joined by the sailing sloop *Jamestown;* the latter's crew had contracted yellow fever at Panama, and they had been ordered to a more temperate climate to recuperate. Soon afterward, the gunboat *Resaca,* the *Jamestown's* relief at Panama, was sent to Alaska for the same reason. "Seward's icebox" seemed well on its way to becoming the convalescent ward for the Pacific Station. Although administration of Alaska was entrusted to the Army, warships were directed to cruise in its waters whenever convenient.

The *Cyane* followed the *Jamestown* and *Resaca* as station ship at

Panama. She did good service during political disturbances on the Isthmus, but after a time yellow fever appeared among her men, and she too was sent to Alaska. Thereafter, no station ship was kept at Panama, but cruising vessels were ordered to touch there frequently.

Shipwreck took a heavy toll of the Pacific Squadrons in the immediate postwar years. First to go was the double-ender *Suwanee*. She was bound for Sitka on 9 July 1868 when she struck an uncharted rock in Shadwell Passage. The swiftly ebbing tide left her hanging on the obstruction, and she broke up some forty minutes after stranding. Officers and men saved such gear as they could in small boats, and all reached the shore safely.

Little more than a month later, the South Pacific Squadron suffered a heavier loss. The storeship *Fredonia* had been moved to Arica, Chile, to escape a cholera epidemic raging at Valparaiso. On 13 August, she was riding at anchor in company with the double-ender *Wateree* when a huge tidal wave engulfed the harbor. The storeship filled and sank with the twenty-seven officers and men on board. The luckier *Wateree* was deposited well above the high-water mark on the beach, losing only one man who had been in a small boat at the time. The *Wateree*'s crew and five men from the *Fredonia* who had been on the beach exerted themselves to succor distressed civilians in the wake of the disaster. The gunboat's hull was badly strained, and it was impracticable to refloat her, so she was sold at public auction sometime later. Meanwhile, she remained in commission, carrying out normal warship routine, except that the small boats normally made fast to her boat booms had been replaced by mules.

Eighteen sixty-nine passed without loss, but the ocean claimed another victim in 1870. The little side-wheeler *Saginaw* was returning from Midway Island when Lieutenant Commander Montgomery Sicard made a slight deviation from his course to check the coral reef known as Ocean Island for castaways. Not desiring to arrive during hours of darkness, Sicard ordered the engines slowed until the paddle wheels were barely turning, and the ship ghosted along under her fore topsail. But a defective compass and unknown currents had set the *Saginaw* much closer to her goal than Sicard realized. At 0300 on 29 October, lookouts reported breakers ahead. The engines were reversed immediately, but steam pressure was too low to give her sternway with the topsail set. The *Saginaw* struck just as the sail was clewed up. Within ten minutes, her hold was flooded, and she broke up in less than an hour. Officers and men made their way to the very island from which they had intended to rescue distressed seamen, and the *Saginaw*'s gig, manned by five volunteers, set out to bring assistance from Hawaii. The 1800-mile passage to Kauai Island was completed in thirty days; then, after one of the epic small boat voyages of maritime history, the gig capsized in the surf, and Coxswain William Halford alone survived. The Hawaiian government immediately sent a relief ship, and Sicard and his men were returned to the United States.

Last in this series of losses was the *Saranac*. The veteran side-wheeler was on passage to Sitka when, on 18 June 1875, she stood into the treacherous Seymour Narrows. Captain Walter W. Queen soon found his ship caught in a whirlpool too strong for her feeble engines, and she was thrown violently against Ripple Rock. Queen immediately headed her for the nearest shore; he and his ship's company managed to save themselves, but the *Saranac* sank in deep water. With this sacrifice, the gods of the sea seemed content—for a time.

Commander George Dewey's *Narragansett* undertook a survey of the major steamship routes along the Mexican and Central American coasts in 1873. While engaged in this useful work, the vessel was also available to protect American interests in adjacent regions. In the same year, the Cuban ship *Virginius,* fraudulently registered in the United States and flying American colors, was captured by a Spanish cruiser while she was running arms to Cuban insurgents. The *Virginius* was taken to Havana, and the Spanish authorities executed a number of her passengers. News of the tension between Spain and the United States over the *Virginius* affair reached Dewey in Mexican waters, and later he stated that he had planned to capture Manila with the *Narragansett* in event of war. What his seniors would think of so foolhardy a scheme, he seems not to have considered. One can only assume that the future "Hero of Manila Bay" gained a more balanced and mature judgment in later years.

Other vessels also were employed in hydrographic work. The *Tuscarora* ran lines of soundings from San Francisco to Honolulu and from San Francisco to Australia. The *Nyack* co-operated with the Navy's Selfridge Expedition which surveyed the Isthmus of

Panama, and her small boats explored rivers of the vicinity. At one time or another, almost every warship on Pacific Station was employed on work of this nature, tedious and wearing in the extreme because of the climate and hard work. Only occasionally was the boredom relieved by some novel incident.

One such occurrence placed an officer of the gunboat *Ranger* in a precarious position. He had been using a red flag to signal a companion while surveying a Central American beach. The color had the traditional effect on a nearby bull, and the officer took refuge in the surf where he had "difficulty in determining the safety line between the sharks, which were swarming in the bay, and the irate animal, pawing sand and bellowing on the beach."[4] One of the ship's launches opportunely passed and picked him up before he had to decide which was the lesser of the two evils.

While unsettled conditions in Central America and Mexico were competing with surveying duties for the attention of the North Pacific Squadron, much the same conditions prevailed in the southeastern Pacific. Political uncertainties in South America and the small number of warships assigned to that region made it impossible for the South Pacific Squadron to visit the islands for long periods, and Australia, westernmost point of the station, was virtually ignored.

By 1875, the South Pacific Squadron had become almost nonexistent. Rear Admiral Reed Werden, ordered to assume the command left vacant by the death of Rear Admiral Napoleon Collins, found that his squadron included only the screw-sloops *Richmond* and *Omaha* and the storeship *Onward*. All were badly in need of overhaul, and their obsolescence was only too apparent when they met the modern warships maintained in that area by Great Britain, France, Prussia, and even some of the Latin American countries. In vain, Werden repeated the requests of his predecessors that his squadron be reinforced, or at least that the *Richmond* receive essential repairs.

So matters stood when, on 2 May 1876, Werden received orders to proceed to the South Atlantic in his flagship to assume command of that station. By trans-Andean telegraph, he acknowledged receipt of the orders, and added that he could not obey until the *Richmond*'s hull, machinery, and sails had been renewed sufficiently to enable her to undertake the mid-winter passage around Cape Horn. If no orders to the contrary were sent, the necessary repairs would be made at Callao.

The work proceeded, and Werden expected to sail within three weeks when, to his surprise, Commodore Charles H. B. Caldwell arrived on 12 July to relieve him. Protesting bitterly at this summary relief, Werden returned to Washington. Secretary Robeson and Admiral David Dixon Porter, senior officer of the Navy, were deaf to his plea that a general court-martial be convened to investigate his conduct. Their refusal was not surprising; a court-martial would reveal their responsibility for the *Richmond*'s poor condition. Rear Admiral Werden realized that his position was hopeless, so he requested, and received, retirement on the ground of ill-health. He was never employed again.

But conditions were not improved on either of the stations. Rear Admiral Alexander Murray's North Pacific Squadron consisted of the screw-sloops *Pensacola* and *Lackawanna* in 1876, while Captain Edward B. Simpson, senior officer in the South Pacific, had only the storeship *Onward* besides his own command, *Omaha*. Rear Admiral George Henry Preble broke his flag in the latter during 1877, but neither squadron was reinforced.

Disturbances reminiscent of the gold rush days and Vigilante activity broke out in San Francisco in 1877. Some Chinese laundries were burned, and a "citizens' protective association" was hurriedly formed to stop the rioting. At the same time, telegraphic appeal for naval aid reached President Rutherford B. Hayes, and soon the North Pacific Squadron (*Pensacola* and *Lackawanna*) was anchored off the city. Its presence was enough; order was restored, and the Governor of California expressed his appreciation to Admiral Murray, together with the opinion that the proximity of the warships was in large part responsible for the tranquillity of hitherto turbulent San Francisco.

A single Pacific Station was re-established in 1878, and Rear Admiral Christopher R. P. Rodgers assumed command of the screw-sloops *Pensacola, Alaska,* and *Lackawanna,* the gunboat *Adams,* and the storeship *Onward.* None of these vessels possessed armor, modern rifled guns, efficient steam engines, or any of the various other improvements introduced since the Civil War. All were built of wood, and none was in good condition. Commander in chief and

Navy Department alike were reluctant to order ships to Mare Island for overhaul, as that yard had a reputation for making such work last as long as possible, and the ship which entered the yard for minor repairs was lost to the squadron for months.[5]

The small force under his command did not prevent Rodgers from carrying out a policy of active cruising. During 1878, vessels of the Pacific Squadron "visited all points along the coast from Puget Sound to Valparaiso as well as Honolulu and Apia, Samoa."[6] Warships sent to assist the wrecked American merchantman *H. N. Carlton* at Molokai found that she had some fifty Chinese passengers in excess of the number certified to have been on board at her port of departure. Obviously she was participating in the illegal trade in Chinese coolies, so orders went out for Asiatic and Pacific Squadrons to intercept American vessels involved in this traffic.

Military forces had been withdrawn from Alaska in 1876, leaving a few customs officials as the only representatives of the United States government in the territory. An occasional visit by a revenue cutter was the only support these gentlemen had; by 1879, "Alaska was absolutely without any form of local government, and was in a condition almost as free from the operation of civil law as the interior of Africa."[7] Quite obviously, something had to be done, and a threatened Indian outbreak in 1879 brought action. No vessel of the Pacific Squadron was immediately available, so HMS *Osprey* was dispatched from the British naval base at Esquimalt on Vancouver Island. The sailing sloop *Jamestown* was hurriedly fitted out and recommissioned at Mare Island, and Commander Lester A. Beardslee took her to Sitka to relieve the *Osprey*. As soon as the situation there was under control, Beardslee sent out parties to bring order to more remote areas. The *Jamestown*'s lack of power was an insuperable handicap; consequently, the tortuous channels and sounds of southeastern Alaska were traversed by the steam launches which she carried.

The screw-sloop *Wachusett* relieved the *Jamestown* in 1881, and a warship was stationed at Sitka continuously until the close of the century. Ships of the Revenue Cutter Service did most of the cruising in western Alaskan and Aleutian waters, but administration of the more populous southeastern region was the responsibility of the warship's commanding officer. Personnel of the Revenue Cutter Service lacked the training and discipline essential for that duty. As before, the ship stationed at Sitka was attached to the Pacific Squadron, but the commander in chief exercised no real control over the station ship, whose commanding officer reported directly to the Navy Department.

Several vessels took their turns at Sitka until 1886 when the iron seagoing tug *Pinta* arrived on the scene. This little ship remained the law in southeastern Alaska for the next eleven years, cruising the inland waters during summer months and spending the period from September to March moored to eight anchors in the inner harbor of Sitka. Officers and men enjoyed the winter sports and took an active part in the simple social life. Duty in the *Pinta* was not wildly exciting, but it had its recompenses.

While threatened violence in Alaska was calling for attention, the always delicate situation in South America had exploded into open warfare. This was the War of the Pacific between Chile, on one hand, and Peru and Bolivia, on the other. No more than the usual interest was shown by the United States Navy until 1881, when Rear Admiral George B. Balch was ordered to take his Pacific Squadron on a round of visits to the ports of the three combatant states. At each port, officers were directed to observe carefully conditions and developments and to make full reports to the Navy Department. No trouble was expected, but it was thought desirable to have a respectable force patrolling the South American coast.

The four old screw-sloops and gunboats with which Balch sailed comprised a force respectable by the standards of the United States Navy at the time, but no foreign naval officer could conceal his scorn for such museum pieces. This fact was borne out by a story, probably apocryphal, current at the time. Kindly old Admiral Balch was attempting to mediate between Chile and Peru, whereupon a senior Chilean naval officer asserted that as soon as he had finished with the Peruvians, he would destroy the American Pacific Squadron and after it the whole United States Navy if necessary. In fact, the Chilean Navy did possess several modern warships which were far superior to the most formidable vessel flying the American flag.

American warships continued their patrol of the South American coast for the rest of the decade, although events elsewhere on the Pacific Station required the attention of the commander in chief as well. The flagship visited other waters after the War of the Pacific ended in 1884, but American interests from Panama to Valparaiso were given somewhat questionable protection by the continued presence of several of the old men-o'-war. The *Wachusett*'s Commander Alfred T. Mahan, who spent two years on this duty, found it extremely dull, and made no complaint when he received orders to take his ship to Mare Island for decommissioning before he joined the faculty of Rear Admiral Stephen B. Luce's new Naval War College.

Events in the Hawaiian Islands eclipsed the South American situation, and Rear Admiral Lewis A. Kimberly hastened there in the flagship *Vandalia* in July 1887, leaving the *Alert, Iroquois,* and *Mohican* to watch Latin American affairs. The immediate cause for concern in Hawaii was a political quarrel between the conservative government and the pro-American faction; the latter was trying to force the adoption of a liberal constitution. American interests had been clearly dominant in Hawaii since ratification of a reciprocity treaty in 1875. This had been renewed in 1884, but the United States Senate held it up until Hawaii granted exclusive use of Pearl Harbor in 1887.

Through the rest of that year, Admiral Kimberly remained at Honolulu with several ships, whose presence probably helped to preserve the peace while the political situation was being resolved by acceptance of the pro-American faction's constitution. Officers from the *Vandalia* put their time to good use in making surveys which enabled the admiral to report on Pearl Harbor's value as a naval base site.

As Kimberly watched conditions in Hawaii, yet another trouble spot on his station was bubbling and threatening to boil over. This was Samoa, more or less considered to be the "Hawaii" of the South Pacific. In 1872, Commander Richard W. Meade of the USS *Narragansett* had concluded a treaty with the "Great Chief" at Pago Pago whereby the United States received the exclusive right to establish a coaling station at that harbor in return for "friendship and protection." Like Thomas ap Catesby Jones's earlier treaties with Tahiti and Hawaii, this died in the United States Senate. Nevertheless, a year later a State Department representative visited Samoa, so it was clear that American interest still existed. Another treaty of

1878 gained the coaling station at Pago Pago in return for a promise that the United States would act as mediator between Samoa and any third power. A shipload of coal was deposited at Pago Pago three years later for the use of the Pacific and Asiatic Squadrons.

Great Britain, whose interest in Samoa was nearly as old as that of the United States, and Germany, an eager newcomer to the Pacific, secured treaty rights in Samoa soon after 1878. The succeeding years witnessed growing tension as consular officials of the three powers conspired against one another, and political conditions approached anarchy. Admiral Kimberly sent the gunboat *Adams* to Samoa in October 1887, and in succeeding months a warship was kept there almost constantly. The admiral complained that Samoa actually required the services of two vessels, as Honolulu was the nearest port where supplies could be obtained. Nevertheless, a man-o'-war was required in Samoan waters because there was no doubt as to German intentions. German forces had been present since August 1887 and were taking an active part in local affairs, having deposed King Malietoa in favor of the pro-German Tamasese. Observers feared that the Germans would resort to force if the latter was not acceptable to the Samoans.

The *Mohican* relieved the *Adams* at Samoa, and Kimberly warned that December to March was the hurricane season; any vessel forced to ride out such a storm in the unprotected roadstead at Apia would be in grave danger. But no hurricane occurred in 1888. Spring, summer, and autumn passed with no more than the usual political disturbances. Kimberly was able to return to San Francisco to welcome a new flagship, the screw-frigate *Trenton*. One of the newest and most formidable American warships then in commission, the *Trenton* was still a ship of the "old" Navy, built of wood, armed with obsolete guns, and boasting full sail rig to supplement a steam engine that was hardly modern.

The flagship was at Panama early in January 1889 when Admiral Kimberly learned that Samoan affairs had flared into open violence. Commander Dennis W. Mullan sent an officer to Auckland, New Zealand, to telegraph the Navy Department that German landing parties had been defeated by Samoans, whereupon the German warships had shelled and burned several villages in retaliation. Mullan's gunboat *Nipsic* was the only American vessel at Samoa, and he joined the American consul in urging that reinforcements be sent.

Kimberly was ordered to Apia to protect American citizens and interests, to assist in restoring peace, and to collect information by which his government could determine the extent of German responsibility for the violence. The storeship *Monongahela* was prepared to take coal and supplies to Apia, so that Kimberly could remain there as long as was necessary.

By the time the *Trenton* and *Vandalia* had joined the *Nipsic* at Apia, it was known that Germany had declared war on Samoa, and the German warships *Olga, Eber,* and *Adler* were preparing to inflict drastic punishment on the Samoans. However, the German government was not desirous of antagonizing the United States, and tension eased slightly as the three interested powers named delegates to attend a conference at Berlin. HMS *Calliope* arrived to represent the Royal Navy in any eventuality; thus, the little anchorage of Apia was crowded with warships as February gave way to March. But February had warned of things to come; during that month, a gale had driven the American barkentine *Constitution* ashore, and her crew was rescued by a boat from the *Nipsic*.

There was still danger of hostilities, but a rising wind and other signs of approaching bad weather caused the various commanding officers to look to the safety of their ships on the afternoon of 15 March. All made preparations for weathering another storm at anchor. But this was no ordinary gale; a hurricane vented its fury on the poorly protected harbor the next day. For a time, the ships were able to steam up to their anchors and so prevent them from dragging, but feeble power plants were unequal to the task.

Whether the *Trenton*'s engines could have saved her will never be known. Her rudder was disabled by heavy seas, and the continuous battering of the gigantic waves washed the stoppers from her hawse-pipes, which were placed below the main deck in order that her forward guns might be trained to fire nearly dead ahead. Tons of water entered her lower deck and soon reached a depth sufficient to extinguish her boiler fires. From that moment she was doomed. Slowly she dragged through the welter of spray and wreck, narrowly avoiding collision with other vessels, German and American, which were also dragging inexorably toward the shore.

As the *Trenton* suffered through her last hours of life, one ship was waging a more successful battle against the storm. HMS *Calliope,* the latest arrival, had been forced to moor farther inshore than the other ships, and she too was unable to ride out the hurricane at anchor. Finally Captain Henry C. Kane slipped his chains, and the *Calliope* stood out for the open sea under every pound of steam that could be coaxed from her straining boilers. It was barely enough. She edged past the helpless *Trenton,* avoiding collision by only a few yards and receiving a cheer from Admiral Kimberly and the undaunted men who could appreciate a good fight even when their own case seemed hopeless.

The first morning light of 17 March 1889 revealed a scene of desolation in Apia Harbor. SMS *Olga* and the USS *Nipsic* had been beached in fair condition, SMS *Adler* was on her beam ends, the USS *Trenton* was on a reef from which she would never be floated, and nearby, masts and a smokestack revealed the last resting place of the USS *Vandalia.* HMS *Calliope* and SMS *Eber* had vanished; the former had won her fight for sea room, while the little German gunboat had carried most of her company to the bottom. American losses numbered fifty officers and men, among them the *Vandalia*'s Captain Cornelius M. Schoonmaker. Heroic exertions by the Samoans and by the *Trenton*'s men had saved most of the *Vandalia*'s crew.

International rivalry had been forgotten in the battle against nature, and all hands turned to at the work of caring for survivors and refloating the *Nipsic* and *Olga.* Despite the opinion of Mullan and some of his men that their ship could not be made seaworthy, Kimberly persisted. Eventually, the battered gunboat, fitted with the *Vandalia*'s stack (her own had been lost), sailed for Auckland in company with the *Alert.* But Mullan's doubts overcame his determination to save his ship, and the two returned to Apia. Kimberly removed the faint-hearted officer from his command, and the *Nipsic* and *Alert* sailed for Honolulu, too much time having elapsed to escape the season of storms in the vicinity of New Zealand. Although the *Nipsic* ran out of fuel and was forced to anchor at Johnston Island while her consort brought a deckload of coal from Honolulu, Hawaii was reached without further untoward event. The *Nipsic* returned to service after receiving extensive repairs.

The disaster at Apia left only the *Alert, Mohican,* and *Monongahela* available for service in the eastern Pacific, and two of these vessels were employed in salvage work at Samoa. However, the commandant at Mare Island notified the Navy Department that he could have the gunboats *Thetis* and *Adams* ready by the end of April, and that the *Iroquois* could be commissioned a month later. So the Pacific Squadron was not completely destroyed at Apia, as has been stated so frequently. The ships commissioned to replace the storm victims were not formidable warships, to be sure, but they would suffice for the Pacific Station.

At Apia, Admiral Kimberly gained deserved respect for his handling of affairs, both diplomatic and naval. He was the senior officer present, and German and English officers alike deferred to his judgment. The decision of the Berlin Conference to leave Samoa in the hands of a three-power condominium, and the willingness of the Samoans to accept the restored King Malietoa, made it possible for Kimberly to depart for Honolulu on 13 September 1889. The admiral, whose best work was done after the disaster, took with him the affectionate wishes of Samoan and foreigner alike. Malietoa even expressed the wish that he could make Kimberly joint ruler of Samoa.

On 27 January 1890, Rear Admiral Kimberly broke his flag in the new cruiser *Charleston* at San Francisco, and later in the day, he was relieved by Acting Rear Admiral George Brown. The ritual of hauling down his flag marked more than the end of Kimberly's eventful cruise. His last flagship was much more akin to HMS *Calliope* than to the USS *Trenton,* and the change of command ceremonies in a modern warship ushered in the era of the "new" Navy on Pacific Station. Some of the obsolete wooden ships continued to serve on all of the stations maintained by the United States, but it is very nearly correct to say that the "old" Navy terminated in the hurricane which wrecked the *Trenton* and *Vandalia.*

10. *A Stagnant Station*

Although Acting Rear Admiral George Brown had a modern cruiser for his flagship, the remainder of his squadron was still a part of the "old" Navy. The *Mohican, Iroquois,* and *Ranger* featured the familiar combination of full sail rig and muzzle-loading guns, and their presence indicated that the transition from "old" to "new" would not be a rapid process, at least on Pacific Station.

Nor was the *Charleston* a formidable warship even by the standards of that day. Her armament was not unimpressive, but in no sense was she intended to take a place in the line of battle. She was too lightly protected for anything other than scouting or commerce raiding, and her eighteen-knot speed was barely adequate for these duties, especially since that speed was largely theoretical. Foreign designers had incorporated such a mixture of old and new ideas in her engines that they were never completely dependable until rebuilt.[1]

Squadron maneuvers, absent from the Pacific Station since 1842, if one excepts the tactical drills carried out in 1883 by Rear Admiral Aaron K. Hughes, were impossible with so heterogeneous a squadron. But the formation of the "Squadron of Evolution" on the Atlantic coast in 1889 presaged a new awareness of the value of such maneuvers throughout the United States Navy.

Had the recommendations made to Secretary of the Navy Benjamin F. Tracy in 1889 by Commodore James A. Greer, head of the Board on Organization, been put into effect at that time, the Pacific Squadron would soon have received enough modern warships to make tactical maneuvers practicable. Greer held that the effective fighting ships should be gathered in fleets based on the Atlantic and Pacific coasts, while detached small squadrons or single ships per-

143

formed the police duties presently the major concern of the Navy. He added:

> This method, with the flag officer commanding having stated head-quarters, would lead to a better management of the naval force at the disposal of the government. At present, for example, in the Pacific, the flag officer commanding is often of little assistance to the Department in disposing his force to advantage because of his inability to communicate promptly with the Dept. and with vessels of his command.[2]

The advantages of this organization were obvious, but the fact was that there were not enough effective warships to put it into operation immediately. Even after the Navy had obtained these, the recommended reorganization was not realized in the Pacific Ocean until after the turn of the century.

Admiral Brown's first success on Pacific Station was in the field of Navy regulations. Since his permanent rank was that of commodore, he was decidedly junior to the commandant of the Mare Island Navy Yard, Rear Admiral Andrew E. K. Benham. When Brown's flagship first visited the yard, her saluting battery boomed out the thirteen-gun salute due Benham's flag, but the old *Independence* answered with only eleven guns. Brown protested in vain; he was only a commodore in Benham's eyes. An exchange of letters with the Navy Department followed, and Benham was informed that he was wrong. Accordingly, some three months later the *Charleston* again arrived at Mare Island, and was received with a thirteen-gun salute. This was in answer to Brown's earlier salute; consequently, the cruiser's guns did not reply. The Pacific Squadron had emerged victorious from the battle of the regulations.

Like his predecessors, Admiral Brown found it necessary to spend much of his time at Honolulu, and there he was when a revolution broke out in Chile in 1891. Chilean adherents of congressional government were attempting to block President Balmaceda's assumption of dictatorial powers and needed arms for that purpose. These were obtained in the United States, and arrangements were made for the steamer *Itata* to load them at San Diego. This was protested by Balmacedist sympathizers in the United States; hence, the ship was seized and placed in custody of a deputy marshal. However, the vessel left San Diego on 6 May 1891, landed the American officer, and stood to the southward after loading the arms from a schooner at sea.

The USS *Charleston,* no longer carrying Brown's flag, was ordered in pursuit, and for a time it was feared that she might have to fight the Chilean cruiser *Esmeralda,* thought to be escorting *Itata. But* the *Charleston* was unable to intercept the merchant vessel before the latter's arrival at Iquique, Chile. Authorities there surrendered her readily, and she headed back toward the United States, escorted by the *Charleston.* Although the Congressionalist officials at Iquique had acted properly with a minimum of unpleasantness, the incident added another to the grievances held against the United States by ambitious Chileans.

As it was impossible to communicate rapidly with Brown at Honolulu, Rear Admiral William P. McCann, commanding the South Atlantic Squadron, was ordered to the coast of Chile in his flagship *Pensacola* when the revolution began. The waters south of Callao were added to the South Atlantic Station temporarily. McCann was reinforced by the modern cruiser *Baltimore* from the Atlantic, and Rear Admiral Brown in the new *San Francisco* joined him soon afterward. McCann transferred the command to Brown in July and returned to his station in a merchant vessel. The *Baltimore* remained at Valparaiso, while the *Pensacola* was sent to San Francisco.

More tension resulted from Admiral Brown's visit to Quinteros Bay to observe troop landings and to watch a battle developing there. The Congressionalists, now obviously winning, accused the American officer of giving information and encouragement to their foes, although there seems to have been little basis for the accusations.

At any rate, the feeling toward Americans was very unfriendly when Captain Winfield S. Schley, commanding the *Baltimore,* decided to grant liberty to his men at Valparaiso. About one hundred and fifteen sailors entered the city on 16 October 1891, and a few hours later were involved in a series of riots in which the police also proved to be decidedly anti-American. Two American enlisted men were killed, and eighteen others were wounded. Whether or not the sailors were drunk (Chileans and Schley could not agree on this point), Schley had acted unwisely in granting liberty when he was acquainted with the temper of the Chileans. He then allowed himself to become involved in a rather pointless argument about the sobriety of his men, and the situation seemed extremely grave.

It appeared very likely that the United States might go to war with Chile in December 1891. The Chilean government was extremely slow in accepting responsibility for the *Baltimore* incident, and the whole tone of the correspondence relating to it seemed to be leading up to hostilities. As Brown had returned to Californian waters before the incident occurred, Schley was warned to be ready for any eventuality, and the modern gunboat *Yorktown* was ordered from the Atlantic to join him.

American naval preparations were much more extensive than was commonly realized at the time. An informal strategy board, which included Captain A. T. Mahan and officers from the Office of Naval Intelligence, formulated plans for operations in southeastern Pacific waters. Negotiations with Peru for obtaining a naval base site on Chimbote Bay had been conducted sporadically since the end of the War of the Pacific in 1884 and with more interest after 1889, but the American desire for exclusive territorial jurisdiction had prevented any agreement. Hence there were no coaling facilities in the region which American warships could rely on, and Admiral Brown pointed out that a fleet of steam colliers would be required in addition to all of the modern men-o'-war to ensure success. Perhaps Secretary Tracy was more excited about the possibility of war than any of his advisers; he even urged that the uncompleted monitor *Monterey,* still without her armor at San Francisco, be rushed to sea as soon as her guns could be mounted and steam raised in her boilers.

Fortunately for all concerned, cooler heads prevailed. The *Yorktown*'s Commander Robley D. Evans showed unexpected diplomatic skill, together with his usual firmness, in handling the situation at Valparaiso; and the Chileans became somewhat more reasonable after Captain Schley departed in the *Baltimore.* President Benjamin Harrison's bellicosity was curbed by Secretary of State James G. Blaine, while the Chileans were coming to realize that they could not hope to wage successful war against a nation more than twenty times their superior. Accordingly, the Chilean Foreign Minister sent an apology early in 1892, and the families of the murdered sailors were ultimately paid some $75,000. The war scare subsided quickly thereafter, but Chile did not forget her humiliation, and the citizens of the Pacific coast states had been made fully aware of their vulnerability.

Another duty which came the way of the Pacific Squadron in 1891 was that of enforcing the *modus vivendi* for the regulation of pelagic sealing reached by a Paris tribunal. The United States had been alarmed at the rapid depletion of the herds of fur seals which bred on the Pribilof Islands in the Bering Sea. Warships and revenue cutters had occasionally cruised in these waters for their protection after 1869, and in 1889 orders had been issued that schooners participating in the hunt anywhere in the Bering Sea were to be seized. Most of these sealers were Canadian, and their government, supported by the Court of St. James, had protested vigorously at this American attempt to transform the Bering Sea into a *mare clausum*. The tribunal decided that the United States must pay damages for the vessels so seized and outlined some rather ineffectual rules governing the conduct of the sealers.

The United States and Royal Navies were assigned the duty of enforcing these regulations, but the majority of the patrolling was carried out by Americans. The *Thetis* sailed from San Francisco for this purpose on 17 June 1891, and the *Mohican, Marion,* and *Alert* soon followed. Every summer thereafter for the remainder of the century some of the older and smaller ships of the Pacific Squadron, together with revenue cutters operating under the orders of the senior naval officer, cruised the Bering Sea to watch the activities of the sealing schooners. It was hard, uncomfortable, and unrewarding work, and their base at Unalaska provided nothing beyond coal and the most essential supplies. Small wonder it came to be regarded as duty fit only for outcasts.

There is a story of an officer who called at the Bureau of Navigation in Washington to request assignment to a vessel fitting out for a cruise with the popular and socially desirable European Squadron. He informed the Bureau chief that he had been at sea for many years on Pacific Station, his last cruise having been in the Bering Sea. "I'm sorry," the old admiral replied, "but officers who cruise in the Behring [*sic*] Sea are not the ones we send to Europe. Good-morning."[3]

After 1900, this duty was performed almost entirely by vessels of the Revenue Cutter Service, and the fur seal herds were saved from extinction by agreement of the United States, Japan, Russia, and Great Britain in the North Pacific Sealing Convention of 1911.

In September 1892, the Pacific Station received evidence that it was still of secondary importance in the eyes of the Navy Department. Admiral Brown acknowledged an order to transfer his flag to the old *Mohican* in order that his erstwhile flagship might join a Special Service Squadron being formed under the command of Rear Admiral Bancroft Gherardi. This was to include the modern warships *Baltimore, San Francisco, Charleston, Boston,* and *Yorktown;* the Pacific Squadron was left with the *Mohican, Alliance, Adams, Ranger,* and *Thetis,* all obsolete and inefficient. However, the *Boston*'s presence was required at Honolulu, so she did not join Gherardi's flag. She was reassigned to the Pacific Squadron in 1893.

The Special Service Squadron left San Francisco in the autumn of 1892, and made its leisurely way down the coast, exercising in fleet tactics and routine drills. A novel and presumably noisy facet of the night maneuvers was the use of steam whistles for transmission of Morse code signals. Admiral Gherardi's ships visited the various ports on the Central American and South American coasts before passing through the Strait of Magellan to join the North Atlantic Squadron.

The situation which had called Admiral Brown to Honolulu just before the outbreak of the Chilean revolution, and later had kept the *Boston* from sailing with the Special Service Squadron, resulted from the death of the irresolute Hawaiian King. His strong-willed and anti-American sister Liliuokalani succeeded to the throne early in 1891. Two-thirds of the taxable real estate in the kingdom belonged to a little group of Americans, and they feared for their property. The United States government too was interested because of its right to the naval station site at Pearl Harbor.

Two years after assuming the throne, Liliuokalani was ready to act. She staged a *coup d'etat,* ousted her few American advisers, and imposed an autocratic constitution on the kingdom. This action did not catch the local American leaders off guard. A revolution was quickly organized, and United States Minister John L. Stevens was asked to lend his support. He arranged with Captain Gilbert C. Wiltse to land more than one hundred and fifty sailors and Marines from the *Boston* to protect American lives and property. With this reinforcement, the Americans definitely had the upper hand, and Stevens recognized the revolutionary government on 17 January 1893, one day after the *Boston*'s men landed. A commission hastened to Washington to arrange for American annexation, and on 1 February, Stevens proclaimed Hawaii an American protectorate.

Washington and American public opinion were favorable to immediate annexation, but President-elect Grover Cleveland requested that the Senate postpone action on the treaty until after his inauguration. He then withdrew the treaty from the Senate, and sent ex-Congressman James H. Blount to make a thorough investigation of Hawaiian affairs. Georgian Blount was greeted in Honolulu by the Royal Hawaiian band playing "Marching through Georgia," an air hardly calculated to make an ex-Rebel look with favor on things Hawaiian.

Blount ordered the landing force re-embarked in the *Boston,* had the American flag hauled down, and found that a majority of the populace was not in favor of annexation. Blount's report led Cleveland to order Liliuokalani restored to her throne on the condition that the revolutionists be treated leniently. She retorted that their heads, as well as their lands, would be removed. Under the circumstances, the revolutionists could not be expected to surrender peaceably; moreover, their army was in control of the situation. As Cleveland could not use force to restore the deposed queen, he accepted the situation by recognizing the Hawaiian Republic in 1894.

An impartial student of the Hawaiian revolution has concluded that it could not possibly have succeeded without the presence of the *Boston*'s landing force, most of which was disposed in positions calculated to intimidate the Queen and some distance from the American property it was supposedly guarding. The account published by an officer of the *Boston* makes it very evident that Wiltse and his subordinates were strongly opposed to Liliuokalani's rule and sympathetic to the aims of the revolutionists.

Clearly the naval forces were guilty of unneutral conduct in this instance. But it need not be concluded that they were governed by motives highly improper in naval officers. For some years the Navy, and the American public as well, had been swayed by the arguments of Captain Mahan that Hawaii in foreign hands would be a definite threat to the west coast of the United States, as well as to the Central American region where one day a canal linking Pacific and Caribbean might be constructed. In addition, it cannot be doubted that many features of Liliuokalani's rule were repugnant to the American naval officers.

However, there can be no doubt as to the significance of the rejection of the treaty of annexation for the Pacific Squadron. Honolulu would continue to be a focal point of the whole Pacific Station until Hawaii was finally annexed.

The Pacific Squadron which Brown turned over to Rear Admiral John Irwin in 1893 was almost devoid of modern ships, but the monitor *Monterey,* a ship which had been many years a-building, was commissioned at San Francisco soon afterward. Fitted only for coast defense duties, she was of doubtful value to the squadron. The protected cruiser *Philadelphia* came out to carry Irwin's flag, and in 1894 the new gunboat *Bennington* arrived from the Atlantic coast. The *Charleston* and *Yorktown* also were under orders for the Pacific, but Rear Admiral Lester A. Beardslee assumed command only of the *Philadelphia, Monterey, Bennington,* and some older ships in 1895.

Soon after taking command of the Pacific Squadron, Beardslee was informed that the Navy Department wished him to assemble such vessels as could be spared from other duties for squadron maneuvers at least every six months. But the composition of his squadron made it impossible that much value should result from tactical evolutions. One cruiser, a gunboat, and a monitor could never form an effective tactical unit, and the older ships were too slow and weak to participate in most drills. However, the commander in chief replied that he would carry out maneuvers before cruising to the southward to visit Californian and Mexican ports.

In the last days of 1895, President Cleveland's handling of the British Guiana–Venezuela boundary controversy brought into sharp focus the weakness of the Pacific Squadron. His message to the Congress in mid-December virtually threatened the British government with war if it attempted to enforce its claims upon Venezuela without resort to arbitration. With Anglo-American relations almost at the breaking point, there was fear of attack in the Puget Sound region by torpedo boats from the Royal Navy's base at Esquimalt in

British Columbia. The only vessel of the Pacific Squadron available for defense of that area was the monitor *Monterey,* and Beardslee revealed that she required repairs before undertaking such service. Moreover, the distinctive qualities of her type—low speed, poor maneuverability, and low freeboard—made her peculiarly liable to capture by boarding and vulnerable to torpedo attack, although it now appears that reports of British torpedo boats at Esquimalt were erroneous.

The senators and congressmen of the three coastal states memorialized Secretary of the Navy Hilary A. Herbert with regard to the lack of protection for the Pacific coast. Herbert replied that the Pacific Squadron would soon be strengthened by the commissioning of the monitor *Monadnock.* This was not the Civil War monitor, but a ship built to replace her with the funds allotted for repairs to the original. This was known as "administrative rebuilding" since there was no authority to build a new vessel. This second *Monadnock* was under construction for more than twenty years. The Secretary also advised the west coast representatives that the battleship *Oregon,* nearing completion at the Union Iron Works, would be placed in commission if Congress would appropriate enough money to provide a crew for her.

Even with the Pacific Squadron so reinforced, it is well that diplomacy and Afro-European affairs made Great Britain averse to an American war. Among Her Majesty's vessels in the eastern Pacific in 1896 were the armored cruiser *Imperieuse* and the cruisers *Royal Arthur* and *Icarus,* none so formidable as the *Oregon,* but the battleship could hardly have become an efficient fighting unit in less than six months. The *Monterey* and *Monadnock* carried heavier guns than the Britons, but would have been effective only under the most favorable conditions. However, the only warlike message received by Beardslee was that ordering him to keep his vessels fully coaled and ready for sea, and soon the tension eased.

For some time Americans had feared that the Japanese might attempt to gain control of the Hawaiian Islands, and this feeling was intensified in 1897 by reports that the government of Japan was undertaking a slow "mongolization" of the islands by the many Japanese settling there. Accordingly, the commander in chief of the Pacific Squadron was ordered there to remain as long as necessary.

Beardslee protested that this order had the effect of isolating him from the rest of his station as communication with Honolulu was completely dependent on mail steamers, but the Department replied that his presence was necessary in Hawaiian waters. As the Japanese cruiser *Naniwa* at Honolulu was rumored to be loaded with arms for Japanese nationals, the State Department told its representative there to be prepared to meet force with force and to proclaim an American protectorate if Japanese occupation was attempted.

So matters stood when Rear Admiral Joseph N. Miller arrived in the *Baltimore* to assume command of the Pacific Station later in 1897. He remained at Honolulu, and such attention as other parts of the station received was from warships operating virtually independent of the commander in chief.

While the Hawaiian situation was yet undecided, events far to the eastward were moving steadily toward the Spanish-American War. The destruction of the USS *Maine* in Havana Harbor on 15 February 1898 must have prepared naval officers for the occurrences which followed. Early in March, Secretary John D. Long left Assistant Secretary Theodore Roosevelt temporarily in charge of the Navy Department, and the latter took full advantage of the opportunity to prepare the Navy for the war he desired so ardently. To Mare Island went orders to load the old *Mohican* with ammunition for Commodore George Dewey's Asiatic Squadron. This was transshipped to the flagship *Baltimore* at Honolulu, and she departed for Hong Kong as soon as Miller had transferred his flag to the *Mohican*.

At this time, the battleship *Oregon* was being docked at the Puget Sound Naval Station. That base had been formally established at Bremerton, Washington, in 1891, but so slowly had it been developed that almost its only facility was the dry dock completed in 1896.[4] The battleship was undesirably large for docking at Mare Island and had been sent to Bremerton. But, with war threatening, the most powerful warship in the eastern Pacific had no offensive power at all, unless she employed the collision tactics suggested by her ram bow, for her ammunition was safely stored at Mare Island, distant some eight hundred miles by sea. Orders went out for her to be undocked and sailed to San Francisco with utmost dispatch. She arrived on 9 March, and coal and ammunition were hastily taken on board, while Captain Charles E. Clark relieved Captain Albert Barker as her commanding officer. The gunboat *Marietta* at Panama was ordered to arrange for a supply of coal at Callao and more southerly ports where the battleship would touch on her way to the Atlantic via the Strait of Magellan. The *Oregon* stood out through the Golden Gate on 19 March, bound for a more active role in the Spanish-American War than any of her less fortunate sisters of the Pacific Squadron.

Midway through April, Roosevelt favored his superior with a view of the preparation of the Pacific Squadron:

The Commander-in-Chief of the Pacific Station should be at once ordered to return to San Francisco. He should then undertake the protection of the Pacific coast, using his own discretion, but providing that the *Monterey* and *Monadnock* with their scouts should protect San Fransisco [*sic*] and Puget Sound, and that one of the vessels should be kept at San Francisco to cruise up and down the coast wherever needed; that if possible a war vessel should protect southern California, and that at least five vessels, with their headquarters at Unalaska and Sitka, should be used in protecting the coal piles and Yukon trade from the mouth of the Yukon to Puget Sound.[5]

Secretary Long ordered Miller to return to San Francisco with his staff on 19 April, but the inevitable communications delay prevented the admiral from complying for some weeks. He finally arrived in the mail steamer on 10 May. Meanwhile, provisions for the defense of the Pacific coast were put into effect as the *Monadnock* steamed north to Puget Sound, while the *Monterey* remained at San Francisco. With the declaration of war on 25 April, an Auxiliary Naval Force composed of revenue cutters, armed yachts, and other hastily converted vessels, manned in part by the Naval Militia, came into being. At first its ships in the Pacific were placed under Admiral Miller, but that officer was still isolated from his squadron and from rapid communication with the Navy Department. Accordingly, Captain John R. Bartlett, commanding the Auxiliary Naval Force in the Atlantic, received command of the Pacific section also, with Lieutenant William E. Gunn as his assistant in California. Such a separation of command was inherently faulty, and in fact Admiral Miller exercised direction of all the naval forces on Pacific Station after he arrived in San Francisco.

Commodore Dewey's decisive victory at Manila Bay on 1 May relieved the Pacific coast from any immediate danger so the Pacific Squadron became a reservoir from which the more actively engaged forces could draw additional vessels. The cruiser *Charleston* was hastily recommissioned at Mare Island and escorted transports to the Philippines. The monitors *Monterey* and *Monadnock* departed to join Dewey's flag in June, and the Fishery Commission's oceanographic vessel *Albatross* became flagship of the Pacific Squadron. The remainder of Miller's force included four revenue cutters, three tugs, and the gunboat *Wheeling*. The latter, the squadron's only warship, was ordered to Alaskan waters by the Department and so was not available to Miller. The gunboat *Bennington* was at Honolulu, and joined the flag at San Francisco when relieved by the *Mohican.*

When the Navy Department requested a copy of Miller's war plans, he replied that he had indeed prepared such plans, but detachment of ships from his force had made them meaningless almost before they could be completed:

Now with the present force . . . it is only possible to patrol the harbors on the Coast which are mined, and to keep these few poorly armed vessels ready for any service of convoy or patrol work which may be required of them. The *Perry* is in Puget Sound and will be used for patrol work in that locality, the *Corwin* will leave in a day or two for San Diego Bay to protect the mines there; the *Grant* and *Rush* are here, and the *Albatross* will not be ready for about a week. When the *Bennington* returns and is ready for service, she will be kept here unless the Department otherwise directs. The three tugs are not yet ready, but work is being pushed on them. In this connection I would state that there is no apprehension among commercial people on this Coast as to danger from the enemy, and that practically there is no insurance war risk.[6]

Miller went on to say that, if the war continued and events took an unfortunate turn, he would concentrate on defense of the San Francisco region.

Rumors that a Spanish privateer was operating in the Puget Sound vicinity sent the *Bennington* to the northward in July to investigate, but her commander found nothing. When the United States consul at El Salvador expressed fears that Spanish sympathizers might try to seize one of the Pacific Mail steamers in the same manner as that attempted by Confederates during the Civil War, the

Navy Department felt it necessary to take no steps beyond warning the Pacific Mail Steamship Company. No more concise indication of the lack of actual danger to the Pacific coast, or of the diminished importance of the Panama route, could be needed than this calmness of the Department. At the same time, it was realized that the Spaniards might send a raiding force to this undefended area and ships of other squadrons were supplied with charts to enable them to operate in the eastern Pacific if necessary.

Agitation for annexation of Hawaii, continuing sporadically ever since Cleveland had prevented it in 1893, was given a powerful assist by Dewey's victory at Manila Bay. The commodore became the hero of his country, and almost no one denied that he should be supported in every way. It was desirable that communications with the Asiatic Squadron should be ensured, and this could be accomplished by taking possession of the important island group almost directly on the route from the United States to the Philippine Islands. Actually this was unnecessary because the Hawaiian Republic had consistently violated its neutrality to aid the United States in every way. At any rate, both sides were eager for annexation, and President William McKinley signed a joint resolution of Congress putting it into effect on 7 July 1898.

Admiral Miller, thus far excluded from the events in which more fortunate officers were gaining fame, was ordered to Hawaii to participate in the annexation ceremonies. He could hardly go in the little *Albatross,* probably still smelling of fish; therefore, the Hawaiian Islands remained nominally independent until the Mare Island Navy Yard could recommission the cruiser *Philadelphia* to carry his flag to Honolulu.

The formal transfer of the Hawaiian Islands to American sovereignty took place on 12 August, with one of the *Philadelphia*'s men hoisting the flag. Ordinarily this duty would have fallen to the chief quartermaster, but he bore the very un-American name of Czarnicke, so a sailor named Winters was selected instead. Later it developed that Winters was an assumed name; he had taken it in order to reenlist after deserting during his first cruise. His true name? Murphy!

The Spanish-American War terminated on the same day, and most of the unwarlike vessels of the Pacific Squadron returned to their former occupations. The purchased tugs *Active, Iroquois,* and *Vigi-*

lant were retained for future use in the Navy, and the Pacific Squadron received additional warships as the fleets of Dewey and Sampson were reduced.

The role of the Pacific Squadron in the Spanish-American War was even smaller than it had been in the Civil War. In its supporting part, Admiral Miller's force did well, but almost the only shots fired by the ships under his command were involved in the twenty-one gun salutes with which they greeted the news of the victories at Manila Bay and Santiago de Cuba.

The return of peace brought no new developments so far as the Pacific Squadron was concerned. Commodore Albert Kautz, who relieved Miller in October 1898, had only the flagship *Philadelphia* and the gunboats *Bennington* and *Yorktown* under his command. To be sure, his responsibilities had been diminished by American annexation of the Hawaiian Islands. His immediate predecessors had been forced to remain at Honolulu for long periods, but now there was little need to maintain a naval force there. The old *Mohican* was assigned as station ship and was available for annual cruises through the islands to discourage infringements on American rights, particularly by Japanese nationals.

Early in 1899, reports of trouble in Samoa caused Secretary Long to order Kautz to proceed to that area in the *Philadelphia*. The terms of the Berlin Agreement of 1889 had included provision for the selection of a "king" to succeed Malietoa. Upon his death, on 22 August 1898, trouble had arisen when rival factions each chose a new leader and refused to accept the decision of the Samoan chief justice about which should be Malietoa's successor. As usual, the consuls present were involved, the Briton and the American supporting the chief justice, while their German counterpart was strenuously opposed to his decision.

Kautz, as senior naval officer present, took charge and worked out a settlement, but this was unacceptable to most of the Samoans. In April, the *Philadelphia* joined with British warships in a punitive bombardment of villages in protest against the local intransigence and the arrogance of the German consul. Samoans ambushed an Anglo-American landing force in retaliation, and sporadic fighting continued until the arrival of a joint commission in the USS *Badger* in May.

International tension rose over the Samoan crisis, but an armed clash was averted by an agreement among the three powers. The German Minister in Washington had proposed that the islands be divided among the United States, Great Britain, and Germany, but the British were not in agreement with this proposal. After further negotiations, it was agreed, on 9 November 1899, to divide the island group between the United States and Germany, with Great Britain accepting from Germany her rights in Tonga and certain areas in the Solomon Islands and in West Africa. Germany took the large islands Upolu and Savaii, while the United States annexed the islands east of 171° West longitude. These included Tutuila with its Pago Pago Harbor, already the site of a coaling station, and the smaller Manua and Rose Islands.

This disposition ended the Samoan difficulties once and for all, but there was less than unanimous opinion as to the wisdom of the American action. Rear Admiral Arent S. Crowninshield, Chief of the Bureau of Navigation, had already protested that the United States had no need of a base in those remote waters, valuable only as a way station on the route to Australia. Moreover, it was unlikely that the Pacific Squadron would be large enough to spend time cruising in that area. Unfortunately for his argument, Crowninshield prefaced it with an admission that the matter was beyond the scope of his duties, and it received scant notice from the Navy Department.

The collier *Abarenda* had been sent out to serve as station ship at Pago Pago even before the annexation, and when, on 1 February 1900, all of American Samoa was placed under Navy Department administration, the *Abarenda*'s Commander Benjamin F. Tilley added to his duties that of territorial governor. His instructions read:

While your position as Commandant will invest you with authority over the islands in the group embraced within the limits of the Station, you will at all times exercise care to conciliate and cultivate friendly relations with the natives.

A simple, straightforward method of administration, such as to win and hold the confidence of the people, is expected of you, by the Dept.[7]

This duty as station ship was one of the most uneventful to which a vessel could be assigned. The *Abarenda* spent her time moored at Pago Pago while her men worked on the new naval station; or she cruised through the waters of her station, surveying or carrying the

legal authority to the smaller islands. Occasionally she went to New
Zealand for docking, but generally she stayed in the vicinity of
American Samoa. The *Abarenda* and her successors were officially
attached to the Pacific Squadron most of the time, but they rarely
came in contact with the flag officer commanding on Pacific Station.

In the years following the war with Spain, the Philippine insurrection caused the retention of a sizable number of warships in the
Asiatic Squadron, with consequent neglect of the Pacific Squadron.
For the most part, the latter consisted of a few protected cruisers
and gunboats with a battleship attached occasionally. However, the
large ship rarely remained in the eastern Pacific for long, and her
presence merely reduced the tactical unity of the Pacific Squadron.
Such maneuvers as were held were hardly more than useless because no two ships possessed even similar characteristics. And few
maneuvers were held—the number of vessels assigned to the Pacific
Station was too small to permit them to gather without neglecting
duties of more immediate importance.

The *Oregon*'s long voyage to join the North Atlantic Squadron
vividly demonstrated the necessity for a canal across Central
America. American acquisition of Hawaii, Puerto Rico, and base
sites in Cuba made this more practical, for the United States was
now in a position to dominate both the Pacific and the Caribbean
approaches to such a canal. The probability that it would be built
either in Nicaragua or in Panama led to increased interest in those
localities. A revolution in Panama in 1901 caused the landing of
Marines from the USS *Iowa* of the Pacific Squadron to ensure safe
rail transit across the Isthmus. A continuation of the trouble in the
following year brought American warships to both Panama City and
Colón, the whole force commanded by Rear Admiral Silas Casey,
commander in chief of the Pacific Squadron. Casey withdrew his
landing forces as Colombian troops demonstrated their ability to keep
the railroad in operation, and then he called a conference between
government and revolutionary leaders on board the flagship *Wisconsin*. Under his supervision, the Colombian terms were not unduly
harsh, and the revolutionists accepted them on 21 November 1902.
Admiral Casey sailed for San Francisco on the following day to receive the approbation of the Department for his tactful handling of
a delicate situation.

Almost a year later the Pacific Squadron's cruiser *Boston* was ordered to Panama on a similar mission. But this time American warships helped to prevent Colombian forces from interfering in the revolution that was to make Panama independent and to lead directly to construction of the Panama Canal. The *Boston*'s part in this affair was very small. Only on the Caribbean coast did the Colombian troops attempt to land, and they were dissuaded by a shrewd mixture of bribes and threats from the American men-o'-war at Colón. No one gained any honor in this incident, but President Theodore Roosevelt had cleared the last political obstacle to construction of the canal and could now "make the dirt fly."

During the period immediately following 1903 the composition of the Pacific Squadron remained about the same. The battleships *Iowa* and *Wisconsin* had been withdrawn, the former to Atlantic waters and the latter to the Asiatic Squadron. The armored cruiser *New York* carried the flag and was supported by the familiar protected cruisers and gunboats. The new monitor *Wyoming* was also assigned to the squadron and proved nearly as difficult to fit into any tactical formation as her older sisters had been.

Something new appeared in the Pacific when the submarine torpedo boats *Grampus* and *Pike* were commissioned at Mare Island on 28 May 1903. They were not a part of the Pacific Squadron; in fact, many felt that they really were not a part of the United States Navy. It has become fashionable to scorn the mossbacks whose conservatism blinded them to the value of the new weapons, but in truth only a visionary could have foreseen a very brilliant future for these strange craft. Usually one commanding officer was assigned to the two boats since only one was available for service at a time, and often both were laid up for alterations and repairs. Their cruising radius almost restricted them to San Francisco Bay, and their infrequent dives were made in the shallow waters of San Pablo Bay near Mare Island.

Lieutenant Arthur MacArthur, Jr., the first commanding officer of the *Pike* and *Grampus,* believed in the submarines, and bent his mind to finding the best way to make them useful to the Navy. Recognizing the difficulty of procuring a suitable mooring site and the limitations imposed by the short cruising range of the primitive submersibles, he recommended that a tug or other small surface vessel be assigned to serve as their tender. She could carry fuel, stores, and spare parts, and provide berthing facilities for their crews. Thus any harbor could serve as a base of operations so long as the tender was present, and she could even tow them from port to port if their gasoline supplies would not permit them to cruise under their own power. Perhaps this idea of a submarine tender was not original with MacArthur, but its value has been demonstrated in two wars.

MacArthur was relieved by Ensign Stanley Woods in 1905. This young officer had an even greater faith in the ability of the submarines to participate actively in naval operations. He obtained permission to go to San Diego with the boats and their tender, the tug *Fortune,* to take part in maneuvers with the Pacific Squadron.

Unfortunately, Woods was more daring than some of the men who served under his command, and they lost confidence in his ability to handle the submarines. When ordered to demonstrate the military value of one of the boats to the Western Board of Inspection and Survey in 1905, several of the most important control operators indicated their unwillingness to dive with him. Woods wished to continue the tests with other men, but the Board members felt that it would be unwise to station inexperienced men at the diving controls. Ensign Woods was therefore relieved of his command, and the enlisted men were assigned to other submarines.[8]

The submarines were not the only torpedo craft on Pacific Station at this time. The need for surface torpedo boats had been emphasized by the Spanish-American War, and several had been built by private shipyards on the Pacific coast. These boats were grouped in the Torpedo Flotilla based at Mare Island. Owing to lack of funds, only one was kept in commission, but her crew took the other boats out occasionally, and they could have been commissioned readily had the need arisen. Like the early submarines, the torpedo boats were very small and could carry only limited amounts of coal, fresh water, and supplies. Since they could not operate as cruising units of the Pacific Squadron, the *Farragut, Davis,* and *Fox* were under a separate command, but joined the larger vessels periodically for maneuvers.

The larger torpedo-boat destroyers *Perry, Preble,* and *Paul Jones* were attached to the Pacific Squadron in 1904. During operations in

Panamanian waters, they proved to have a range of about twenty-six hundred miles at ten knots and were especially valuable as dispatch boats. But life in the little ships was hardly attractive. Virtually all boilers and engines, they would have been hot even in Arctic waters when steaming on all four boilers, and in tropical heat they were unbearable. They were painted black for lower visibility during night torpedo attacks, although most American naval vessels of the time wore the white coats so welcome in tropical waters. Rear Admiral Henry Glass, commanding the Pacific Squadron, recommended that the destroyers also be painted white, and this alleviated the discomfort of their personnel to some extent.

Despite the apparent usefulness of the destroyers to the Pacific Squadron, the Navy Department could not decide to assign them to that force permanently. Even its commander in chief was occasionally in doubt about whether or not the Torpedo Flotilla was under his command, a graphic example of the uncertainty as to the proper tactical use of destroyers.

The first disaster to strike the Pacific Squadron since 1889 occurred on 21 July 1905 when an explosion on board the gunboat *Bennington* at San Diego killed one officer and sixty-five men. The monitor *Wyoming* had lost her starboard screw, and the gunboat was raising steam to go to her assistance when two boilers exploded. The *Bennington* sank at her moorings, but was later raised under the direction of Naval Constructor Holden A. Evans of Mare Island. He also undertook the defense of her commanding officer and chief engineer at the subsequent courts-martial and won their acquittal by proving that defective material in one boiler had caused the original explosion. This incident and the subsequent inquiries brought to light the palpable indifference toward engineering in the United States Navy—the *Bennington*'s chief engineer was an ensign who had never stood an engine-room watch before being assigned to his post—and led to increased emphasis on the training of officers for engineering duty.

For the most part, the Pacific Squadron busied itself with the routine duties of cruising; maneuvers and target practice on the "drill ground" at Magdalena Bay, Mexico; surveying; observing conditions in the region of Panama where the canal was under construction; and establishing coaling stations in Alaska and the Aleutians. And the squadron was hardly large enough even for these prosaic tasks. Rear Admiral Caspar F. Goodrich wrote in 1905:

The Panama station requires practically the undivided attention of two vessels, leaving but three others available for Squadron work during such brief periods as they may be out of the navy yards. Their advanced years and feebleness render their visits to these most useful, if at times somewhat exasperating, adjuncts to naval power, not only frequent, but prolonged.[9]

He went on to ask that six of the militarily worthless, but tactically identical, *Tacoma*-class cruisers be assigned to his squadron in order that his officers might improve their tactical skill and that some of the more remote waters of the station might be visited. But the Department replied that commitments in West Indian and Asiatic waters made it impossible to reinforce the Pacific Squadron; Goodrich would have to be satisfied with his old and slow cruisers and gunboats, no two of which were similar in anything but age.

That they had some value, however, was demonstrated when Admiral Goodrich at Long Beach received a wireless message informing him of the San Francisco earthquake and fire of 18 April 1906. He got the flagship under way immediately, ordered the *Marblehead* to follow, and raced to the northward. The admiral disembarked from the *Chicago* to find that the commandant at Mare Island had sent his tugs to aid in fighting fires, while the destroyer *Preble* and other vessels brought Marines and sailors. The Navy established a waterfront patrol in addition to rendering aid wherever required. The last of the naval forces were re-embarked in the *Boston* and *Princeton* on 10 May, leaving the San Francisco area in the hands of army and militia personnel. It would be impossible to evaluate the assistance given to the populace of San Francisco by naval personnel on this occasion, nor is it necessary to do so. It was simply another instance of the ability of a naval force to be of great assistance to fellow-countrymen even in time of peace.

In December 1906, Captain Alfred T. Mahan's doctrine of fleet concentration was approaching reality. With few exceptions, American battleships had been concentrated in the North Atlantic Ocean to form the Atlantic Fleet. The Asiatic Squadron possessed a strong and homogeneous group of cruisers in addition to the necessary gunboats, but most of the old distant stations had been discontinued.

Only the Pacific Squadron seemed to have been forgotten; however, better things were promised it in a letter received by its commander in chief in the waning days of 1906. This informed him that the force under his command would be reorganized on 1 January 1907. The First Division of the First Squadron was to include the new first-class (partially armored) cruisers *Charleston* and *Milwaukee,* the protected cruiser *Chicago,* and the gunboat *Yorktown.* The protected cruiser *Boston* and the gunboat *Princeton* would form the Second Division, and the Fourth Torpedo Flotilla—the destroyers *Preble* and *Paul Jones*—would also be attached to the Pacific Squadron. This relatively imposing organization was somewhat less powerful in reality, for the *Milwaukee* had not completed her trials. This merely meant that only the two destroyers were tactically identical; a situation by no means unusual for the Pacific Squadron.

Civilian interest in naval affairs continued to be great on the Pacific coast, and it was encouraged by reports that the Navy Department intended to form the long-desired "Pacific Coast Fleet" containing at least eight of the most modern warships. The editor of the *Seattle Post-Intelligencer* sought to confirm the rumors by a telegram to Secretary of the Navy Victor H. Metcalf on 5 February 1907. Metcalf replied:

Press despatch misleading. Dept. simply contemplates placing all vessels in Pacific Ocean under one command, same as present force in Atlantic. Eventually all vessels in Pacific can be repaired on our own coast, moving by divisions from Asiatic waters. No present change in distribution of vessels.[10]

The Secretary's answer seemed to presage the end of the old Pacific Station, but it was destined to return.

11. The Armored Cruiser Squadron

Official confirmation of the planned organization of a Pacific Fleet which would include all of the United States naval forces in that ocean came on 27 February 1907. Rear Admiral William T. Swinburne, Commander in Chief, Pacific Squadron, was informed that he would report to Commander in Chief, Asiatic Squadron, for duty as Commander, Second Squadron, Pacific Fleet, upon receipt of telegraphic orders. These arrived on 13 April, and Swinburne reported accordingly to Rear Admiral James H. Dayton, who became Commander in Chief, Pacific Fleet, on 15 April 1907.

The new fleet was made up of three squadrons and two torpedo flotillas. The First and Second Squadrons consisted of fairly efficient fighting ships, while the Third Squadron contained a heterogeneous force of gunboats not suitable for tactical exercises. It was intended for detached duty in Chinese and Philippine waters, with headquarters at Cavite, and would necessarily operate as an almost independent force. The five destroyers of the First Torpedo Flotilla were also in Asiatic waters and continued to serve in that area.

The Second Squadron was almost identical with Swinburne's old Pacific Squadron and continued to cruise on the former Pacific Station. It was considered to be detached from the Pacific Fleet for special service until 1908.

In short, the only real change brought about by creation of the Pacific Fleet was that Admiral Dayton brought the four armored cruisers and four protected cruisers of his First Squadron from Asiatic waters to the west coast of the United States. Under his personal supervision, these vessels could devote their time to the endless drills and maneuvers necessary to transform them into an efficient fighting force, while Swinburne's Second Squadron performed its usual duties in the accustomed waters, and Rear Admiral Giles B. Harber directed the

164

activities of his Third Squadron from Cavite. It was expected that
the First Squadron would visit most of the areas bordering on the
Pacific Ocean, but in fact much of its time was spent in the eastern
Pacific.

During 1907, the protected cruisers of Squadron One were replaced by four armored cruisers, and Squadron Two became a fairly
homogeneous unit including the big first-class cruisers *Charleston,
Milwaukee,* and *St. Louis,* the protected cruiser *Albany,* and the
gunboat *Yorktown.* This was far and away the most formidable naval
force ever assembled in the eastern Pacific, and for the first time it
became possible to hold tactical drills and maneuvers that would be
something other than a farce.

Neither the armored cruisers nor the big *Charlestons* have fared
well at the hands of naval historians—they sacrificed far too much
in the way of armament and protection to gain an extra few knots
of speed—but they seem to have been suitable for service in the eastern Pacific.

The only possible major threat in the Pacific Ocean could have
come from Japan. It was hardly likely that the Pacific Fleet would
have attempted to protect American possessions in the Far East for
the cruisers would have had to face a much heavier force operating
almost in its home waters, while there was no large United States
base nearer than Mare Island.

On the other hand, any Japanese fleet with hostile intent toward
Hawaii or the American Pacific coast would have had to operate at
the end of a long and vulnerable line of communications. The armored cruisers still could not have hoped to accomplish much
against battleships, but they should have presented a serious threat
to the auxiliary vessels supporting the enemy fleet. With their great
cruising radius, the big cruisers could have operated from the Hawaiian and Aleutian Islands, and even from the ports on the long
Pacific seaboard. Using their superior speed to avoid action with the
more heavily armed ships, the cruisers should have forced the Japanese admiral to divert so many of the battleships to guard his supply
line as to handicap seriously the main fleet.

Mahan might frown on such guerrilla warfare, but only two factors would have made it impractical. The armored cruisers were virtually the only scouting force possessed by the United States Navy,

and it might have been considered undesirable to risk the "eyes" of the battleship fleet before the latter could arrive in the Pacific Ocean. And the successful raiding operations of the armored cruisers depended on the availability of fueling stations. The United States had many suitable sites, particularly in the Aleutians which flanked the great circle route from Japan, but most of these were undeveloped or at best had facilities and supplies only for the revenue cutters and small warships cruising in the Bering Sea.

Nevertheless, the mere presence of a fast and homogeneous squadron in the eastern Pacific must have acted as a deterrent to the Japanese high command had there been any tendency toward an adventurous policy in the waters to the eastward of the 180th meridian of longitude.

There was very definite tension in American-Japanese relations in 1907. Despite Japanese displeasure at the American annexation of Hawaii, relations between the two nations had been amicable until after the Russo-Japanese War of 1904-5. American public opinion had been pro-Japanese during that conflict, and the United States had acted correctly toward the few Russian ships which made their way to American ports. But President Theodore Roosevelt's efforts to conclude the war, advantageous to Japan though they probably were, had aroused Japanese antagonism.

In addition, there were conflicting interests in Manchuria, and then San Francisco, rebuilding after its 1906 earthquake and fire, forced children of Oriental descent to attend segregated schools. Japanese newspapers promptly protested against this discrimination, and anti-American feeling ran high in Japan. Roosevelt was highly indignant at this foolish attitude on the part of the Californians and unleashed the full fury of his vocabulary against them. But the westerners were not impressed and retorted that their real enemy might well be an "unpatriotic President." Roosevelt finally solved the difficulty by arranging a visit of the San Francisco school board to Washington. The school officials agreed to rescind their segregation order in return for a promise that coolie immigration would be restricted. This was accomplished by the Gentlemen's Agreement of 1907-8 in which the Japanese government promised to issue no more passports to laborers going directly to the continental United States.

However, the "Rough Rider" President was afraid that the Japanese would take his efforts on their behalf as evidence that he feared them. To demonstrate American power, he decided to send the Atlantic Fleet around the world. It was announced in July 1907 that the fleet would visit the Pacific coast, and on 27 August, the various bureaus of the Navy Department were informed that the battleships and a destroyer flotilla would sail for San Francisco, the small vessels departing not later than 1 December and the capital ships before 16 December.

This brought a storm of protest from easterners who saw that the Atlantic seaboard would be left unprotected, but the President pointed out that the Pacific coast was just as emphatically the national interest and so was entitled to a visit from the fleet. He even expressed the hope that the fleet might be shifted to the Pacific Ocean every year or two until the completion of the Panama Canal made such a transit much simpler.

The fleet sailed on schedule and proceeded down the Atlantic coast of South America, through the Strait of Magellan, and northward in the Pacific, meeting with a vociferous welcome wherever it touched. Reaching Magdalena Bay, Mexico, two days ahead of schedule, the battleships paused for target practice, and then went on to San Francisco. Here, the fleet was joined by two more battleships and the armored cruisers of the Pacific Fleet. The whole vast armada entered San Francisco Bay together and anchored simultaneously with flying moors, a method in which a ship uses two anchors, dropping the first while making considerable headway. Mooring in an assigned berth with this method requires superb seamanship.

A round of parades and banquets followed, after which the fleet was divided for docking, with the battleships going to Bremerton or to Hunter's Point at San Francisco, while the smaller vessels were accommodated at Mare Island. Various Pacific coast ports were visited, and then the fleet reassembled at San Francisco before sailing westward on its voyage of circumnavigation. The battleships *Alabama* and *Maine,* replaced in the fleet by the *Wisconsin* and *Nebraska,* proceeded independently to the Atlantic via the Suez Canal. The fleet was greeted as enthusiastically in Japan as elsewhere, and there can be no doubt but that Roosevelt's bold stroke was an outstanding success.

Among other things, the cruise revealed a serious lack of colliers. It was obvious that many more of these vessels would be necessary were the fleet sent to the Pacific in wartime—it was largely dependent on chartered foreign colliers on its round-the-world voyage— but the building programs of the next few years indicated that no alarm was felt on this point. The United States Navy remained seriously in need of all types of auxiliaries right up to World War I.

Lieutenant Hutchinson I. Cone's destroyer flotilla did not accompany the Atlantic Fleet when it left San Francisco, but was added to the torpedo force temporarily attached to the Pacific Fleet. The nine destroyers and five torpedo boats were grouped in three flotillas as the Eleventh Fleet with the former hospital ship *Solace* as tender. This force constituted a separate command, but joined the Pacific Fleet for annual maneuvers and was placed under the Commander in Chief, Pacific Fleet, permanently in 1913.

The old and small torpedo boats were of doubtful value. The Department suggested that they might make occasional cruises northward to Puget Sound, but their commanding officer pointed out that they would be endangered in rough weather north of San Francisco. The only ports which could offer refuge south of the Columbia River were Coos Bay, Oregon, and Humboldt Bay, California, and these could not be entered when the seas were breaking over their bars. The torpedo boats might be towed by the larger destroyers, but the latter were so lightly constructed that the practice resulted in damage to engines and hulls. The 420-ton "flivver" destroyers were subject to enough ills without forcing them to tow the outmoded torpedo boats. The desirability of concentrating the flotilla for maneuvers made it impossible to disperse the boats at strategic Pacific coast ports, and Mare Island was the only place where they could be kept up in reserve. So at Mare Island they stayed, except for an occasional short coastwise cruise.

San Diego was a persistent claimant as a base site for all or part of the torpedo flotillas. Many naval officers found its climate much pleasanter than that of San Francisco and sought to have it developed as a naval base, but the Navy Department would not divert funds from the stations already in existence, and it could not compete with San Francisco's more central location. San Diego's citizenry had to remain content with an occasional visit from ships of the Pacific Fleet for the next several years.

After the Atlantic Fleet left the eastern Pacific, the Pacific Fleet continued its usual cruising and target practice. Rear Admiral Swinburne took his armored cruisers and some of the destroyers on a cruise to Samoa and Honolulu later in 1908. The large vessels towed the destroyers part of the distance to save coal, and the experience revealed a few of the difficulties that might have been expected. Hawsers parted occasionally, but in a smooth sea it was an easy matter to retrieve the tows. One division of the cruisers with its destroyers stopped at Pago Pago while the others touched at Apia, receiving an enthusiastic welcome from the inhabitants of that German outpost.

In 1909, Rear Admiral Uriel Sebree cruised in western Pacific waters with the armored cruisers. Calling at Japan nearly a year after the battleship fleet's visit, his ships were received with comparable joy and probably helped to maintain the amicable feeling then manifested toward Americans by the Japanese populace.

In no sense, however, were these cruises merely intended to impress foreigners. Regardless of their destination, the ships were continually engaged in maneuvers and tactical drills. The succeeding commanders in chief of the Pacific Fleet strove to increase the fighting efficiency of their vessels, and something of their enthusiasm was instilled in the captains, junior officers, and enlisted men under their command. The deficiencies of the armored cruiser type were not yet widely realized. To those who served in the big white ships with their distinctive four funnels, they were the dashing cavalry of the sea, an elite force which boasted the highest morale. The tradition of the "Armored Cruiser Squadron" has not yet disappeared entirely from the United States Navy.

The *Tennessee* and *Washington,* the heaviest armored cruisers in the Pacific Fleet, were detached for duty in the Atlantic early in 1910. The *Washington*'s departure was delayed by smallpox among her crew and the smaller *South Dakota* was sent in her place. The latter returned to the Pacific Fleet upon being relieved in Atlantic waters by the *Washington,* and the six ships remaining in the Pacific were divided into two divisions of three ships each, still large enough for effective tactical use.

One of these vessels, the *Pennsylvania,* was to take part in two important experiments early in 1911. After Mare Island workmen erected a temporary platform above her stern, she was moored in San Francisco Bay, and on 18 January 1911, Eugene Ely, a civilian pilot, landed a Curtiss biplane on this "flight deck," the first such landing to be attempted. Onlookers were aware of the significance of his feat, but the masking of the cruiser's after eight-inch mount by the temporary structure caused the Secretary of the Navy to express interest in a float-equipped airplane which could be carried by warships unencumbered by platforms. Glenn Curtiss was already at work on such a machine, and on 17 February landed his hydro-airplane alongside the *Pennsylvania* in San Diego Bay. The cruiser's boat crane hoisted aircraft and pilot on board and then returned them to the water, whence Curtiss flew back to his base on North Island. While the success of these experiments augured well for the future of naval aviation, its development was not rapid. A few vessels of the Atlantic Fleet received aircraft in 1914 and 1915, but apparently no aviation unit was assigned to a ship of the Pacific Fleet before 1917.

By 1910, notwithstanding the fact that it was desirable to have all American naval forces in the Pacific Ocean under one command, it had become apparent that the area was simply too vast for the commander in chief to wield effective control over the whole station. The Third Squadron had been acting under direct orders of the Navy Department ever since the formation of the Pacific Fleet and so had never been a true part of that organization. Accordingly, the Asiatic Fleet was re-established as a separate command in 1910, and a few years later the Pacific Fleet's cruising ground was defined as an area almost identical with the old Pacific Station. But the Pacific Fleet was much stronger than the Pacific Squadron had ever been. Rear Admiral John Hubbard's Asiatic Fleet received only the few old cruisers and gunboats which had been assigned to the Third Squadron. Even as reduced, the Pacific Fleet was still the strongest American naval force after the immeasurably superior Atlantic Fleet.

Regardless of the strength of the Pacific Fleet, it was not well fitted in every respect for its normal duties. The recurrent Central American difficulties had to be dealt with by armored cruisers, and this was not the proper use of those vessels. They were too large to enter many of the ports on the Central American Pacific coast, and large as their coal bunkers were, their furnaces seemed to have an even larger capacity for consuming coal. Smaller cruisers and gunboats were needed for such duties, but these were few in number and so decrepit that most of them should long since have been stricken from the *Navy Register*. The "reign of Roosevelt" had resulted in a navy of large ships, and President William H. Taft's Navy Department was unable to relieve the almost desperate need for light craft and auxiliaries. To be sure, the number of battleships authorized was reduced during Roosevelt's second term, but there was no comparable increase in the construction of smaller vessels.

As a result, every new crisis in Central America called the armored cruisers away from the maneuvers which alone could keep them an effective squadron. Life in these ships and in the little old gunboats may well be imagined. Day after day they rode at anchor in the tropical heat, rolling monotonously in the ever-present ground swell. Refrigeration facilities were small or nonexistent, and only limited supplies of fresh food could be obtained from the shore. Evaporators were barely efficient enough to keep the boilers supplied with fresh feed water, so the grime and dust which accompanied every coal-burning vessel could be removed only with salt water. Despite their white paint (most American warships were painted grey after 1910, but some vessels on duty in tropical waters retained their white coats), the living quarters and engineering spaces of the ships reached notably high temperatures under the tropical sun. Nor was there much relief when finally empty coal bunkers and supply lockers forced the vessel to depart for replenishment, usually in San Diego. Of course, there would be mail and perhaps liberty, but first all hands, including junior officers, turned to at the incredibly dirty and hard task of coaling ship. This completed and the ship washed down to remove the coal dust which penetrated every crack and covered every square inch of her topsides, there might be time for leisure. Too often, however, the coaling gear and hoses were stowed only to be followed by orders to unmoor and return to the area whence the ship had just come.

One of the crises which were such a trial to the Pacific Fleet occurred in the form of the Nicaraguan revolution of 1911. American interests were endangered, and although the Panama route had been chosen for the isthmian canal, some Americans feared that an un-friendly foreign power might seize control of the Nicaragua route and build a canal which would weaken our strategic position. So long as the United States controlled the only canal, any foreign naval force would have to make the long passage around South America in order to threaten the Pacific coast. With a Nicaraguan canal, however, an unfriendly fleet might be able to arrive in the Pacific before the American Atlantic Fleet, which would have to take the slightly longer way through the Panama Canal.

Therefore, warships in the Caribbean and the Pacific were fre-quently in Nicaraguan waters, and when President Adolfo Diaz in-vited intervention for protection of American citizens in 1912, the gunboat *Annapolis* promptly arrived at Corinto and sent a landing force of sailors and Marines to Managua. They helped to keep fight-ing to a minimum in Managua and kept the railroad to the Pacific coast open. Rear Admiral William H. H. Southerland hastened to the scene in his flagship *California* to take command of the American forces, and additional men were landed from warships on both coasts. Major Smedley Butler's Marines from Panama were also dis-patched to Nicaragua, and within two months United States forces in the Central American republic numbered some twenty-seven hun-dred men. Southerland's Marines and sailors captured the last rebel stronghold, León, on 6 October, and the violence was ended. Soon thereafter the Americans were withdrawn, leaving only a legation guard of Marines at Managua.

An unfortunate corollary of the Nicaraguan intervention was its effect on Latin American public opinion. Combined with the other and smaller interventions in the past, it was hardly calculated to in-still a feeling of friendliness in the inhabitants of those areas toward the United States Navy. Their animosity did not ease the task of American sailors and Marines when, soon afterward, Mexican affairs became the overriding concern of the Pacific Fleet.

President Taft's exceptionally able Secretary of the Navy, George von Lengerke Meyer, was essentially a businessman, and his strong desire for efficiency was immeasurably helpful to the service. Among other reforms, he introduced scheduled visits of warships to the navy yards so that the latter maintained fairly constant work loads. Thus some of the ships were unavailable for service at all times, but no longer would an entire fleet be immobilized for overhaul at one time with a resulting strain on yard facilities. Nowhere was this more important than in the Pacific, where only Mare Island and the poorly equipped Puget Sound yard were available to keep the fleet in repair. There were no less than nine navy yards on the east coast, several with better facilities than those at Mare Island.

Up to this time, decommissioned ships had been laid up at navy yards and allowed to deteriorate at their moorings. Meyer instituted a system of reserve fleets which contained the more effective of these vessels. They were kept in reduced commission with nucleus crews which were occupied with the upkeep of the ships. Occasionally each vessel's complement would be supplemented from those of the others, and she would go to sea on a short training cruise. Thus the personnel was kept at a fair state of efficiency, and defects in the material condition of the vessels were revealed.

Most of the ships assigned to the Pacific Reserve Fleet were based at Bremerton. They included two armored cruisers, the old battleship *Oregon,* two first-class cruisers, three protected cruisers, two torpedo boats, two submarines, and a submarine tender. Rear Admiral Alfred Reynolds commanded this force with his flag in the armored cruiser *Pittsburgh* (ex-*Pennsylvania*). Sometimes vessels of the Pacific Fleet would be transferred to the Reserve Fleet when they were due for major overhauls, but usually such work required that they be placed out of commission entirely. Generally, however, the more modern warships alternated between active service with the Pacific Fleet and idleness with the Pacific Reserve Fleet.

By 1913, the United States Navy was experiencing a serious personnel shortage, obvious to naval officers, but overlooked by Secretary of the Navy Josephus Daniels and most other civilians. In the absence of any attempts to remedy this deficiency, it was natural that the officer and enlisted complements of the reserve fleets should have been reduced to man fully the ships in full commission. This policy resulted in deterioration of the reserve vessels, and soon they were in little better condition than those which were decommissioned and laid up. In 1916, the Pacific Reserve Fleet staff engineer, a lieutenant, was commanding two 14,000-ton armored cruisers in addition to his staff duties. In fact, he was the only commissioned officer assigned to the two ships. The beneficial aspects of Meyer's system disappeared soon after its progenitor left the Navy Department.

The end of violence in Nicaragua was followed closely by the outbreak of disorder in Mexico which required the presence of American warships in the Pacific coast ports of that republic. President Woodrow Wilson had refused to recognize the government of Victoriano Huerta, who had declared himself provisional president of Mexico, and succeeding events culminated in the arrest of an American naval boat party in Tampico on 9 April 1914. President Wilson then ordered a blockade of Mexican harbors and the seizing of the customhouse at Veracruz. There was some fighting in this city, and later in April, five American battleships arrived in the harbor. However, the further spread of hostilities was prevented when a joint arbitration proposal by Argentina, Brazil, and Chile was accepted. The cities near the seaboard of western Mexico had sizable American "colonies," and American investments in mines, railroads, and oil wells were valued at hundreds of millions of dollars. However, the situation had not called for active intervention by the Pacific Fleet, although some American property at Manzanillo had been destroyed before a warship could arrive. Usually the mere presence of a cruiser or a gunboat had been enough to guarantee the safety of foreign residents and property.

After the outbreak of World War I, some anxiety was felt lest German agents gain a controlling voice in Mexican affairs, and this added to the necessity of keeping ships in or near the western harbors. The armored cruisers in commission were first on the scene, but they were soon joined by smaller vessels operating directly under Navy Department orders at first. By 1915, however, the Pacific Fleet included five protected cruisers and two gunboats in addition to its three armored cruisers and the torpedo flotillas. The conditions under which the Mexican coastal operations were carried out were no more attractive than those which had characterized the earlier Central American patrol duties, and the ships remained the same except that their increasing years made themselves felt in aggravated material defects.

Gradually conditions became more tranquil, and on 7 May 1915, Admiral Thomas B. Howard advised the Department that the continued presence of his warships in Mexican ports would serve only to irritate public opinion in Mexico. Further, he warned that American citizens wished to detain the vessels in those harbors for purposes other than protection. Few of the cities enjoyed radio or cable connections with the interior or with the United States; therefore, the merchants were availing themselves of the radio facilities of the men-o'-war to communicate with those points. Instead of keeping a ship constantly in each major harbor, Howard set up a patrol system whereby each port would be visited periodically by a warship.

Later in 1915, Howard's fleet was reduced drastically. Only one armored cruiser was retained in commission to serve as his flagship. His request that more small vessels be commissioned for duty in Mexican waters received little notice, and his desire for information as to the expected role of the Pacific Fleet in event of war with a major power seems to have been ignored also. A few months earlier, the Pacific Fleet had been advanced to a dignity comparable to that of the Atlantic Fleet when the former's commander in chief was authorized to break an admiral's four-starred flag at his flagship's main truck. This was the only similarity between the two fleets; that in the Atlantic was made up of the most modern dreadnought battleships, while its Pacific counterpart contained only one obsolete armored cruiser.

Nor were conditions any better in the Pacific Reserve Fleet. Rear Admiral William F. Fullam, appointed to that command in 1915, found it in a sadly neglected state. The inadequate personnel had done its best, but the ships were badly run down, and it was impossible to carry out the desired training exercises. The facilities of the Bremerton yard were not adequate for the upkeep of several large ships, and Fullam absolved its commandants of any blame for the deterioration.

A lesser man might have accepted the situation and contented himself with routine work and explanations, but not Fullam. Innumerable letters, reports, and requests crossed his desk, and he spent hours inspecting the ships, encouraging the disheartened junior officers and enlisted men whose best efforts hitherto had been unappreciated. He bombarded the Navy Department with demands for more men and appropriations for repairs. Under this leadership, something had to happen, and happen it did. The Pacific Reserve Fleet eventually became what George von L. Meyer had intended— an effective addition to the Pacific Fleet when needed.

Admiral William B. Caperton assumed command of the Pacific Fleet in 1916 and lost no time in asking for reinforcements. He thought that some of the ships of the Pacific Reserve Fleet might serve in Mexican waters, and at the same time Fullam was request- ing that four of the older pre-dreadnought battleships be sent to the Pacific for use as training ships by his men since the armored cruisers were still immobilized. The desires of both men were met by a Navy Department order authorizing the use of Pacific Reserve Fleet vessels on active service, but without placing them in full commission. Their complements would be increased only to the minimum required for sustained operations, and the ships would not be considered as units of the Pacific Fleet although cruising under Caperton's orders. Soon the latter was demanding that all routine reports of these ves- sels be sent to him, but Fullam insisted that they were still a part of his command and he must be the recipient of such reports. Fullam was undoubtedly correct in this stand, but it is impossible to escape the conclusion that all warships cruising actively in Mexican waters should have been attached to the Pacific Fleet.

Fullam lost no time in preparing some of the armored cruisers for this service, and even more defects came to light when they put to sea. The *West Virginia* sailed in spite of the bad condition of her main engines, controlled by hand gear aft because her steering engine was inoperative, and passing engine orders through voice tubes since her annunciators refused to function properly. She spent five months on Mexican patrol before receiving essential repairs at Mare Island.

Nor were all of the Pacific Fleet vessels in good material condi- tion. While the small cruiser *Chattanooga* was bound for San Diego early in 1916, damage to her starboard high pressure cylinder caused her engineering force to compound the engine. There was no time for repairs at San Diego, and she sailed for Mexican waters once more with her starboard engine running at seriously reduced effi- ciency. The *Chattanooga* met the larger *Milwaukee* at Guaymas, and the latter's repair force worked around the clock for four days to cast and machine the necessary parts to return the cylinder to use. The general decrepitude of the ships was surpassed only by the ingenuity and hard work of the repair forces which kept them at sea long after navy yard refits seemed imperative.

Although the Navy Department had ordered that two of the Pacific Reserve Fleet ships should be in Mexican waters at all times, that organization received no corresponding increase in personnel for some months. And when the Reserve Fleet complements were increased to fifty per cent of normal in February 1917, Admiral Caperton expressed his dissatisfaction because the men had not been sent to the Pacific Fleet instead. Fullam's reply is not known, but he might well have repeated the words earlier attributed to a sailor of the Reserve Fleet: "If we need a rest we will go into the active fleet."[1]

There is some evidence of friction between the two admirals somewhat earlier. Late in October 1916, the *Maryland* required relief, and Caperton had no vessel available for that assignment. Fullam advised him that the Reserve Fleet flagship *Colorado* was ready for sea, only to be told that the commander in chief did not wish him to go to Mexican waters. The irate rear admiral informed Admiral William S. Benson, Chief of Naval Operations:

> I expressed my willingness to go to Mexico and relieve the *Maryland,* and shall still be glad to do so if necessary; but Caperton informs me that he prefers that *I* should not go there at present! Why? Is he or is the Department afraid of me? I should gladly go as a passenger in the *Colorado,* but I do not wish to be compelled to shift my flag again, having shifted it five times in one year.[2]

Eventually the Department authorized Caperton to man and recommission the old cruiser *New Orleans* as the *Maryland*'s relief. No reason for Caperton's refusal of the *Colorado* appears in official correspondence.

It would be strange if this period of active cruising by worn-out and undermanned ships had ended without a disaster, but when that did occur, it was not attributable to the afore-mentioned deficiencies. A division of submarines was proceeding southward along the coast early in January 1917, when one of them, *H-3,* grounded near Humboldt Bay, California, owing to a navigational error. The *Milwaukee* and the monitor *Cheyenne* (ex-*Wyoming*), both serving as submarine tenders, were ordered to her assistance. The *H-3*'s crew was removed by surfmen from the Humboldt Bay Coast Guard Station, and civilian salvage firms were asked for estimates on the cost of refloating the submarine. However, these were considered to be unduly high, and the Navy decided that the two surface vessels should attempt to pull the *H-3* off.

On 12 January, the *Milwaukee* steamed into position and passed a towing hawser, while the *Cheyenne* took a line from the cruiser's bow to assist in keeping the latter perpendicular to the beach. The first effort was unsuccessful, so the *Milwaukee* anchored and kept a strain on the hawser while awaiting the next flood tide. But during the night, her anchors dragged, and the current swung the cruiser into the surf, broadside on. The Coast Guardsmen removed her crew in the morning, just in time to escape a storm which drove the stranded warship even more firmly onto the beach. It was obvious that she would never be refloated; the removable gear was salvaged, and the *Milwaukee*'s hulk was abandoned to the surf. Ironically enough, the *H-3* was later returned to service after having been refloated by one of the salvage firms whose bid had been rejected previously.

It might be argued that the slow and weakly armed cruiser was no real loss to the United States Navy, but the sight of her disintegrating hulk was certainly an embarrassment for some time. However, just as the *Levant*'s disappearance was all but forgotten in the excitement attending the preliminaries to the Civil War, so the events leading up to 6 April 1917 soon drove the *Milwaukee*'s fate from the minds of American citizens.

12. *Pacific Fleet in the Atlantic Ocean*

There had been plans, before 1917, for the employment of the Pacific Fleet in the event of hostilities, but they had not progressed beyond the planning stage and had had relatively little effect on the operations of the Pacific Fleet and the Pacific Reserve Fleet. The first attempt at a War Plans Portfolio for the Pacific seems to have been made in 1904; however, the first comprehensive plan was not made until 1913. Naturally, the Pacific Fleet plans were most concerned with Japan and Mexico. War Plans Orange and Green envisioned wars with those nations, respectively.[1]

War Plan Orange apparently provided for withdrawal of most of the United States naval forces from Asiatic and western Pacific waters as far to the eastward as Pearl Harbor and for the mobilization of all effective warships on the Pacific coast. No serious offensive operations seem to have been contemplated until such time as the battleships of the Atlantic Fleet could arrive in Pacific waters, but this moment would be facilitated greatly by the opening of the Panama Canal, then approaching completion. The state of defenses of American island possessions was so poor that it would have been futile to try to hold them. The 1909 decision that Pearl Harbor should be the westernmost major base meant that it would be defended, although development of its facilities and defenses lagged far behind the plans of the strategists. But political realities had to be considered, and there was no likelihood that large sums would be voted for the protection of far-distant island possessions.

Available records yield no hint that the armored cruisers were to have been used offensively against Japanese communications before American battleships arrived on the scene. Nor could this have been expected. Many of the armored cruisers were in reserve and could hardly have been readied for service before the Atlantic Fleet arrived in the Pacific Ocean. And despite their obvious obsolescence, they were virtually the only cruisers available to the United States Navy.

Plainly, the role of the Navy in a Mexican war would be much less important, and War Plan Green seems to have been concerned only with a blockade of the Mexican coast and the occupation of some of the more important seaports. Any invasion other than that by land across the Texas border probably would have been supported by forces in the Gulf of Mexico, for the important regions of Mexico are much more accessible from that coast than from the Pacific seaboard. The Pacific Fleet thus would have had a much less spectacular, but nevertheless important, part in a conflict with Mexico.[2]

Also in 1913, the then Captain Fullam, aide for inspections to Secretary Meyer, submitted a memorandum on steps to be taken in anticipation of war with Japan. His paper was concerned with the preparation of all units and facilities in order that mobilization might proceed without confusion. It is interesting to note that no less than five of the eight points proposed by Fullam were concerned with personnel procurement. Little more than two years later he was to have reason to wish that some of his suggestions had been acted on by the Department.

The opening of the Panama Canal to traffic in 1914 ended the comparative isolation of the Pacific coast and cleared away the main obstacle to a division of the battleship fleet. Even the archexponent of concentration, Theodore Roosevelt, had thought that a number of the capital ships should be stationed in the Pacific as soon as the canal was in use, because it would make strategic concentration possible even with vessels on both coasts. But the Navy Department had no intention of dividing the fleet in 1914, and even the Pacific coast states made no demand that additional warships be assigned to the Pacific Fleet.[3] Despite American neutrality in the war that had just come to Europe, both the government and the public felt that the greatest danger lay in the German High Seas Fleet. If it evaded or defeated the British Grand Fleet, it would menace the Atlantic coast of the United States; consequently, the modern warships were retained in the Atlantic Fleet almost by unanimous consent. Few men outside the Navy seemed to realize that the German vessels could not operate thousands of miles from a base, particularly with the Grand Fleet intact in their wakes. Even if the Grand Fleet were defeated, it was inconceivable that the High Seas Fleet would emerge from such a battle unscathed and ready for a transatlantic campaign, but this fact too was overlooked. In 1915, the older battleships of the Naval Academy Practice Squadron did pass through the canal, but they returned to the Atlantic at the conclusion of their cruise.

During the first two years of World War I, the United States Navy continued on its peaceful course, outwardly content with Secretary Daniels' assurances of its readiness for any eventuality. Many officers, including those commanding in the Pacific, doubted this, but their demands for preparedness measures fell on deaf ears. Secretary Daniels has received praise for his conduct of naval affairs, but it seems evident that the Daniels program did not contribute immediately to the readiness of the United States Navy for entry into the conflict in 1917.

Admiral Caperton was informed in 1916 that some of his ships would be required for service in the Atlantic in event of hostilities with Germany. He was ordered to dispatch the armored cruiser *San Diego* (ex-*California*), the first-class cruiser *Milwaukee,* and the protected cruisers *Raleigh* and *Albany* to the fleet rendezvous in Chesapeake Bay as soon as the mobilization order was received.

In October 1916, the President of the Associated Chambers of Commerce of the Pacific Coast informed Daniels that he had been directed to protest against the rumored transfer of the armored cruisers to the Atlantic, and the Chief of Naval Operations replied that no such change was contemplated. Whether or not Secretary Daniels realized it, to his senior officers in the Pacific it was inconceivable that the obsolete, but still powerful, armored cruisers should remain on the west coast if Germany became an enemy. At the beginning of 1917, the large ships had been withdrawn from Mexican waters, and Admiral Fullam thought they should be detached from further patrol duty in order that they might rehearse in company the scouting role to which they were likely to be assigned. Nevertheless, as late as 27 March 1917, Admiral Benson informed Caperton that it was the intention of the Navy Department gradually to withdraw almost all of the smaller cruisers, gunboats, and destroyers for use on the Atlantic coast patrol, leaving the armored cruisers to guard the

Pacific coast. Of the latter, the *Huntington* (ex-*West Virginia*) would also be ordered to the eastern seaboard if her aviation unit could be installed in time.

Early in March 1917, the destroyer *Hopkins* was ordered to carry out a careful reconnaissance of the coast of Lower California to detect German agents reported to be active in that region, but her commanding officer found nothing to confirm the reports.

As international tension mounted, the Department issued another order whereby the Pacific Fleet torpedo vessels were to be prepared for departure eastward when so ordered. In the closing days of March, most of the effective warships on the Pacific coast were in commission and fairly well prepared for service, due in large part to the efforts of Rear Admiral Fullam, but no definite information as to the contemplated employment of the Pacific Fleet seems to have been received.

When the mobilization order was issued on 6 April 1917, the flagship of the Pacific Fleet was not among its addressees; nevertheless, the vessels of that command proceeded to their assigned stations. At least one commanding officer had little idea as to whom he should look for fuel, supplies, and further orders—the commanding officer of the *Yorktown* made inquiries for such to Admiral Caperton on 12 April. And six days later, Fullam added a postscript to his report to Admiral Benson:

> By the way, what am I?
> 1. Commander of Reserve Force?
> 2. Commander of Scout Force?
> or 3. 2nd in command on the Pacific?
> All Reserve Ships are now in full commission! Understand, my dear Benson, makes no difference to me *what* I am, just so I have something to do that will utilize my time. . . .[4]

A month later, some order was emerging from the initial uncertainty. The Pacific Reserve Fleet was abolished early in May, and Fullam shifted his flag from the *Pueblo* (ex-*Colorado*) to break it in the *San Diego* as Commander, Patrol Force, Pacific Fleet. And on 9 May, Caperton was informed that he would command the *Pittsburgh, Pueblo, South Dakota,* and *Frederick* (ex-*Maryland*) on distant service.

The distant service for which Caperton's scouting force was destined was a patrol of the South Atlantic Ocean within the following geographical limits:

From the Brazilian coast at Latitude 5° South, east to Longitude 30° West, thence south (true) to Latitude 15° South, thence in general parallel to the South American coast to Latitude 35° South, Longitude 35° West, thence west to the mouth of the Rio de la Plata.

He was advised that French naval forces would operate in the area to the northward and westward, while British warships would be cruising to the southward. His mission was "to search for and capture or destroy all enemy vessels within your area of operations, and to cooperate with the forces of the Entente Allies in all possible ways to the same end." Caperton was to assume that Brazilian and Uruguayan ports would be open to his ships, and coal would be supplied by colliers sailing regularly from Hampton Roads. In addition, his orders read:

You will retain the rank and title of Admiral, Commander-in-Chief of the Pacific Fleet, but on account of the wide separation of your forces from the Pacific coast, the administration of the forces remaining in the Pacific will be left to the Commander of the Pacific Patrol Force.[5]

Admiral Caperton proceeded to Balboa, Canal Zone, with three ships, and there he was joined by the *Frederick* bringing welcome drafts of men for the other cruisers. She also brought less welcome German measles and mumps, and all of the ships were quickly infected. The measles epidemic ran its course in ten weeks, but the sick bays of the cruisers contained sailors suffering from mumps as late as December 1918.

Before passing through the canal, the armored cruisers were docked at Balboa. Their progress was so leisurely that they did not arrive at Bahia, Brazil, until 14 June 1917, and there a base was established for the *Pueblo* and *South Dakota*. The *Pittsburgh* was to operate out of Rio de Janeiro and the *Frederick* from Montevideo. The patrol area of 1,000,000 square miles was large enough in all conscience for only four ships. Although the auxiliary cruisers *Steuben* and *DeKalb* originally had been assigned to Caperton, they were employed as transports and never joined his flag. Caperton's plans called for each of his four ships to spend ten days on station cruising at five knots. The passages to and from the patrol area were to require five days each, with the vessels ordered to proceed at ten knots by day and five knots during hours of darkness. These speeds would be dangerously low if U-boats were in the area, but coal consumption at higher speeds would reduce the endurance of the armored cruisers to an undesirable extent.

Before the patrols were established, Admiral Caperton used his ships to foster the friendship of Latin America for the United States. He had indicated his belief that the mission of his fleet was in part "to assist bringing the South American Republics into an open espousal of the policies of the United States and to promote the solidification of the South American countries in their mutual relations."[6]

At Rio de Janeiro, the armored cruisers were accorded a tumultuous welcome, and their reception at Montevideo was just as cordial. The Argentine government asked that Caperton touch at Bahia Blanca, an ocean port, probably hoping to avoid such incidents as might be caused by the large German populace of Buenos Aires. However, the admiral insisted on visiting the capital.

In addition to the unfriendly feeling which might manifest itself at Buenos Aires, the voyage to that city was not without danger. It is located on the broad and shallow Rio de la Plata, some one hundred miles from Montevideo. For the most part, the depth of the estuary was somewhat less than the minimum amount of water necessary to float the big armored cruisers, but several feet of soft mud blanketed the river bottom. Moreover, it was the pampero season, and that offshore wind had been known to lower the river level to such an extent that ships in mid-channel had grounded. Even if the warships did not run aground, they would be certain to suck so much mud into their condenser main injections as to impair seriously the functioning of the main engines. Fortunately, the fleet engineer pointed out that the condensers could be cross-connected, with one overboard discharge substituted for both main injections. This obviated the difficulty; the armored cruisers were almost the only vessels in the United States Navy in which this arrangement was possible.

The run up the Rio de la Plata was made without incident at twelve knots, with the ships plowing furrows in the mud on the channel bottom. They received a cordial welcome at Buenos Aires, and officers and men alike were entertained most hospitably. It was noted that the armored cruisers were the largest vessels which had ever visited the Argentine capital.

However valuable the Buenos Aires visit may have been from the diplomatic standpoint, one cannot escape the feeling that Admiral Caperton was most unwise in risking his ships in the Rio de la Plata. To be sure, they suffered no damage other than losing much of the paint from their bottom strakes, but there were not a few wrecks concealed in the mud at the channel bottom, and it requires little imagination to envisage the effect had one of the armored cruisers struck a submerged wreck at twelve knots, although the ships might well have been unmanageable at a lower speed under such conditions. When it is considered that the United States was at war and that Caperton's force was so small, the good will gained from the visit must count little compared with the loss of material and prestige had even one cruiser been stranded.

Having completed its diplomatic duties, the Pacific Fleet settled down to the routine of patrolling the South Atlantic. The cruising proceeded without incident, and no sign of enemy raiders was seen. By November 1917, the Navy Department had found it desirable to place Caperton's ships under the orders of the Commander in Chief, Atlantic Fleet, but the armored cruisers retained their identity as the Pacific Fleet. Soon after the Armistice was declared on 11 November 1918, the *Pueblo, South Dakota,* and *Frederick* were assigned to Rear Admiral Albert Gleaves's Transport and Cruiser Force and helped to ferry American troops from Europe. In their stead, Caperton received three old and small cruisers and an obsolete gunboat. The cruiser *Chicago* became his flagship in place of the *Pittsburgh* which was detached for duty in European waters.

Meanwhile, the portion of the Pacific Fleet which remained in that ocean suffered the tribulations common to naval forces in a backwater far from the war zone. Since Fullam had expressed repeatedly his view that there was virtually no danger of German activity in the eastern Pacific, it is not surprising that his force was reduced quickly. (The Patrol Force originally included the armored cruisers *San Diego* and *Saratoga,* the battleship *Oregon,* the protected cruiser *Marblehead,* the gunboats *Vicksburg* and *Yorktown,* and the destroyers *Perry* and *Lawrence.* The submarines and their tender *Cheyenne* composed a separate command, but Fullam exercised general supervision.) The flagship *San Diego* and the *Saratoga* were detached for duty in the Atlantic as were the destroyers, and Fullam broke his flag in the *Oregon*. The submarines based at Pearl Harbor and San Pedro were also sent to the war zone with the exception of some of the older *F*- and *H*-type boats which were retained in the Pacific primarily for use in training crews for the new submarines building in west coast yards.

The Patrol Force was abolished in July 1917, and its ships were redesignated as Division Two, Pacific Fleet. Fullam was retained in command, and in addition, continued to hold supervisory authority over the submarines and the Pacific coast naval districts. He was also senior officer of Allied naval forces in the eastern Pacific, but exercised little actual control over ships of foreign navies. The extent of his authority is not clear; at most he seems to have served in a coordinating capacity with the right to request British or Japanese vessels to perform duties for which no American warships were available.

A few small and weak extemporized men-o'-war maintained a loose patrol of Mexican waters, but their commanding officers had strict orders to avoid any incidents that might cause Mexican officials or private citizens to take offense. The major fueling base for these vessels was at Pichilinque, and supplies of gasoline and lubricating oil were landed at Corinto, Nicaragua, and Amapala, Honduras, for the use of the 110-foot wooden submarine chasers assigned to patrol those waters. In each case, the government concerned had offered the use of the port, and Fullam ordered that the supplies be left unguarded until losses proved that guards were necessary. He felt that the presence of Marines might be an irritant to local authorities, and was determined to avoid friction if possible.

The heavy ships of Division Two, the *Oregon* and *Cheyenne,* were relatively inactive. The latter served as submarine tender at San Pedro where her two twelve-inch guns were virtually the only harbor defense, while the old battleship which had starred in the Spanish-American War now contented herself with unspectacular supporting roles. She remained at San Francisco for a time to defend that port, went to San Diego to serve as Fullam's flagship, and cruised along the coast occasionally to stimulate recruiting and bond-selling campaigns.

There were the usual nervous citizens who saw German U-boats off the Pacific coast, but none of their reports was found to be correct. More persistent were rumors of German surface raiders operating in the eastern Pacific, and one such in November 1917 led the Navy Department to ask that the Imperial Japanese Navy send a cruiser in search of a raider supposedly operating in the Honolulu area. Needless to say, the Japanese complied readily, but no enemy vessel was found. Admiral Fullam was humiliated by this incident, and he requested permission to arm the colliers *Nanshan* and *Brutus* as auxiliary cruisers so he would have ships of his own to dispatch in search of German raiders in waters near American possessions.

The nearest thing to a German raider encountered by Fullam's ships was the absurdly small and slow American gas schooner *Alexander Agassiz*. Reports of her suspicious character reached naval officers from Mazatlán, whence it was feared that she would sail to capture a merchantman that might be converted for raiding activity. The officers found it somewhat difficult to take the would-be raider seriously, but when she stood out of Mazatlán on 18 March 1918, the gunboat *Vicksburg* was in the offing and took possession as soon as the *Agassiz* cleared neutral waters. The prize had no registration papers, and boarding officers found a German flag and a few small arms. This was enough to warrant her seizure, but added little glory to the record of Division Two, Pacific Fleet.

Of all the naval forces on the Pacific coast, probably the bases made the most important contribution in World War I. Destroyers, submarines, and submarine chasers were built, commissioned, and sent to the war zone in considerable numbers. Many of the steel cargo ships built on the west coast for the Emergency Fleet Corporation were taken over by the Naval Overseas Transport Service, and to the naval districts in which they were built went the duty of outfitting and manning these vessels, all of which went to the Atlantic also. Both the Mare Island and the Puget Sound Navy Yards built small warships, and the former was at work on the superdreadnought *California,* the first battleship, and the last, built at a Pacific coast navy yard.

The most serious loss suffered in the eastern Pacific came on 17 December 1917 when the submarine *F-1,* cruising in company with several sisters, collided with one of them and sank with nineteen men. Among other less serious accidents, the Coast Guard cutter *McCulloch* was sunk in collision off Port Hueneme, California, with the loss of one life.

The cessation of hostilities came as a surprise to the Pacific coast, as to the rest of the country. Shipyards, government and private, were really just hitting their stride, and would have shown an even more astonishing capability for building and fitting out vessels of all types had the war continued. No plans for cutting back production had been made, and the Armistice threw the whole program into confusion.

So the record of the Pacific Fleet in World War I was little more spectacular than that compiled by the Pacific Squadron in conflicts since the Mexican War. But its duties were performed adequately, and Admiral Fullam proved himself an able leader in spite of his undistinguished position.

13. "And Here Our Navy Is"

The end of World War I found the United States with the second largest navy in the world, and the completion of ships then building or authorized would make the United States Navy the most powerful ever seen. Of the existing navies, it was obvious that only the British Royal Navy and the Imperial Japanese Navy could be its serious competitors, and in 1919, a Navy Department Planning Committee reported that the only two powers likely to be rivals of the United States were Great Britain and Japan. While Anglo-American amity had cooled immediately after the Armistice and the commercial policies of Great Britain made it possible that tension between the two western powers might arise in the future, for the present there was no real danger of such a development.

Japanese-American relations, however, were such that difficulty might be anticipated in the near future. The Far Eastern possessions of the United States, always vulnerable to attack by Japan, were rendered more precarious by the Japanese occupation of the former German islands north of the Equator. These flanked the American line of communications to the Philippines and all but surrounded the potential naval base on Guam. Moreover, Japanese policy toward China seemed particularly apt to involve the United States in differences which might lead to war in the western Pacific. Further to complicate matters, there was the Anglo-Japanese Alliance. It was doubtful that Great Britain would fulfill her treaty obligations in the event of a Japanese-American War, but the possibility could not be ruled out.

By the time this realistic appraisal of the situation had been completed, the Navy Department had already decided to depart from the traditional policy in its peacetime fleet dispositions. The Atlantic and Pacific coasts were to receive approximately equal fleets. Secre-

189

tary Daniels pointed out that the Panama Canal made it possible to unite the fleet quickly and insisted that the planned annual joint maneuvers would give adequate opportunity for the two forces to become accustomed to working together. In short, he believed that this division of the major warships into two fleets would not violate the principle of strategic concentration at all, and further, that the assignment of equal forces to the Atlantic and Pacific Fleets would result in a healthy spirit of competition that could not fail to bring about increased efficiency in all vessels concerned.

On 18 June 1919, the Planning Committee had submitted its recommendation for the assignment of ships to the Atlantic and Pacific Fleets. It was governed by the principle that ships of similar characteristics should be kept together for tactical unity, and by the logistic reality that a large amount of good coal was available on the eastern seaboard, while the Pacific coast, which lacked steam coal, had a plentiful supply of fuel oil. The order that the two fleets be nearly equal meant that some coal-burning pre-dreadnoughts would have to go to the Pacific, but all of the dreadnoughts tentatively assigned to the west coast had oil-fired boilers. This resulted in a certain inequality—the coal-burning dreadnoughts were older and weaker ships—so in compensation, the Atlantic Fleet received an additional pre-dreadnought.

Division along the lines suggested by the Planning Committee seems to have been both logical and practical, but it was not adopted. Instead, four of the eight dreadnoughts assigned to the Pacific Fleet burned coal, while an equal number of those retained in the Atlantic were much newer vessels using oil fuel. This did result in two fleets as nearly equal as possible, except that the Atlantic Fleet was stronger in pre-dreadnought battleships with seven to the Pacific Fleet's six, and of the seven, two were the *South Carolina* and *Michigan,* sometimes considered the first American dreadnoughts.

No explanation of this departure from the recommendation has been found, but it is impossible to escape the conclusion that political considerations were again allowed to outweigh strategic and logistic principles. A presidential election was fast approaching, and it was obvious that the Democratic Party would have to grasp at every straw if it were to remain in power. The political importance of the Atlantic coast far eclipsed that of the western seaboard, so it was not desirable to alienate the voters of the former section by assigning the older warships to the Atlantic Fleet. This cannot be proven, but it must have been of some importance; indeed, it seems likely that the decision to retain half of the Navy's battleship strength in the Atlantic Ocean was based on political motives. Certainly few responsible men would have held that the Royal Navy presented a threat equal to that of the Japanese men-o'-war. However, strategy is apt to emerge a poor second from any encounter with politics, at least in peacetime.

While the redistribution of the major warships was being planned, a Pacific Fleet of sorts was still in existence. Admiral Caperton struck his flag in the *Chicago* upon reaching retirement age in 1919, and Rear Admiral Clarence S. Williams was ordered to relieve him, but without being advanced to the rank of admiral. The few old ships of his command—the *Chicago, Denver, Tacoma,* and the gunboat *Machias*—were designated as Division One, Pacific Fleet, and Williams did not assume the title of commander in chief.

Williams's vessels were still on the east coast, so the work of demobilization in the Pacific was carried on under the direction of Rear Admiral Fullam. It was no more spectacular than the wartime activities of his force had been. A ship was sent to Alaska to assist in helping the victims of the 1918 influenza epidemic. The patrol of Mexican and Central American waters was continued by the old gunboats and the submarine chasers as the requisitioned vessels were returned to their previous services or owners. The fitting out of cargo ships for the Naval Overseas Transport Service was halted, and many reservists and other enlisted men were discharged to civil life. Warship building programs were curtailed on the west coast, as elsewhere in the country.

Rear Admiral Fullam struck his flag upon reaching retirement age on 20 October 1919, but his part in directing Pacific Fleet activities had come to an end even earlier. The first ships of the new Pacific Fleet had reached Californian waters early in August under the command of Admiral Hugh Rodman. Their arrival was made the occasion for a mammoth naval review for which the veteran *Oregon* was hastily recommissioned. After this final association with her younger sisters, the proud old battleship was again retired and in 1925 was turned over to the state whose name she bore for preservation as a naval monument, supposedly in perpetuity. (The *Oregon* was requisitioned by the government in 1943 and, stripped of armor and superstructure, was moored at Apra, Guam, for use as an explosives barge. A typhoon drove her on a reef, and there she rested until her hulk was sold to a Japanese scrap company in 1956. She was broken up in Japan during 1957.)

The power of the Pacific Fleet was in the eight dreadnoughts and six older battleships. They were supported by fifty-four active destroyers with the scout cruiser *Birmingham* as force flagship, fourteen submarines with two tenders, a mine force consisting of two minelayers and twelve minesweepers, and a fleet train of twenty-eight auxiliary vessels. In addition, fifty-four destroyers were retained in reserve with the scout cruiser *Salem* as flagship.

It will be noted that no cruisers except the destroyer force flagships were included in the Pacific Fleet organization. This omission indicates the United States Navy's most serious deficiency at that date. There simply were no effective cruisers, although ten modern scouts of the *Omaha* class were building. The first of these, however, was not commissioned until 1923, and even when all were completed, they were too few to relieve the shortage. Most of the hopelessly obsolete armored cruisers were assigned to squadrons in Asiatic and European waters, but eventually some served in the eastern Pacific once more. The old and ineffectual smaller cruisers of the aforementioned Division One also joined Rodman's flag, but were useful only for the patrol of Central American waters.

By any standard, however, Admiral Rodman's Pacific Fleet was a powerful force, and its presence on the west coast revealed the extent to which the facilities of the Mare Island and Puget Sound Navy Yards had been expanded. The former was a well-equipped yard in every respect, but it was considered undesirable to dock large ships there because of the shallow and restricted waters surrounding the island. Completion of the 32,000-ton battleship *California* proved that Mare Island could build large vessels, but her launching on 21 November 1919 demonstrated one of the dangers of such practice. The "Prune Barge" slid down the ways as planned and then resisted all efforts to stop her until she had crossed the channel and smashed some twenty-five feet of a Vallejo ferry landing. Needless to say, this had not been planned. Thereafter, Mare Island built only cruisers and smaller ships.

The Puget Sound Navy Yard at Bremerton, Washington, was notably free from Mare Island's shortcomings, but its development had been so slow that there was no thought of having big ships built there. As late as 1909, the major warships sent there for docking had first to unload their ammunition for storage in Mare Island's magazine because Puget Sound had no storage facilities other than open lighters. The political weakness of the Pacific Northwest was never more clearly revealed than by the failure of its congressmen to get funds appropriated for the construction of adequate facilities at the only navy yard in the region. But the serious shortage of ships during World War I resulted in a rapid expansion of the Puget Sound Navy Yard, and finally it was no longer necessary to send to the more amply equipped southern yard for workmen and tools when a major job was ordered. Since Mare Island was unable to offer docking facilities for battleships, the assignment of fourteen vessels of that type to the Pacific Fleet assured a busy future for the Puget Sound Navy Yard.

The third major fleet base in the Pacific Ocean was at Pearl Harbor—the Navy Department had decided to establish a large naval station there in 1909. For a time, more rapid progress was made on its development than on that of the Puget Sound yard, but Congress was not enthusiastic about appropriating the necessary funds, and the construction of a large dry dock was delayed by the action of subterranean springs which wrecked it early in 1913. This disaster slowed the development of the entire Pearl Harbor base, and its commandant found mainly deficiencies on which to report in 1918. Four years later, Pearl Harbor remained the "Gibraltar of the Pacific" on paper only, but work on its facilities and defenses was in progress.[1]

Other bases and shore facilities to support the Pacific Fleet were located principally on the southern California coast. San Diego finally achieved its desire to become an important naval base when a large recruit training center was established there in the course of World War I. It was destined also to become the site of destroyer and submarine bases, while its North Island Naval Air Station was soon to train the pilots for the first carrier air groups. The main operating base for the heavy ships was located in the Long Beach–San Pedro area. Finally, the whole Pacific coast was linked together by naval radio stations at strategic points. The west coast seemed rapidly to be approaching equality with the Atlantic seaboard in its naval bases and facilities.

But the outlook was not entirely bright. The large scale discharge of enlisted men resulted in a personnel problem for the United States Navy as a whole, and in the Pacific Fleet it caused many warships to be so undermanned that they were handicapped as cruising units. Some of the smaller vessels had to be placed in reserve and their crews transferred to the large ships to enable the latter to operate efficiently.

Mexican conditions remained unsettled, and the government of that republic assumed a defiant attitude distinctly alarming to American investors, particularly those interested in Mexican oil fields. These investors pressed for American intervention to protect their holdings, and War Plan Green was dusted off once more. For a time in 1919, it seemed very likely that intervention would become a fact. Naval and military commanders were ordered to prepare for a campaign in Mexico, and Admiral Rodman promulgated tentative assignments for his ships if hostilities were ordered. Momentarily the issue was undecided, but cooler heads prevailed. The threat to American property in Mexico was averted temporarily without recourse to arms, and few private citizens of the United States realized how narrowly armed intervention had been avoided.

One of the most onerous of the duties of the Pacific Fleet was removed from its jurisdiction in 1920 when the Special Service Squadron was organized under the command of Rear Admiral H. F. Bryan. To this "Banana Squadron," consisting of the old cruisers *Des Moines, Galveston, Cleveland, Denver,* and *Tacoma,* and the gunboats *Dolphin, Sacramento, Asheville,* and *Niagara,* was assigned the responsibility for patrolling Central American waters in the Caribbean Sea and the Pacific Ocean. It was based on the Canal Zone so that its vessels could be dispatched to either coast without delay. It was ridiculous that one of the world's strongest navies should have had to rely on such a decrepit force for this duty—the flagship *Dolphin,* no less than thirty-five years of age, was one of the vessels of the original "Squadron of Evolution" of 1889, and only the gunboats *Sacramento* and *Asheville* were relatively modern warships—but it did leave the men-o'-war of the Atlantic and Pacific Fleets free for more important duties.

Early in 1921, the two fleets met for joint maneuvers in the Pacific off the Canal Zone, and concluded their training with a cruise to ports on the west coast of South America. These had been largely neglected since the completion of the Panama Canal, for its construction had deprived the southeastern Pacific area of much of its strategic importance to the United States. This fact also reflected the relative stability of the political situation on the South American Pacific coast as compared with Mexico and Central America, although it must be stated that American investments in the latter regions were much greater than those in the countries farther south.

At the conclusion of the cruise in February 1921, the two fleets separated and proceeded to their respective bases. However, the United States Navy was becoming ever more concerned with conditions in the Pacific. At the Naval War College in 1919 and 1920, the major emphasis had been on problems in that ocean; and the war game board was largely occupied with a war between Orange (Japanese) and Blue (American) forces. Almost no one of authority in the Navy Department doubted that the next war would be fought against Japan.

Already protests had been voiced against the separation of the Atlantic and Pacific Fleets. Civilian writers pointed out that the annual maneuvers were not of sufficient duration to permit the warships to operate in company efficiently and warned against undue reliance on the Panama Canal as a means of reinforcing either fleet in time of need. The canal had already been blocked temporarily by slides, and Canal Zone engineers could not guarantee that service would not be interrupted in the future. Moreover, the locks were peculiarly liable to damage by sabotage, and there were not a few who predicted that the opening move in a Japanese-American war would be the explosion of a Japanese freighter in one of the locks.[2]

The noted British authority Hector C. Bywater also wrote that the American Pacific Fleet, inferior to the Imperial Japanese Navy, would not loom large in Japanese eyes as a deterrent force even if it could count on immediate reinforcement from the Atlantic in the event of war. The only sufficient deterrent might well be the entire

American fleet stationed in the Pacific Ocean, because of the Oriental psychology which counted it dishonorable to retreat before any force not clearly superior. Bywater concluded that it would be nothing less than foolhardy for the United States Navy to continue its two-fleet policy.

On 5 June 1921, the *New York Times* announced that the Navy's General Board had recommended a reorganization of the fleet to include the creation of a permanent major fleet in the Pacific Ocean; many naval officers supposedly felt that Secretary Daniels had made "a serious tactical error" in dividing the fleet in 1919. Although it was realized that the United States had little to fear from Europe, there was no thought of transferring all of the capital ships to the Pacific. Such a course would leave the eastern navy yards without employment and would place an intolerable burden on the Pacific coast bases.

Some two weeks later, it was stated that the existing fleets were to remain equal as to the number of warships in each, but that the Pacific Fleet was to consist of modern oil-burning superdreadnoughts, while eight older ships would be assigned to the Atlantic. The major reason was one of economy—a saving of nine dollars per ton of fuel would be realized by the reorganization.[3]

Soon thereafter, the Conference on Limitation of Armament began its deliberations in Washington. The reductions in total capital ship tonnages are too well known to require consideration here, but the importance of the Armament Limitation Treaty's Article XIX must not be overlooked. By it, the United States, Great Britain, and Japan agreed to abstain from fortifying and developing most of their outlying insular possessions in the Pacific Ocean. This meant in effect that the Philippine Islands, Guam, and other islands held by the United States in the western and central Pacific could not be prepared for use as naval bases. In the event of a Japanese attack on these unprotected areas, the American fleet would have no major base closer than Pearl Harbor, while the enemy could operate from home bases without difficulty. With such a disadvantage, even the entire American fleet would not be more than equal to the nominally inferior Japanese Navy. Moreover, the Anglo-Japanese Alliance was dissolved by the accompanying four-power treaty signed by the United States, Great Britain, Japan, and France, so it was clear that the British would be unable to deter their former ally from offensive action against American possessions.

Yet another facet of the dissolution of this alliance was the fact that it invalidated once and for all the argument earlier advanced for retaining half of the American battleships in the Atlantic Fleet. Great Britain was no longer bound to support Japan in any war against a third power, and it was almost inconceivable that the British would side with the Oriental power against the United States. Thus, danger from Europe had become nearly nonexistent, but the situation in the western Pacific would be much graver if Japan failed to honor her Washington Treaty commitments.

Against this background appeared General Order Ninety-four which was promulgated on 6 December 1922 by Secretary of the Navy Edwin Denby. By this order, the two major fleets were combined to form the United States Fleet consisting of four divisions: Battle Fleet, Scouting Fleet, Control Force, and Fleet Base Force. The United States Fleet was to be used in either ocean in time of need, but ordinarily the Scouting Fleet and the Control Force were to be based on the Atlantic seaboard, while the Battle Fleet and the Fleet Base Force would be stationed in the eastern Pacific. Since the Battle Fleet was to contain all of the modern battleships, it was obvious that a major change in American naval strategy had occurred. However, the Secretary made no mention of the outstanding strategic reasons for the fleet reorganization. He attributed the "merger" of the fleets merely to a desire to promote "a closer coordination of effort and unity of practice which are so necessary to the most effective operation of our fighting forces."[4]

At any rate, the various divisions of the United States Fleet met for joint maneuvers in the Bay of Panama in March 1923, and upon the conclusion of the exercises, Vice Admiral John D. MacDonald, Commander, Scouting Fleet, in the *Wyoming,* led the five oldest dreadnoughts and the new *Maryland* back to the Atlantic Ocean. The remainder of the battleships, eleven superdreadnoughts in all, gathered in Los Angeles Harbor in mid-April, with Admiral Hilary P. Jones, previously commanding the Atlantic Fleet, flying his flag in the USS *Pennsylvania* as Commander in Chief, United States Fleet.[5] (Admiral Edward W. Eberle, former Commander in Chief, Pacific Fleet, reverted to vice admiral as Commander, Battle Fleet,

United States Fleet, with his flag in the *California*. The *Maryland* returned to the Atlantic coast for completion of the installation of her fire control system and minor modifications before joining the Battle Fleet.)

This realization of the ideal contained in General Order Ninety-four may be considered to have signified the end of the United States Navy's Pacific Station. The primary mission of Admiral Jones's United States Fleet differed almost as much from that outlined in Captain John Downes's sailing orders as did Jones's flagship from the USS *Macedonian*. For the next few decades, at least, the waters traversed by the ships of the old Pacific Squadron would be the cruising ground of the most formidable American naval force.

And since navies are merely agents of national policy, this transfer of naval strength indicated a corresponding reorientation of national policy. In the future, for a time, American naval thinking was to follow the directive laid down for it by Commodore Downes in 1833.

Downes and his successors in command of the United States Naval Forces on Pacific Station were responsible in a large sense for the westward emphasis. The cruises of his *Macedonian* and the men-o'-war which sailed in her wake resulted in significant additions to the fund of hydrographic, meteorologic, and economic knowledge of the eastern Pacific area. The mere presence of the warships encouraged commercial expansion—based in part upon this information—by lessening the dangers to life and cargo, and the naval vessel was able to provide many types of assistance to speed the merchantman upon her appointed way. The businessman was more willing to invest in Latin American republic or Pacific island with the Pacific Squadron as partial guarantor of the investment, and the diplomat found his task the easier because of the silent assurance given by American war vessels showing the flag in the waters of the country to which he was accredited. In many cases, the visit of a unit of the Pacific Squadron led to more amicable relations between the United States and the country visited, although the natural tendency of sailors to disport themselves in time-honored fashion ashore caused difficulty on occasion.

The total lack of sea battles on the Pacific Station has caused the Navy's role in expanding the territorial limits of the United States in that region largely to be overlooked. California was acquired without any major engagements, but in such battles as did occur, most of the fighting was done by seamen and Marines of the Pacific Squadron, led by officers from their ships. While it was not possible for men-o'-war to contribute significantly to the acquisition of the Pacific Northwest or of Alaska, units of the Pacific Squadron acted as agents of American imperialism in helping to bring the Hawaiian Islands, American Samoa, and certain other islands under the United States flag.

Naval personnel helped to maintain order in California in the absence of effective civil government, and the Army welcomed the assistance of warships during the Indian troubles on the shores of Puget Sound. For nearly a generation, naval officers governed Alaska and performed a like function in American Samoa for an even longer time. In the event of natural catastrophe, men-o'-war were usually early on the scene, and their officers and men proved themselves outstanding in relief work.

Through these and other services—often unspectacular, but generally laudable—the Pacific Squadron demonstrated the power and versatility of naval force.

Admiral Hilary P. Jones, standing on the flag bridge of the USS *Pennsylvania* in 1923, might well have thought of Commodore John Downes's statement of ninety years earlier:

Everything conspires to render the Pacific of great interest to the people of the United States at the present time. Our future sea fights are as likely to take place here as on the Atlantic Ocean, for here we are acquiring a preponderating commercial interest, and here must be our navy also.

And Admiral Jones might well have made a signal to that officer in the USS *Potomac:* "And here our Navy is!"

Notes

CHAPTER 1

Distant Stations

1. Howard I. Chapelle, *The History of the American Sailing Navy* (New York: W. W. Norton and Co., 1949), p. 340, intimates that some sloops were designed specifically for duty on Pacific Station, but gives no authority for this intimation.

CHAPTER 2

The Cruise of the Macedonian

1. Charles Gauntt, "Journal of the Cruise of the USS *Macedonian,* 29 July 1818—18 June 1821."

CHAPTER 3

From Ship to Squadron

1. General J. Paroisien to Robinson, 3 March 1822, "Correspondence relating to the Cruises of *Cyane, Franklin, Ontario, Peacock,* and *United States,* January 1818—May 1827." While a gentleman's agreement may have been made with the Patriots regarding Pezuela, there seems to be no evidence of any formal commitment on Ridgely's part.
2. Fletcher Pratt, *Preble's Boys* (New York: William Sloane Associates, 1950), p. 339.
3. Rodgers to Smith Thompson, 22 December 1821, "Board of Navy Commissioners' Letters to the Secretary of the Navy, April 1815—August 1842," I, 561.
4. Testimony of Captain James Biddle, *American State Papers, Naval Affairs* (Washington: Gales and Seaton, 1834-1861), II, 513.
5. Letter written by Lieut. Andrew H. Foot, 15 September 1824, "Area Nine File, 1814-1910."
6. Allan Westcott, "Captain 'Mad Jack' Percival," *U.S. Naval Institute Proceedings,* LXI (1935), 315. Dudley W. Knox, Captain, USN, *A History of the United States Navy* (New York: G. P. Putnam's Sons, 1936), pp. 102 and 150, holds that *Dolphin* was the second American warship to visit Honolulu. However, his candidate for the honor, the prize *Sir Andrew Hammond,* was not a man-o'-war at all, so I cannot consider her visit in 1814 as that of a warship.
7. Southard to Hull, 24 June 1825, "Letters to Officers, Ships of War, March 1798—September 1868," XVI, 58.
8. Hull to Southard, 24 April 1827, "Isaac Hull Letter Book No. 1, 25 October 1823—2 July 1827."
9. Rodgers to Branch, 17 September 1830, "Board of Navy Commissioners' Letters to the Secretary of the Navy, April 1815—August 1842," IV, 7-8.

10. Southard to President J. Q. Adams, 2 December 1826, *American State Papers, Naval Affairs,* II, 728.

CHAPTER 4

Aground on Her Own Beef Bones

1. Dickerson to Ballard, 20 December 1837, "Letters to Officers, Ships of War, March 1798—September 1868," XXV, 28.
2. Captain Daniel Turner's correspondence, 2 and 3 February 1840, "Letter Books of Officers of the United States Navy at Sea, March 1778—July 1908."
3. Paulding to Claxton, 9 May 1839, "Letters to Officers, Ships of War, March 1798—September 1868," XXIV, 431-439.
4. Louis N. Feipel, "The United States Navy in Mexico, 1821-1914," *U.S. Naval Institute Proceedings,* XLI (1915), 44, puts this visit in 1841. It is true that *St. Louis* was at Monterey in May 1841, but George P. Hammond, ed., *The Larkin Papers* (Berkeley: University of California Press, 1951-1955), I, 45-46, and Hubert H. Bancroft, *The History of California* (San Francisco: A. L. Bancroft and Co. and The History Co., 1884-1890), IV, 36, make it clear that the following incident occurred in 1840. The rank of commander replaced the cumbersome title of master-commandant.
5. Aulick to Turner, 11 May 1841, "Turner's Letter Book."
6. Warrington to Badger, 8 May 1841, "Board of Navy Commissioners' Letters to the Secretary of the Navy, April 1815—August 1842," VII, 39.

CHAPTER 5

The Flying Welshman

1. Simms (Navy Department) to Jones, 22 March 1841, "Letters to Officers, Ships of War, March 1798—September 1868," XXX, 313. It must be remembered that news of Claxton's death had not reached Washington at this time.
2. Jones to Upshur, 22 March 1842, "Letters from Officers commanding Squadrons, Pacific Squadron, February 1841—November 1886." Hereafter cited as "Pacific Squadron Letters."
3. Upshur to Jones, 10 December 1841, "Letters to Officers, Ships of War," XXXI, 381.
4. Herman Melville, *White Jacket* (New York: Harper and Bros., 1850), p. 261. Melville's *Neversink* was in fact *United States.*
5. Jones to Upshur, 18 June 1842, "Pacific Squadron Letters."
6. *Ibid.*
7. Jones to U.S. Minister at Court of Mexico, 22 October 1842, copy, *ibid.*
8. Jones to Upshur, 16 January 1843, *ibid.*
9. Jones to Dallas, 22 November 1843, *ibid.*
10. Dallas to Secretary of the Navy, 23 February 1844, *ibid.*
11. Sloat to Bancroft, 29 July 1845, *ibid.*
12. Bancroft to Sloat, 24 June 1845, "Record of Confidential Letters," I, 141.
13. Sloat to Bancroft, 17 March 1846 and 6 May 1846, "Pacific Squadron Letters."
14. Sloat to Mervine, 18 May 1846, "Area Nine File, 1814-1910."

15. Sloat to Bancroft, 30 April 1846, "Pacific Squadron Letters."
16. Sloat to Bancroft, 6 June 1846, *ibid.*

CHAPTER 6

Too Many Commodores

1. Larkin to Montgomery, 7 July 1846 (duplicate of Sloat's order of previous day, sent by courier), "Area Nine File, 1814-1910."
2. Sloat to Bancroft, 31 July 1846, "Pacific Squadron Letters."
3. Stockton to Sloat, 23 July 1846, "Letter Books of Officers of the United States Navy at Sea, March 1778—July 1908."
4. See p. 72, *supra.*
5. See p. 75, *supra.*
6. Allan, Nevins, *Frémont, The West's Greatest Adventurer* (2nd ed.; New York: Harper and Bros., 1928), I, 324.
7. *Ibid.,* I, 324.
8. Stockton to Bancroft, 22 August 1846, "Stockton Letter Book."
9. Stockton to Polk, 26 August 1846, *ibid.*
10. Proclamation of blockade, 19 August 1846, "Area Nine File, 1814-1910."
11. Stockton to Mervine, 19 September 1846, "Stockton Letter Book."
12. Chapelle, *op. cit.,* p. 358, says *Warren* became a storeship in 1840, but actually she served actively as a cruiser during the early months of the Mexican War.

CHAPTER 7

The Gold Mania

1. Jones to Secretary of the Navy, 25 October 1849, "Pacific Squadron Letters."
2. For a vivid account of the dangers of Puget Sound, see Comdr. George F. Pearson to McCauley, 18 July 1851, "Pacific Squadron Letters."
3. This account is based on Trial 1187, "Records of the Office of the Judge Advocate General, Records of Courts-Martial and Courts of Inquiry," LX.
4. McCauley to Secretary of the Navy, 25 August 1850, "Pacific Squadron Letters."
5. McCauley to Magruder, 7 October 1850, *ibid.*
6. Dobbin to Dulany, 3 January 1854, "Confidential Letters Sent, September 1843—December 1879," III, 125.
7. Graham to Sloat, 27 January 1852, "Letters of Officers, Ships of War," XLVI, 359-362, and Charles O. Paullin, "Naval Administration, 1842-1861," *U.S. Naval Institute Proceedings,* XXXIII (1907), 1453.
8. For the details of Mare Island's development, see Arnold S. Lott, Lt. Cdr., USN, *A Long Line of Ships* (Annapolis: U.S. Naval Institute, 1954).
9. Dobbin to Mervine or Senior Officer Present, San Francisco, 2 August 1856, "Confidential Letters," III, 382-384.
10. Montgomery to Toucey, 13 February 1861, "Area Nine File, 1814-1910."

CHAPTER 8

Guarding the Gold Steamers

1. Welles to Montgomery, 27 April 1861, "Confidential Letters Sent, September 1843—December 1879," V, 49.

2. Dudley W. Knox, Captain, USN, *op. cit.,* p. 195, states that all but three American steam warships were recalled to the Atlantic coast on the outbreak of the war, but this is in error as none of Montgomery's steamers left the Pacific in 1861.
3. Bell to Welles, 4 April 1862, "Pacific Squadron Letters."
4. *Ibid.*
5. Bell to Welles, 10 March 1862, "Area Nine File, 1814-1910."
6. Welles to Pearson, 4 October 1864, "Letters to Officers commanding Squadrons or Vessels, September 1861—May 1886," IV, 338-339.
7. Arnold S. Lott, Lt. Cdr., USN, *op. cit.,* pp. 85-86. Lott spells the monitor's name "Comanche," but all contemporary records read "Camanche."
8. Telegram, Welles to McDougal, 15 April 1865, "Area Nine File, 1814-1910."

CHAPTER 9

Economy and Decline

1. Charles E. Clark, Rear Admiral, USN (Ret.), *My Fifty Years in the Navy* (Boston: Little, Brown and Co., 1917), pp. 123-124, believes that the French threat brought about the reinforcement, but Rodgers' orders make no mention of this. Welles to Rodgers, 26 July 1865, "Area Nine File, 1814-1910."
2. Harold and Margaret Sprout, *The Rise of American Naval Power, 1776-1918* (Princeton: Princeton University Press, 1939), quoted on p. 166.
3. Robeson to Winslow, 21 March 1871, "Letters to Officers commanding Squadrons or Vessels, September 1861—May 1886," VII, 87.
4. Clark, *op. cit.,* p. 247.
5. See Sprout, *op. cit.,* pp. 191-192, for general discussion of inefficiency in navy yards.
6. Secretary of the Navy, *Annual Report, 1878,* p. 39.
7. Henry Glass, Comdr., USN, "Naval Administration in Alaska," *U.S. Naval Institute Proceedings,* XVI (1890), 2.

CHAPTER 10

A Stagnant Station

1. John D. Long, *The New American Navy* (New York: Outlook Co., 1903), I, 39.
2. Greer to Tracy, 5 October 1889, "Area Nine File, 1814-1910."
3. Henry A. Wiley, Rear Admiral, USN (Ret.), *An Admiral from Texas* (New York: Doubleday, Doran & Co., 1934), p. 63.
4. C. S. Freeman, Rear Admiral, USN, "The Puget Sound Navy Yard," *Historical Transactions, 1893-1943* (New York: Society of Naval Architects and Marine Engineers, 1945), p. 32.
5. Roosevelt to Long, 18 April 1898, "Area Nine File, 1814-1910."
6. Miller to Long, 15 June 1898, *ibid.*
7. Acting Secretary of the Navy Allen to Tilley, 17 February 1900, *ibid.*
8. This was the "Navy Mutiny of 1905" described in Holden A. Evans, *One Man's Fight for a Better Navy* (New York: Dodd, Mead and Co., 1940), pp. 158-160. My account is based largely on a letter from Admiral

Arthur J. Hepburn to me, 28 November 1955. Both Hepburn and Evans
were members of the Board.

9. Goodrich to Secretary of the Navy, 26 November 1905, "Area Nine File,
1814-1910."

10. Secretary of the Navy Metcalf to Editor, *Seattle Post-Intelligencer,* 5 February 1907.

CHAPTER 11

The Armored Cruiser Squadron

1. Fullam to Caperton, 30 October 1916, "W. F. Fullam Papers."
2. Fullam to Benson, 26 October 1916, *ibid.*

CHAPTER 12

Pacific Fleet in the Atlantic Ocean

1. War Plans for 1913 are still classified so this discussion is based on unclassified correspondence referring to War Plans Orange and Green.

2. It must be noted that this is largely speculation. The sources open to me contained few references to War Plan Green, but these would seem to support my supposition.

3. The Commander in Chief, Pacific Fleet, did point out the danger inherent in the weakness of his force, but his letter seems to have elicited no reply. Howard to Daniels, 15 April 1915, "General Correspondence of the Office of the Secretary of the Navy."

4. Fullam to Benson, 12 April 1917, "W. F. Fullam Papers."

5. Daniels to Caperton, 9 May 1917, "Office of the Secretary, Confidential Correspondence, 1917-1919 (Declassified)."

6. Caperton to Daniels, 21 June 1917, "General Correspondence."

CHAPTER 13

"And Here Our Navy Is"

1. Paul A. Stevens, Capt., USN, "Pearl Harbor and Its Relation to the United States Navy," *Historical Transactions, 1893-1943* (New York: Society of Naval Architects and Marine Engineers, 1945), pp. 25-26.

2. David Hannay, "Sea Power in the Pacific," *Edinburgh Review,* CCXXXIV (July–October, 1921), 127. Hannay scoffed at fears that the Japanese might block the canal.

3. *New York Times,* 5 June 1921, p. 19.

4. Secretary of the Navy, *Annual Report, 1923,* p. 3.

5. *Los Angeles Times,* 12 April 1923, II, 1.

Appendices

Sailing Orders to Captain Downes

Sept. 2, 1818

Captain John Downes
  U.S. Ship Macedonian
    Boston, Mass.

Sir,

The United States Ship Macedonian, under your command, having been equipped for service, you are hereby ordered to proceed to sea immediately, and shape your course for the Brazil Coast, and thence round Cape Horn into the Pacific Ocean.

One of the principal objects of the expedition of this ship, is to afford to the persons and property of the citizens of the United States protection and security, consistently with the laws of nations, and the respect due to all existing authorities, wherever and whenever such protection may be needed, and can be afforded.

You are directed to put into the Port of Pernambuco, and make a demand of the Governor of that place, for the release of seven American Seamen, whose names are signed to a petition, a copy of which is herewith enclosed. The Consul, Mr. Rea, has not been able to effect this of the Brazillian [sic] Government, and should you not succeed, you will make a report upon the subject to the U.S. Minister, Mr. Sumpter, at Rio Janeiro [sic], to enable him to pursue the subject at that Court;—these men, if released, you may deliver over to the Consul, or leave at liberty to go where they please.

You will thence proceed to Rio Janeiro, and deliver the despatches from the Department of State, to Mr. Sumpter, with a statement of the issue of your application for the above mentioned Seamen. Making as short a stay as possible at Rio Janeiro, proceed thence to Rio de la Plata, and place the ship in the safest moorings in the Bay or River, with a view to remain as long there as the favorable season to double Cape Horn will admit.

It is Wished by the President of the United States, that you find or make an occasion to pass the most or great part of your time on shore at Buenos Ayres, observing the state of affairs there, and especially the movements of any agents, avowed or otherwise, of any European Power who may be there;—and you are requested to make report to this De-

207

partment, of every circumstance interesting to the United States, that may fall within your notice.

After passing Cape Horn, and in pursuing your course through the South Sea, you will endeavor to ascertain whether any interruption has been given to our Whale Fishery or Merchant Ships in that quarter; and after touching at such ports for refreshments as may be convenient, endeavor to fall in with the above mentioned ships, and convoy them, if necessary, to friendly ports.

It is particularly recommended to you, to show every mark of respect to the existing governments of the several places you may visit, and observe the usual Salutes and etiquette to all ships of war of a friendly nation; and while in port permit no violation of the rights of hospitality and punish all offences which may be committed by officers or men, on shore, by a total prohibition of that indulgence afterwards.

To your good judgment and experience, are committed the health and lives of your crew; and you will endeavor to furnish them, upon the best terms, with all the necessary provisions and refreshments, the country you visit may afford.

You will have opportunities by the several whale ships returning home, to transmit frequent information to the Department of the events which shall occur during your cruize [*sic*], which may be extended according to circumstances, and the state of your ship, to the full term of the crew's enlistment.

The U.S. Ship Hornet is intended to be equipped when she shall return from her present cruize, and will be ordered to join you in the Pacific Ocean, and be attached to your command;—you will therefore leave a letter at Valparaiso, to notify the Commander where to meet you.

Enclosed you have letters of authority to draw upon this Department as occasion may require, for Provisions, Contingent, and other expenses.

In case of meeting with the U.S. Ship Ontario, Captain James Biddle, you have an order to him, herewith to transfer Surgeon Hoffman to your ship, in exchange for Surgeon Edgar.

With sincere wishes for your health and success,

I am, very respectfully,
Sir, your most ob: Servant,

B. W. Crowninshield

Officers Commanding United States Naval Forces on Pacific Station

Captain John Downes, 1818-20
Captain Charles Goodwin Ridgely, 1820-21
Commodore Charles Stewart, 1821-24
Commodore Isaac Hull, 1824-26
Commodore Jacob Jones, 1826-29
Commodore Charles C. B. Thompson, 1829-31
Commodore John Downes, 1832-34
Commodore Alexander Scammell Wadsworth, 1834-36
Commodore Henry E. Ballard, 1837-39
Commodore Alexander Claxton, 1839-41
Captain Daniel Turner, 1841-42
Commodore Thomas ap Catesby Jones, 1842-43
Commodore Alexander James Dallas, 1843-44
Captain James Armstrong, 1844
Commodore John Drake Sloat, 1844-46
Commodore Robert Field Stockton, 1846-47
Commodore William Branford Shubrick, 1847
Commodore James Biddle, 1847
Commodore William Branford Shubrick, 1847-48
Commodore Thomas ap Catesby Jones, 1848-50
Commodore Charles Stewart McCauley, 1850-53
Commodore Bladen Dulany, 1853-55
Commodore William Mervine, 1855-57
Flag Officer John Collins Long, 1857-59
Flag Officer John Berrien Montgomery, 1859-62
Flag Officer Charles Henry Bell, 1862-64
   (Acting Rear Admiral, 15 September 1862)
Rear Admiral George Frederick Pearson, 1864-66
North Pacific Squadron
Rear Admiral Henry Knox Thatcher, 1866-68
Rear Admiral Thomas Tingey Craven, 1868-69
South Pacific Squadron
Rear Admiral George Frederick Pearson, 1866-67
Rear Admiral John Adolphus Bernard Dahlgren, 1867-68
Rear Admiral Thomas Turner, 1868-69
Pacific Station

Rear Admiral Thomas Turner, 1869-70
Rear Admiral John Ancrum Winslow, 1870-72
North Pacific Station
Rear Admiral Alexander Mosely Pennock, 1872-74
Rear Admiral John Jay Almy, 1874-76
Rear Admiral Alexander Murray, 1876-78
South Pacific Station
Rear Admiral Charles Steedman, 1872-73
Rear Admiral Napoleon Collins, 1874-75
Rear Admiral Reed Werden, 1875-76
Commodore Charles Henry Bromedge Caldwell, 1876
Rear Admiral George Henry Preble, 1877
Pacific Station
Rear Admiral Christopher Raymond Perry Rodgers, 1878-80
Rear Admiral Thomas Holdup Stevens, 1880-81
Rear Admiral George Beall Balch, 1881-83
Rear Admiral Aaron Konkle Hughes, 1883-84
Rear Admiral John Henry Upshur, 1884-85
Rear Admiral Edward Yorke McCauley, 1885-87
Rear Admiral Lewis Ashfield Kimberly, 1887-90
Rear Admiral George Brown, 1890-93
Rear Admiral John Irwin, 1893-95
Rear Admiral Lester Anthony Beardslee, 1895-97
Rear Admiral Joseph Nelson Miller, 1897-98
Commodore Albert Kautz, 1898-1901
Rear Admiral Silas Casey, 1901-3
Rear Admiral Henry Glass, 1903-5
Rear Admiral Caspar Frederick Goodrich, 1905-6
Rear Admiral William Thomas Swinburne, 1906-7
Pacific Fleet
Rear Admiral James Henry Dayton, 1907-8
Rear Admiral William Thomas Swinburne, 1908-9
Rear Admiral Uriel Sebree, 1909-10
Rear Admiral Giles Bates Harber, 1910
Rear Admiral Edward Buttevant Barry, 1910-11
Rear Admiral Chauncey Thomas, 1911-12
Rear Admiral William Henry Hudson Southerland, 1912-13
Rear Admiral Walter Cleveland Cowles, 1913-14
Rear Admiral Thomas Benton Howard, 1914-15
    (Admiral, 11 March 1915)
Admiral Cameron McRae Winslow, 1915-16
Admiral William Banks Caperton, 1916-19
Admiral Hugh Rodman, 1919-21
Admiral Edward Walter Eberle, 1921-23

Annual Composition of United States Naval Forces on Pacific Station

This information is taken from the *Navy Register* and lists vessels assigned as of 1 January unless otherwise stated. The *Register* sometimes included ships coming out from the Atlantic coast or returning home; hence the actual number of vessels on station occasionally was smaller than this list would make it appear.

After 1915, the composition of the Pacific Fleet varied rapidly, and the *Register* ceased to give information as to fleet composition. Therefore, it was considered impractical to extend the list beyond 1 January 1915.

(F) indicates the flagship of the commander in chief, (f) squadron or division flagship. Vessels serving in Asiatic waters (Third Squadron, Pacific Fleet) and torpedo flotillas when operating as independent commands, are not listed.

1818-20
Macedonian	Capt. John Downes

1821
Constellation	Capt. Charles G. Ridgely

1822-23
Franklin (F)	Commo. Charles Stewart
Dolphin	Lieut. David Conner

1824-26
United States (F)	Commo. Isaac Hull
Peacock	M-Cdt. William Carter
Dolphin	Lieut. John Percival

1827-29
Brandywine (F)	Commo. Jacob Jones
Vincennes	M-Cdt. William B. Finch
Dolphin	

1830-31
Guerrière (F)	Commo. Charles C. B. Thompson

| *St. Louis*
Dolphin | M-Cdt. John D. Sloat |

1832-33

Potomac (F)	Commo. John Downes
Falmouth	M-Cdt. Francis H. Gregory
Dolphin	Lieut. John C. Long

1834

Vincennes (F)	Commo. Alexander S. Wadsworth
Fairfield	M-Cdt. Elie A. F. LaVallette
Dolphin	Lieut. Ralph Voorhees

1835-36

Brandywine (F)	Commo. Wadsworth
Vincennes	M-Cdt. John H. Aulick
Dolphin	Lieut. Voorhees
Boxer	Lieut. Hugh N. Page

1837

| *North Carolina* (F) | Commo. Henry E. Ballard |
| *Boxer* | Lieut. Page |

1838

North Carolina (F)	Commo. Ballard
Lexington	Capt. John H. Clack
Falmouth	Comdr. Isaac McKeever
Enterprise	Lieut. William M. Glendy
Boxer	Lieut. William C. Nicholson

1839

Constitution (F)	Capt. Daniel Turner
Lexington	Capt. Clack
Falmouth	Capt. McKeever
Boxer	Lieut. Nicholson

1840

Constitution (F)	Capt. Turner
Lexington	Capt. Clack
Falmouth	Capt. McKeever
St. Louis	Comdr. French Forrest
Shark	Lieut. Abraham Bigelow
Boxer	Lieut. Nicholson

1841

| *Constitution* (F) | Capt. Turner |
| *St. Louis* | Comdr. Forrest |

| *Shark* | Lieut. Bigelow |
| *Relief* | Lieut. John S. Nicholas |

1842
United States (F)	Capt. James Armstrong
St. Louis	Comdr. Forrest
Cyane	Comdr. Cornelius K. Stribling
Yorktown	Capt. John H. Aulick
Dale	Comdr. Charles Gauntt
Shark	Comdr. Thomas A. Dornin
Relief	Lieut. Nicholas

1843
United States (F)	Capt. Armstrong
Cyane	Comdr. Stribling
Yorktown	Lieut. J. S. Nicholas
Dale	Comdr. T. A. Dornin
Shark	Lieut. Henry Eagle
Relief	Lieut. Isaac S. Sterett

1844
Savannah (F)	Capt. Andrew Fitzhugh
United States	Capt. Armstrong
Warren	Comdr. Joseph B. Hull
Cyane	Comdr. Stribling
Levant	Comdr. Hugh N. Page
Shark	Lieut. Eagle
Relief	Lieut. Sterett
Erie	Lieut. Nathaniel W. Duke

1845
Savannah (F)	Capt. J. Armstrong
Warren	Comdr. Hull
Levant	Comdr. Page
Portsmouth	Comdr. John B. Montgomery
Shark	Lieut. Neil M. Howison
Relief	Lieut. Henry K. Hoff

1846
Savannah (F)	Commo. John D. Sloat
Constitution	Capt. John Percival
Congress	Commo. Robert F. Stockton
Portsmouth	Comdr. Montgomery
Levant	Comdr. Page
Warren	Comdr. Hull

Cyane	Capt. William Mervine
Shark	Lieut. Howison
Erie	Lieut. Charles C. Turner
Relief	Lieut. Robert G. Robb

1847

Independence (F)	Capt. Elie A. F. LaVallette
Savannah	Capt. W. Mervine
Congress	Commo. Stockton
Portsmouth	Comdr. Montgomery
Warren	Comdr. Hull
Cyane	Comdr. Samuel F. DuPont
Dale	Comdr. William W. McKean
Preble	Comdr. William F. Shields
Erie	Lieut. Turner
Lexington	Lieut. Theodorus Bailey
Southampton	Lieut. Robert D. Thorburn

1848

Ohio (F)	Capt. William V. Taylor
Independence	Commo. W. Branford Shubrick
Portsmouth	Comdr. Montgomery
St. Mary's	Comdr. Jacob Crowninshield
Warren	Lieut. Joseph Lanman
Cyane	Comdr. DuPont
Dale	Comdr. Thomas O. Selfridge
Preble	Comdr. Shields
Lexington	Lieut. Bailey
Southampton	Lieut. Thorburn

1849

Ohio (F)	Comdr. Cornelius K. Stribling
Independence	Commo. Shubrick
St. Mary's	Comdr. Crowninshield
Warren	Comdr. Andrew K. Long
Dale	Comdr. John Rudd
Preble	Comdr. James Glynn
Lexington	Lieut. Frederick Chatard
Southampton	Lieut. Edward L. Handy
Fredonia	Lieut. Frederick A. Neville

1850

Savannah (F)	Comdr. Zachariah F. Johnston
Vandalia	Comdr. William H. Gardner
Falmouth	Comdr. Thomas Pettigru

Vincennes	Comdr. William L. Hudson
Warren	Lieut. Charles W. Pickering
Supply	Lieut. Charles H. A. H. Kennedy
Massachusetts	Lieut. Samuel R. Knox

1851
Savannah (F)	Capt. Hugh N. Page
Raritan	Capt. Charles Gauntt
St. Mary's	Comdr. George A. Magruder
Vandalia	Comdr. Gardner
Falmouth	Comdr. George F. Pearson
Vincennes	Comdr. Hudson
Warren	Lieut. Pickering
Supply	Lieut. Kennedy
Southampton	Lieut. Peter Turner
Massachusetts	Lieut. Knox

1852
Raritan (F)	Comdr. William W. McKean
St. Lawrence	Capt. Bladen Dulany
Portsmouth	Comdr. Thomas A. Dornin
St. Mary's	Comdr. Magruder
Vandalia	Comdr. Gardner
Vincennes	Comdr. Hudson
Warren	Lieut. Henry Moor
Lexington	Lieut. William Radford
Southampton	Lieut. Turner
Massachusetts	Lieut. Knox

1853
St. Lawrence (F)	Commo. Bladen Dulany
Portsmouth	Comdr. Dornin
Warren	Lieut. Fabius Stanly
Southampton	Lieut. Junius J. Boyle

1854
St. Lawrence (F)	Comdr. William W. Hunter
Portsmouth	Comdr. Dornin
St. Mary's	Comdr. Theodorus Bailey
Decatur	Comdr. Isaac S. Sterett
Warren	Lieut. Stanly
Fredonia	Lieut. J. D. Johnston

1855
Independence (F)	Capt. Josiah Tattnall
St. Mary's	Comdr. Bailey

John Adams	Comdr. Edward B. Boutwell
Decatur	Comdr. Sterett
Massachusetts	Lieut. Richard W. Meade
Warren	Lieut. David McDougal
Fredonia	Lieut. Johnston

1856

Independence (F)	Capt. Tattnall
St. Mary's	Comdr. Bailey
John Adams	Comdr. Boutwell
Decatur	Comdr. Guert Gansevoort
Massachusetts	Comdr. Samuel Swartwout
Warren	Lieut. McDougal
Fredonia	Lieut. William Nelson

1857

Independence (F)	Comdr. Henry K. Hoff
St. Mary's	Comdr. Charles H. Davis
John Adams	Comdr. Boutwell
Decatur	Lieut. Edward Middleton
Massachusetts	Comdr. Swartwout
Warren	Lieut. McDougal
Fredonia	Lieut. Nelson

1858

Merrimack (F)	Comdr. R. B. Hitchcock
Saranac	Capt. John Kelly
St. Mary's	Comdr. Davis
Decatur	Comdr. Henry K. Thatcher
Fredonia	Lieut. William H. Ball

1859

Merrimack (F)	Comdr. Hitchcock
Saranac	Capt. Kelly
St. Mary's	Comdr. Robert D. Thorburn
Vandalia	Comdr. Arthur Sinclair
Decatur	Comdr. Thatcher
Cyane	Comdr. Samuel Lockwood
Fredonia	Lieut. Ball

1860

Lancaster (F)	Capt. John Rudd
Saranac	Capt. Robert Ritchie
Cyane	Comdr. Lockwood
Levant	Comdr. William E. Hunt

St. Mary's	Comdr. William D. Porter
Wyoming	Comdr. John K. Mitchell
Narragansett	Comdr. Timothy A. Hunt
Fredonia	Lieut. James M. Watson
Warren	Lieut. Junius J. Boyle

1861

Lancaster (F)	Capt. Rudd
Saranac	Capt. Ritchie
Levant	Comdr. W. E. Hunt
St. Mary's	Comdr. Porter
Wyoming	Comdr. Mitchell
Narragansett	Comdr. T. A. Hunt
Cyane	Comdr. Simon B. Bissell
Fredonia	Lieut. Watson
Warren	Lieut. Boyle

1862

Lancaster (F)	Capt. Henry K. Hoff
Narragansett	Comdr. Fabius Stanly
Saranac	Capt. Joseph Lanman
Cyane	Comdr. Bissell
St. Mary's	Comdr. Edward Middleton
Warren	Lieut. W. Winder Pollack
Fredonia	Lieut. Henry C. Kean

1863

Lancaster (F)	Capt. J. Lanman
Cyane	Comdr. Bissell
St. Mary's	Comdr. Middleton
Narragansett	Comdr. Stanly
Fredonia	Lieut. Kean

1864

Lancaster (F)	Capt. Lanman
Saranac	Capt. Charles H. Poor
St. Mary's	Capt. Middleton
Narragansett	Comdr. Selim E. Woodworth
Saginaw	Comdr. William E. Hopkins
Cyane	Comdr. Paul Shirley
Fredonia	Comdr. Roger Perry
Farallones	Actg. Master C. C. Wells

1865

Lancaster (F)	Comdr. Henry K. Davenport
Saranac	Capt. Poor

St. Mary's	Capt. Middleton
Wateree	Comdr. Frank K. Murray
Cyane	Lt. Cdr. John H. Russell
Saginaw	Comdr. Hopkins
Fredonia	Comdr. Perry
Farallones	Actg. Master Nelson Provost

1866

Lancaster (F)	Comdr. Davenport
Saranac	Capt. G. H. Scott
St. Mary's	Comdr. George M. Colvocoresses
Wateree	Comdr. Murray
Mohongo	Comdr. J. W. A. Nicholson
Suwanee	Comdr. Paul Shirley
Cyane	Lt. Cdr. Leonard Paulding
Saginaw	Lt. Cdr. Robert W. Scott
Nyack	Lt. Cdr. L. H. Newman
Fredonia	Comdr. Thomas M. Brasher
Farallones	Master Provost

1867 North Pacific

Vanderbilt (F)	Comdr. J. P. Sanford
Pensacola	Capt. John L. Worden
Saranac	Capt. Scott
Lackawanna	Capt. William Reynolds
Suwanee	Comdr. Shirley
Mohican	Comdr. Edward Simpson
Resaca	Comdr. Joseph M. Bradford
Mohongo	Comdr. James A. Greer
Saginaw	Lt. Cdr. Samuel R. Franklin
Jamestown	Lt. Cdr. Charles J. McDougal

1867 South Pacific

Powhatan (F)	Capt. Theodore P. Greene
Tuscarora	Capt. Fabius Stanly
Dacotah	Comdr. Egbert Thompson
Wateree	Comdr. Leonard Paulding
Nyack	Lt. Cdr. Austin Pendergrast
Fredonia	Comdr. Brasher

1868 North Pacific

Pensacola (F)	Comdr. Paul Shirley
Ossipee	Capt. George F. Emmons
Saranac	Capt. James M. Frailey
Lackawanna	Capt. Reynolds

Mohican	Comdr. Simpson
Resaca	Comdr. Bradford
Suwanee	Comdr. Richard L. Law
Cyane	Comdr. John Watters
Saginaw	Lt. Cdr. John G. Mitchell
Jamestown	Lt. Cdr. McDougal

1868 South Pacific

Powhatan (F)	Capt. David McDougal
Dacotah	Comdr. William F. Spicer
Wateree	Comdr. James H. Gillis
Nyack	Comdr. Pendergrast
Fredonia	Capt. Brasher

1869 North Pacific

Pensacola (F)	Capt. George H. Preble
Lackawanna	Capt. Edward Middleton
Ossipee	Comdr. L. C. Sartori
Mohongo	Comdr. Stephen B. Luce
Resaca	Comdr. R. F. R. Lewis
Cyane	Comdr. Watters
Saginaw	Comdr. R. W. Meade

1869 South Pacific

Powhatan (F)	Capt. McDougal
Kearsarge	Comdr. James S. Thornton
Tuscarora	Comdr. Walter W. Queen
Nyack	Lt. Cdr. C. A. Babcock

1870 Pacific Fleet

Saranac (F)	Lt. Cdr. S. Dana Greene
Mohican	Comdr. William W. Low
Kearsarge	Comdr. Thornton
St. Mary's	Comdr. Thomas C. Harris
Jamestown	Comdr. William T. Truxton
Onward	Comdr. Milton Haxton
Resaca	Comdr. Lewis
Cyane	Lt. Cdr. Alfred Hopkins
Saginaw	Lt. Cdr. Montgomery Sicard
Nyack	Lt. Cdr. T. H. Eastman
Ossipee (f)	Commo. William R. Taylor, North Squadron
Guerrière (f)	Commo. David McDougal, South Squadron

1871

Pensacola (F)	Capt. Paul Shirley
California	Capt. J. M. B. Clitz

Mohican	Comdr. Low
St. Mary's	Comdr. Harris
Jamestown	Comdr. Bancroft Gherardi
Cyane	Comdr. Hopkins
Saginaw	Comdr. Sicard
Resaca	Lt. Cdr. Nathaniel Green
Onward	Lt. Cdr. George B. White
Nyack	Lt. Cdr. S. D. Greene
Saranac (f)	Commo. Taylor, North Squadron
Ossipee (f)	Commo. McDougal, South Squadron

1872

California (F)	Capt. Clitz
Pensacola	Capt. J. H. Spotts
Saranac	Capt. T. S. Phelps
Mohican	Comdr. Low
St. Mary's	Comdr. Harris
Narragansett	Comdr. R. W. Meade
Ossipee	Comdr. Joseph N. Miller
Resaca	Comdr. Green
Onward	Lt. Cdr. White

1873 North Pacific

California (F)	Capt. J. C. P. deKrafft
Benicia	Capt. A. G. Clary
Saranac	Capt. Phelps
Narragansett	Comdr. Meade

1873 South Pacific

Pensacola (F)	Capt. John H. Upshur
Omaha	Capt. John C. Febiger
Tuscarora	Comdr. George E. Belknap
Onward	Lt. Cdr. Edwin White

1874 North Pacific

Richmond (F)	Capt. deKrafft
Saranac	Capt. Thomas Pattison
Benicia	Capt. William E. Hopkins

1874 South Pacific

Pensacola (F)	Capt. Aaron K. Hughes
Omaha	Capt. William K. Mayo
Onward	Lt. Cdr. White

1875 North Pacific

Pensacola (F)	Capt. Bancroft Gherardi
Benicia	Capt. Hopkins
Saranac	Capt. Walter W. Queen
Portsmouth	Comdr. Joseph S. Skerrett
Tuscarora	Comdr. Henry Erben
Narragansett	Comdr. George Dewey

1875 South Pacific

Richmond (F)	Capt. Edmund R. Colhoun
Omaha	Capt. Philip C. Johnson
Onward	Lt. Cdr. White

1876 North Pacific

Pensacola (F)	Capt. Gherardi
Lackawanna	Comdr. James A. Greer
Tuscarora	Comdr. Joseph N. Miller

1876 South Pacific

Richmond (F)	Capt. P. C. Johnson
Omaha	Capt. Edward Simpson
Onward	Lt. Cdr. Edward S. Keyser

1877 North and South Pacific

Pensacola (F)	Capt. John Irwin
Omaha	Capt. Simpson
Lackawanna	Capt. Greer
Onward	Lt. Cdr. Keyser

1878

Pensacola (F)	Capt. Irwin
Alaska	Capt. George Brown
Tuscarora	Comdr. John W. Philip
Adams	Comdr. Frederick Rodgers
Onward	Lt. Cdr. Charles J. Barclay

1879

Pensacola (F)	Comdr. Edward Terry
Lackawanna	Capt. Ralph Chandler
Alaska	Capt. Brown
Tuscarora	Comdr. Philip
Adams	Comdr. Rodgers
Onward	Lt. Cdr. Barclay

1880
Pensacola (F)   Capt. Kidder R. Breese
Lackawanna   Capt. Chandler
Alaska   Capt. Brown
Marion   Comdr. Francis M. Bunce
Adams   Comdr. John A. Howell
Onward   Lt. Cdr. Thomas M. Gardner

1881
Pensacola (F)   Capt. B. B. Taylor
Lackawanna   Capt. James H. Gillis
Alaska   Capt. Brown
Adams   Comdr. Howell
Wachusett   Comdr. Edward P. Lull
Onward   Lt. Cdr. Gardner

1882
Pensacola (F)   Capt. William P. McCann
Alaska   Capt. George E. Belknap
Lackawanna   Capt. Henry Wilson
Adams   Comdr. Edgar C. Merriman
Essex   Comdr. Alexander H. McCormick
Wachusett   Comdr. Henry Glass
Onward   Lt. Cdr. Gardner

1883
Pensacola (F)   Capt. Joseph Fyffe
Alaska   Capt. Belknap
Lackawanna   Capt. Wilson
Hartford   Capt. Charles C. Carpenter
Adams   Comdr. Merriman
Wachusett   Comdr. Frederick Pearson
Iroquois   Comdr. James H. Sands
Onward   Lt. Cdr. Gardner

1884
Hartford (F)   Capt. Carpenter
Shenandoah   Capt. Charles S. Norton
Lackawanna   Capt. Augustus P. Cooke
Wachusett   Comdr. Alfred T. Mahan
Iroquois   Comdr. Sands
Adams   Comdr. Joseph B. Coghlan
Onward   Lt. Cdr. Francis W. Dickins

1885

Hartford (F)	Capt. George H. Perkins
Shenandoah	Capt. Norton
Lackawanna	Capt. Cooke
Wachusett	Comdr. Mahan
Monongahela	Comdr. Henry L. Johnson
Iroquois	Comdr. Yates Stirling

1886

Hartford (F)	Capt. Edward P. Lull
Shenandoah	Capt. Norton
Adams	Comdr. Louis Kempff
Mohican	Comdr. Benjamin F. Day
Iroquois	Comdr. Stirling
Monongahela	Lt. Cdr. George B. Livingston

1887

Vandalia (F)	Capt. Henry L. Howison
Iroquois	Comdr. John C. Watson
Adams	Comdr. Kempff
Mohican	Comdr. Day
Alert	Comdr. James D. Graham
Juniata	Comdr. George T. Davis
Monongahela	Comdr. Samuel H. Baker
Pinta	Lt. Cdr. John S. Newell

1888

Vandalia (F)	Capt. Howison
Iroquois	Comdr. Richard P. Leary
Adams	Comdr. Kempff
Mohican	Comdr. Day
Alert	Comdr. Graham
Juniata	Comdr. Davis
Monongahela	Comdr. Baker
Pinta	Lt. Cdr. Newell

1889

Trenton (F)	Capt. Norman H. Farquhar
Vandalia	Capt. Cornelius M. Schoonmaker
Alert	Comdr. Graham
Mohican	Comdr. Joseph B. Coghlan
Adams	Comdr. R. P. Leary
Nipsic	Comdr. Dennis W. Mullan
Monongahela	Comdr. George E. Wingate
Pinta	Lt. Cdr. Newell

1890

Mohican (F)	Comdr. Coghlan
Adams	Comdr. Edwin T. Woodward
Alert	Comdr. James G. Green
Monongahela	Comdr. Wingate
Iroquois	Comdr. Joshua Bishop
Pinta	Lt. Cdr. Oscar W. Farenholt
Nipsic	Lt. Cdr. Henry W. Lyon

1891

Charleston (F)	Capt. George C. Remey
Mohican	Comdr. Edwin M. Shepard
Iroquois	Comdr. Bishop
Ranger	Comdr. G. E. Wingate

1892

San Francisco (F)	Capt. William T. Sampson
Pensacola	Capt. Albert Kautz
Charleston	Capt. Remey
Boston	Capt. Gilbert C. Wiltse
Baltimore	Capt. Winfield S. Schley
Mohican	Comdr. Charles S. Cotton
Iroquois	Comdr. John J. Read
Yorktown	Comdr. Robley D. Evans

1893

Mohican (F)	Comdr. Henry L. Johnson
Boston	Capt. Wiltse
Alliance	Comdr. William H. Whiting
Adams	Comdr. Thomas Nelson
Ranger	Comdr. Edwin Longnecker

1894

Philadelphia (F)	Capt. Albert S. Barker
Monterey	Capt. Louis Kempff
Charleston	Capt. Henry F. Picking
Yorktown	Comdr. Purnell F. Harrington
Mohican	Comdr. Charles E. Clark
Alliance	Comdr. Timothy A. Lyons
Adams	Comdr. Nelson
Ranger	Comdr. Longnecker

1895

Philadelphia (F)	Capt. C. S. Cotton
Monterey	Capt. Kempff

Mohican	Comdr. Dennis W. Mullan
Bennington	Comdr. Charles M. Thomas
Alert	Comdr. George E. Ide
Ranger	Comdr. Eugene W. Watson

1896
Philadelphia (F)	Capt. Cotton
Monterey	Capt. Theodore F. Kane
Marion	Comdr. D. W. Mullan
Bennington	Comdr. George W. Pigman
Alert	Comdr. Franklin Hanford
Adams	Comdr. E. W. Watson

1897
Philadelphia (F)	Capt. Cotton
Oregon	Capt. Henry L. Howison
Monadnock	Capt. George W. Sumner
Monterey	Capt. Charles E. Clark
Bennington	Comdr. Pigman
Marion	Comdr. James G. Green
Adams	Comdr. Watson
Alert	Comdr. Hanford

1898
Baltimore (F)	Capt. Nehemiah M. Dyer
Oregon	Capt. Albert S. Barker
Monterey	Capt. Clark
Monadnock	Capt. William H. Whiting
Bennington	Comdr. Henry E. Nichols
Alert	Comdr. Eugene H. C. Leutze
Marietta	Comdr. Frederick M. Symonds

1 July 1898
Albatross (F)	(Fisheries Commission)
Bennington	Comdr. Nichols
Corwin	(Revenue Cutter Service)
Grant	(Revenue Cutter Service)
Perry	(Revenue Cutter Service)
Rush	(Revenue Cutter Service)
Mohican	Comdr. George M. Book
Wheeling	Comdr. Uriel Sebree

1899
Philadelphia (F)	Comdr. Edwin White
Badger	Comdr. James M. Miller
Yorktown	Comdr. Charles S. Sperry

1900

Philadelphia (F)	Capt. George C. Reiter
Iowa	Capt. Caspar F. Goodrich
Marblehead	Comdr. Harrison G. O. Colby
Abarenda	Comdr. Benjamin F. Tilley

1901

Iowa (F)	Capt. Philip H. Cooper
Philadelphia	Capt. William W. Mead
Wheeling	Comdr. Albert R. Couden
Farragut	Lt. Cdr. Reginald F. Nicholson
Abarenda	Comdr. Tilley

1902

Wisconsin (F)	Capt. G. C. Reiter
Iowa	Capt. Thomas Perry
Philadelphia	Capt. Mead
Concord	Comdr. William W. Kimball
Farragut	Lieut. Theodore C. Fenton
Abarenda	Capt. Uriel Sebree

1903

New York (F)	Capt. Morris R. S. Mackenzie
Boston	Comdr. Charles P. Perkins
Marblehead	Comdr. Thomas S. Phelps
Ranger	Comdr. William P. Potter

1904

New York (F)	Capt. John J. Hunker
Boston	Comdr. Samuel W. B. Diehl
Marblehead	Comdr. Phelps
Wyoming	Comdr. Vincendon L. Cottman
Bennington	Comdr. Kossuth Niles
Concord	Comdr. C. P. Perkins
Petrel	Lt. Cdr. Benjamin Tappan
Paul Jones	Lieut. Gregory C. Davison
Preble	Lieut. Theodore C. Fenton

1905

Chicago (F)	Capt. Edwin K. Moore
Boston	Comdr. K. Niles
Marblehead	Comdr. Frank H. Holmes
Wyoming	Comdr. Cottman
Bennington	Comdr. Lucien Young
Petrel	Lt. Cdr. Francis H. Sherman

Paul Jones	Lieut. Davison
Perry	Lieut. Frank H. Schofield

1906
Chicago (F)	Comdr. Charles J. Badger
Boston	Comdr. DeWitt Coffman
Marblehead	Comdr. Richard T. Mulligan
Princeton	Lt. Cdr. F. H. Sherman
Paul Jones	Lieut. John F. Marshall, Jr.
Perry	Lieut. Frederick N. Freeman

1907
Charleston (F)	Comdr. Cameron McR. Winslow
Chicago	Comdr. Robert M. Doyle
Milwaukee	Comdr. Charles A. Gove
Yorktown	Comdr. R. T. Mulligan
Boston	Comdr. Coffman
Princeton	Comdr. Arthur W. Dodd

1908 Pacific Fleet
First Squadron, First Division, R. Adm. J. H. Dayton
West Virginia (F)	Capt. Alexander McCrackin
Colorado	Capt. Sidney A. Staunton
Maryland	Capt. Chauncey Thomas
Pennsylvania	Capt. Aaron Ward

Second Division, R. Adm. Uriel Sebree
Tennessee (f)	Capt. Thomas B. Howard
California	Capt. Vincendon L. Cottman
Washington	Capt. Austin M. Knight

Second Squadron, Third Division, R. Adm. W. T. Swinburne
Charleston (f)	Comdr. Frank E. Beatty
Milwaukee	Comdr. Gove
St. Louis	Comdr. Nathaniel R. Usher

Fourth Division
Albany	Comdr. Henry T. Mayo
Yorktown	Comdr. James H. Glennon

Third Squadron and First Torpedo Flotilla in Asiatic waters.
Fourth Torpedo Flotilla
Perry
Preble

1909
First Squadron, First Division, R. Adm. Swinburne
West Virginia (F)	Capt. McCrackin
Colorado	Capt. Charles B. T. Moore

| *Maryland* | Capt. Moses L. Wood |
| *Pennsylvania* | Capt. Frank A. Wilner |

Second Division, R. Adm. Sebree

Tennessee (f)	Capt. Bradley A. Fiske
California	Capt. Cottman
South Dakota	Capt. James T. Smith
Washington	Capt. Knight

Second Squadron, Third Division

| *Milwaukee* | Capt. Charles C. Rogers |
| *St. Louis* | Capt. Albert Gleaves |

Third Squadron and First Torpedo Flotilla in Asiatic waters.
Pacific Torpedo Fleet an independent command.

1910

First Division, R. Adm. Sebree

Tennessee (F)	Capt. Fiske
California	Capt. H. T. Mayo
South Dakota	Capt. Smith
Washington	Capt. C. C. Rogers

Second Division, R. Adm. Edward B. Barry

West Virginia (f)	Capt. John M. Orchard
Colorado	Capt. Valentine S. Nelson
Maryland	Capt. James C. Gillmore
Pennsylvania	Capt. Charles F. Pond
Glacier	Comdr. Robert F. Lopez

1911

First Division, R. Adm. Barry

West Virginia (F)	Capt. Orchard
Colorado	Capt. William A. Gill
Pennsylvania	Capt. Pond

Second Division, R. Adm. Chauncey Thomas

California (f)	Capt. Mayo
Maryland	Capt. Gillmore
South Dakota	Capt. Frank M. Bennett
Glacier	Lieut. Levin J. Wallace

1912

First Division, R. Adm. Thomas

California (F)	Capt. Alexander S. Halstead
Maryland	Capt. John M. Ellicott
South Dakota	Capt. Bennett

Second Division, R. Adm. William H. H. Southerland

| *West Virginia* (f) | Capt. Orchard |
| *Colorado* | Capt. Gill |

Pennsylvania	Capt. Pond
Glacier	Lieut. Wallace

1913
Colorado (F)	Capt. William W. Gilmer
California	Capt. Halstead
Maryland	Capt. Ellicott
South Dakota	Capt. Charles P. Plunkett
Glacier	Lt. Cdr. Richard S. Douglas

1914
Pittsburgh (F)	Capt. W. W. Gilmer
California	Capt. Newton A. McCully
Maryland	Comdr. Philip Andrews

Torpedo Flotilla, Lt. Cdr. Edwin H. Dodd, *Iris* (tender)
First Division, Lieut. M. K. Metcalf
Whipple, Paul Jones, Perry, Stewart, Truxtun
First Submarine Division, Lieut. Charles E. Smith
Alert (tender), *F-1, F-2, F-3, F-4*
Second Submarine Division, Lieut. Henry M. Jensen
Cheyenne (tender), *H-1, H-2*
Glacier	Lt. Cdr. Charles M. Tozer

1915
San Diego (F)	Capt. Ashley H. Robertson
Maryland	Capt. P. Andrews
West Virginia	Lt. Cdr. David F. Boyd
Chattanooga	Comdr. Thomas J. Senn
Cleveland	Comdr. George W. Williams
Denver	Comdr. Henry J. Ziegemeier
New Orleans	Comdr. Noble E. Erwin
Raleigh	Comdr. Thomas P. Magruder
Annapolis	Comdr. Jonas H. Holden
Yorktown	Comdr. Raymond D. Hasbrouck
Glacier	Lt. Cdr. Austin Kautz

Torpedo Flotilla, Lt. Cdr. Dodd, *Iris* (tender)
First Division, Lieut. Metcalf
Whipple, Preble, Paul Jones, Perry, Truxtun
First Submarine Division, Lieut. Smith
Alert (tender), *F-1, F-2, F-3, F-4*
Second Submarine Division, Lieut. Jensen
Cheyenne (tender), *H-1, H-2, H-3*
Third Submarine Division, Lieut. J. V. Ogan
K-3, K-4, K-7, K-8

Characteristics of Ships Serving on Pacific Station

Information gathered from U.S. Navy Ships' Data books; Howard I. Chapelle, *The History of the American Sailing Navy; Jane's Fighting Ships;* Frank M. Bennett, *The Steam Navy of the United States;* and miscellaneous sources. Data are approximate only, and it must be noted that batteries, engines, boilers, and rigs varied from time to time. So far as possible, the characteristics are those while the ships were assigned to the Pacific Station.

Displacement tonnage is given except for the older vessels which were described in terms of old measurement (om) tonnage. Dimensions are given: length x beam x draft. Depth of hold (dh) is listed instead of draft for older ships. Length is over-all unless otherwise noted: (pp) length between perpendiculars, (wl) length on waterline. The date of building is generally that of completion. Ordnance abbreviations are: SB—smooth-bore, MLR—muzzle-loading rifle, BLR—breech-loading rifle, Hzr—howitzer, RF—rapid-firing, 6″/50—six-inch bore, fifty calibers length of gun; similar abbreviations are used to describe all modern breech-loading rifled guns. Boilers are described: SE—single-ended, DE—double-ended, cyl.—cylindrical, B&W—Babcock and Wilcox. Machinery abbreviations are: tr. exp.—triple expansion (vertical inverted unless otherwise noted), hor.—horizontal, inc.—inclined, osc.—oscillating, comp.—compound. All are reciprocating steam engines.

Abarenda

Steel collier built by Edwards S. B. Co., Newcastle, Eng.; acquired by USN 1898. 6,705 tons, 325′ x 42′ x 23′, forty men, two SE boilers, tr. exp. engine, 1,050 IHP, single screw 9 kts., 3,400 tons cargo coal, 813 tons bunker coal, schooner rig. Sold in 1926.

Adams

Wooden gunboat built by Donald McKay, completed at Boston Navy Yard in 1876. 1,400 tons, 187′ (pp) x 35′ x 15′, four IX″ SB, one 8″ MLR, one 60-pdr. MLR, 185 men, four SE boilers, hor. comp. engine, 800 IHP, single screw, 9.8 kts., 141 tons coal, bark rig, one stack.

Alaska

Wooden screw-sloop built by Boston Navy Yard in 1867. 2,394 tons, 250′ (pp) x 38′ x 16′, twelve guns, two hor. engines, single screw, bark rig, two stacks. Sold at Mare Island in 1883.

Albany

Steel protected cruiser built for Brazil at Elswick, Eng.; acquired by USN upon completion in 1898. 3,450 tons, 330′ x 44′ x 18′, six 6″/50, four 5″/50, 300 men, four DE boilers, two tr. exp. engines, 7,500 IHP, twin screws, 20.5 kts., 450 tons coal, two masts, two stacks. Sold at Mare Island in 1929.

Alert

Iron gunboat built by John Roach at Chester, Pa., in 1875. 713 tons, 177′ (pp) x 32′ x 13′, six 4″/40, four 6-pdrs., 143 men, two B&W boilers, hor. comp. engine, 560 IHP, single screw, 10 kts., 197 tons coal, barkentine rig, one stack. Sold in 1922.

Alliance

Wooden gunboat built at Norfolk Navy Yard in 1876. See *Adams* for characteristics.

Annapolis

Composite gunboat built by Lewis Nixon at Elizabethport, N.J., in 1897. 1,010 tons, 203′ x 36′ x 12′, six 4″/40 RF, four 6-pdrs., 156 men, two B&W boilers, tr. exp. engine, 1,227 IHP, single screw, 13.7 kts., 230 tons coal, 3-masted schooner rig, one stack. Sold in 1941.

Badger

Steel merchant vessel built by John Roach & Sons at Chester, Pa., in 1889; acquired for use as auxiliary cruiser by USN in 1898. 4,784 tons, 326′ x 42′ x 19′, six 5″ RF, six 3-pdrs., 235 men, tr. exp. engine, 3,200 IHP, single screw, 16 kts., 836 tons coal, schooner rig.

Baltimore

Steel protected cruiser built by William Cramp & Sons at Philadelphia, Pa., in 1889. 4,413 tons, 327′ (pp) x 49′ x 20′, four 8″/30, six 6″/30, four 6-pdrs., 374 men, eight B&W boilers, two hor. tr. exp. engines, 8,978 IHP, twin screws, 20.1 kts., 1,079 tons coal, brig rig, two stacks. Sold in 1937.

Benicia

Wooden screw-sloop built at Portsmouth Navy Yard in 1864. Generally similar to *Alaska*. Sold at Mare Island in 1884.

Bennington

Steel gunboat built by N. F. Palmer at Chester, Pa., in 1890. 1,700 tons, 230′ (wl) x 36′ x 14′, six 6″/30, two 6-pdr. RF, 187 men, four SE boilers, two hor. tr. exp. engines, 3,436 IHP, twin screws, 17.5 kts., 341 tons coal, 3-masted schooner rig, one stack. Sold in 1910.

Boston (later Despatch)

Steel protected cruiser built by John Roach & Sons at Chester, Pa., in 1887. 3,000 tons, 277′ x 42′ x 17′, two 8″/30, three 6″/30, one 4″/40, 380 men, eight cyl. boilers, hor. comp. engine, 4,030 IHP, single screw, 15.6 kts., 428 tons coal, brig rig, two stacks. Sold in 1946.

Boxer

Wooden schooner built at Boston Navy Yard in 1831. 194 tons (om), 88′ (pp) x 24′ x 10′ (dh), eight 24-pdr. carronades, two long 9-pdrs. Sold at Philadelphia in 1848.

Brandywine

Wooden frigate built at Washington Navy Yard in 1825. 1,726 tons (om), 175′ (pp) x 45′ x 14′ (dh), thirty-three long 24-pdrs., twenty 42-pdr. carronades, 480 men. Burned at Norfolk Navy Yard in 1864.

California

Wooden screw-sloop built at Portsmouth Navy Yard in 1869. 3,953 tons, 313′ x 46′ x 17′, eighteen XI″ SB, one 60-pdr. MLR, two 100-pdr. MLR, two 20-pdrs., two hor. engines, single screw, 3-masted ship rig, two stacks. Sold in 1875.

California (later San Diego)

Steel armored cruiser built by Union Iron Works at San Francisco, Cal., in 1905. 13,500 tons, 502′ x 70′ x 27′, four 8″/45, fourteen 6″/50, 6″ belt armor, 822 men, sixteen B&W boilers, two tr. exp. engines, 23,000 IHP, twin screws, 22 kts., 900 tons coal, two masts, four stacks. Sank after striking mine off Fire Island, N.Y., 19 July 1918.

Camanche

Iron and wood single-turret monitor built by Donahue, Ryan & Secor, assembled at San Francisco, Cal., in 1864. 1,875 tons, 200′ x 46′ x 11′, two XV″ SB, 7 kts. Sold in 1899.

Charleston (I)

Steel protected cruiser built by Union Iron Works at San Francisco, Cal., in 1890. 4,040 tons, 312′ (wl) x 46′ x 20′, two 8″/30, six 6″/30, two hor. comp. engines, 6,666 IHP, twin screws, 18.2 kts., two masts, one stack. Wrecked near Luzon, P. I., 7 November 1899.

Charleston (II)

Steel first-class cruiser built by Newport News S. B. Co. at Newport News, Va., in 1905. 9,700 tons, 423' x 65' x 23', fourteen 6"/50, eighteen 14-pdrs., partial 4" armor belt, 564 men, sixteen B&W boilers, two tr. exp. engines, 21,000 IHP, twin screws, 21.5 kts., 650 tons coal, two masts, four stacks. Sold in 1926.

Chattanooga

Steel protected cruiser built by Crescent Shipyard at Elizabethport, N.J., in 1905. 3,200 tons, 309' x 44' x 16', ten 5"/50, eight 6-pdr. RF, 322 men, six B&W boilers, two tr. exp. engines, 5,398 IHP, twin screws, 16.65 kts., 733 tons coal, two masts, two stacks. Sold in 1930.

Chicago (later *Alton*)

Steel protected cruiser built by John Roach & Sons at Chester, Pa., in 1885. 5,000 tons, 328' x 48' x 23', four 8"/35, fourteen 5"/40, 459 men, six B&W boilers, two hor. tr. exp. engines, 10,000 IHP, twin screws, 19 kts., 940 tons coal, two masts, two stacks. Sold in 1935.

Cleveland

Steel protected cruiser built by Bath Iron Works at Bath, Me., in 1903. See *Chattanooga* for characteristics. Sold in 1930.

Colorado (later *Pueblo*)

Steel armored cruiser built by William Cramp & Sons at Philadelphia, Pa., in 1905. Thirty-two Niclausse boilers. See *California* (*San Diego*) for other characteristics. Sold in 1930.

Columbus

Wooden ship-of-the-line built at Washington Navy Yard in 1819. 2,480 tons (om), 193' (pp) x 52' x 21' (dh), sixty-three long and medium 32-pdrs., twenty-four 32-pdr. carronades, 780 men. Burned at Norfolk Navy Yard in 1861.

Concord

Steel gunboat built by N. F. Palmer at Chester, Pa., in 1891. 1,710 tons, 244' x 36' x 14', three 6"/30, one 4"/40, four 3-pdr. RF, 187 men, four locomotive boilers, two hor. tr. exp. engines, 3,404 IHP, twin screws, 16.8 kts., 354 tons coal, 3-masted schooner rig, one stack. Transferred to U.S. Coast Guard in 1915.

Congress

Wooden frigate built at Portsmouth Navy Yard in 1841. 1,867 tons (om), 179' (pp) x 48' x 23' (dh), forty-two long 32-pdrs., eight 8" shell guns. Destroyed in action with the CSS *Virginia*, 8 March 1862.

Constellation

Wooden frigate built by David Stodder at Baltimore, Md., in 1797. 1,278 tons (om), 164' (pp) x 41' x 13' (dh), twenty-eight long 18-pdrs., ten 24-pdr. carronades, 340 men. Broken up at Norfolk Navy Yard in 1852.

Constitution

Wooden frigate built by Hartt Shipyard at Boston, Mass., in 1797. 1,576 tons (om), 175' (pp) x 43' x 14' (dh), thirty long 24-pdrs., twenty 32-pdr. carronades. Retained as a relic.

Cyane

Wooden sloop-of-war built at Boston Navy Yard in 1837. 792 tons (om), 132' (pp) x 34', eighteen 32-pdr. carronades, four 8" shell guns. Sold in California in 1887.

Dacotah

Wooden screw-sloop built at Norfolk Navy Yard in 1859. 1,369 tons, 198' x 33' x 13', two XI" SB, four long 32-pdrs., two hor. return fire-tube boilers, two hor. engines, single screw, 11.5 kts., bark rig, one stack. Sold at Mare Island in 1873.

Dale

Wooden sloop-of-war built at Philadelphia Navy Yard in 1839. 566 tons (om), 118' (pp) x 34' x 15' (dh), fourteen 32-pdr. carronades, two long 9-pdrs., 150 men. Sold in 1906.

Davis

Steel torpedo boat built by Wolff & Zwicker at Portland, Ore., in 1899. 154 tons, 146' (wl) x 15' x 6', three 1-pdr. RF, three 18" torpedo tubes, 29 men, two Thornycroft boilers, two tr. exp. engines, 1,750 IHP, twin screws, 23.41 kts., 40 tons coal, one mast, two stacks. Sold in 1920.

Decatur

Wooden sloop-of-war built at New York Navy Yard in 1839. See *Dale* for characteristics. Sold at San Francisco in 1865.

Denver

Steel protected cruiser built by Neafie & Levy at Philadelphia, Pa., in 1904. See *Chattanooga* for characteristics. Sold in 1930.

Dolphin

Wooden schooner built at Philadelphia Navy Yard in 1821. 178 tons (om), 86' (pp) x 25' x 10' (dh), ten 12-pdr. carronades, two long 18-pdrs., 80 men. Sold in 1835.

Enterprise

Wooden schooner built at New York Navy Yard in 1831. See *Boxer* for characteristics. Sold at Boston in 1845.

Erie

Wooden storeship built at Boston Navy Yard in 1842. 118′ (pp) x 32′ x 14′ (dh), four 9-pdrs. Sold at New York in 1850.

Essex

Wooden gunboat built by Donald McKay at Boston, Mass., completed by Portsmouth Navy Yard in 1876. Two SE boilers, tr. exp. engine, 505 IHP. See *Adams* for other characteristics. Sold in 1930.

F-1, F-2, F-3, F-4

Steel submarines, *F-1* and *F-2* built by Union Iron Works at San Francisco, Cal., *F-3* and *F-4* built by Moran Bros. at Seattle, Wash., all in 1908. 330 tons (surface), 143′ long, two 18″ torpedo tubes. *F-1* sunk 17 December 1917, *F-2* and *F-3* sold in 1922, *F-4* sunk 25 March 1915.

Fairfield

Wooden sloop-of-war built at New York Navy Yard in 1828. 127′ (pp) x 34′ x 15′ (dh), eighteen 32-pdr. carronades, two medium 32-pdrs. Sold at Norfolk in 1852.

Falmouth

Wooden sloop-of-war built at Boston Navy Yard in 1827. 190 men. See *Fairfield* for other characteristics. Sold at Aspinwall, Panama, in 1863.

Farallones (see *Massachusetts*)

Farragut

Steel torpedo boat built by Union Iron Works at San Francisco, Cal., in 1899. 279 tons, 213′ (wl) x 21′ x 6′, four 6-pdr. RF, two 18″ torpedo tubes, 64 men, three Thornycroft boilers, two tr. exp. engines, 5,600 IHP, twin screws, 30.13 kts., 95 tons coal, one mast, two stacks. Sold in 1919.

Fortune

Iron tug built by James Tetlow at Boston, Mass., in 1865. 450 tons, 148′ x 26′ x 9′, 340 IHP, single screw, 10 kts., 108 tons coal, schooner rig, one stack.

Fox

Steel torpedo boat built by Wolff & Zwicker at Portland, Ore., in 1899. See *Davis* for characteristics. Sold in 1916.

Franklin

Wooden ship-of-the-line built by Humphreys & Penrose at Philadelphia, Pa., in 1815. 2,243 tons (om), 188' (pp) x 50' x 20' (dh), sixty-three long and medium 32-pdrs., twenty-four 32-pdr. carronades, 780 men. Broken up at Portsmouth Navy Yard in 1853.

Fredonia

Wooden merchant vessel purchased for use as storeship in 1846. 800 tons (om), four guns. Wrecked by tidal wave at Arica, Chile, 23 August 1868.

Glacier

Steel refrigerated storeship built by J. L. Thompson & Son at Sunderland, Eng., in 1891; acquired by USN in 1898. 8,325 tons, 389' x 46' x 25', one 3-pdr. RF, 138 men, three DE, 1 aux. boilers, tr. exp. engine, 1,650 IHP, single screw, 12.3 kts., 917 tons coal, schooner rig, one stack. Sold in 1922.

Goldsborough

Steel torpedo boat built by Wolff & Zwicker at Portland, Ore., in 1900. 255 tons, 198' (wl) x 21' x 7', four 6-pdr. RF, two 18" torpedo tubes, 64 men, three Thornycroft boilers, two tr. exp. engines, 5,850 IHP, twin screws, 27.4 kts., 89 tons coal, one mast, two stacks. Sold in 1919.

Grampus (later *A-3*)

Steel submarine built by Union Iron Works at San Francisco, Cal., in 1903. 106 tons, 67' long, one torpedo tube, one Otto four-cylinder gasoline engine, 160 IHP, single screw, 8 kts. surface, electric waterproof main motor, 70 IHP, 7 kts. submerged. Stricken in 1922 and expended as a target.

Guerrière (I)

Wooden frigate built by Joseph & Francis Grice at Philadelphia, Pa., in 1814. See *Brandywine* for characteristics. Broken up at Norfolk in 1841.

Guerrière (II)

Wooden screw-sloop built at Boston Navy Yard in 1867. 319' x 46' x 18', two 100-pdr. MLR, one 60-pdr. MLR, six IX" SB, four 20-pdr. Hzrs., four main, two superheat boilers, two hor. engines, single screw, 13 kts., 3-masted ship rig, two stacks. Sold in 1872.

H-1, H-2, H-3

Steel submarines built in 1914, *H-1* and *H-2* by Union Iron Works at San Francisco, Cal., *H-3* by Moran Bros. at Seattle, Wash. 358 tons surface, 434 tons submerged, 150′ x 16′ x 12′, four 18″ torpedo tubes, two eight-cylinder Nlseco Diesel engines, 480 BHP, twin screws, 14.1 kts. surface, two Electric Dynamic Co. motors, 600 HP, 10.6 kts. submerged. *H-1* wrecked at Magdalena Bay, Mexico, March 1920. *H-2* and *H-3* stricken in 1930.

Hartford

Wooden screw-sloop built at Boston Navy Yard in 1859. 2,900 tons, 225′ (pp) x 44′ x 18′, one 8″ MLR, twelve IX″ SB, two Martin boilers, two hor. engines, 940 IHP, single screw, 9.5 kts., 241 tons coal, 3-masted ship rig, one stack. Retained as relic, sank at Norfolk in 1956.

Hopkins

Steel destroyer built by Harlan & Hollingsworth at Wilmington, Del., in 1903. 408 tons, 249′ x 23′ x 6′, two 3″/50, five 6-pdrs., two 18″ torpedo tubes, 78 men, four Thornycroft boilers, two tr. exp. engines, 8,456 IHP, twin screws, 29.02 kts., 143 tons coal, one mast, four stacks. Sold in 1920.

Hull

Steel destroyer built by Harlan & Hollingsworth at Wilmington, Del., in 1903. See *Hopkins* for characteristics. Sold in 1920.

Independence

Wooden ship-of-the-line built by E. Hartt & J. Barker at Charlestown, Mass., in 1814; razeed to a frigate in 1836. 188′ (pp) x 51′ x 15′ (dh), fifty-four guns. Sold at Mare Island in 1912 and burned for her metal in 1914.

Iowa

Steel battleship built by William Cramp & Sons at Philadelphia, Pa., in 1897. 11,410 tons, 360′ (wl) x 72′ x 28′, four 12″/35, eight 8″/30, 486 men, 18″ armor belt, three DE, two SE boilers, two tr. exp. engines, 11,000 IHP, twin screws, 16.5 kts., 625 tons coal, one mast, two stacks. Sunk as a target in 1923.

Iris

Iron merchant vessel built by A. Leslie & Co. at Newcastle, Eng., in 1885; acquired by USN for use as supply and repair ship in 1898. 6,100 tons, 321′ x 39′ x 24′, 124 men, two DE, one aux. boilers, comp. engine, 1,320 IHP, single screw, 10 kts., 300 tons coal, brigantine rig, one stack.

Iroquois

Wooden screw-sloop built at New York Navy Yard in 1858. 1,575 tons, 199′ (pp) x 34′ x 15′, two 8″ MLR, four 60-pdr. MLR, one 60-pdr. BLR, two Martin boilers, hor. engine, 1,202 IHP, single screw, 10.7 kts., 128 tons coal, 3-masted ship rig, one stack. Transferred to Marine Hospital Service in 1899.

Jamestown

Wooden sloop-of-war built at Norfolk Navy Yard in 1844; converted to storeship at Mare Island in 1865. 1,150 tons, 163′ x 32′ x 17′ (dh), armament and complement as storeship unknown. Transferred to Marine Hospital Service in 1892.

John Adams

Wooden sloop-of-war built at Norfolk Navy Yard in 1830. See *Fairfield* for characteristics. Sold at Boston in 1867.

John Hancock

Wooden tug built by Samuel Pook at Boston, Mass., in 1850; lengthened and refitted in 1853. 382 tons (om), 164′ x 22′ x 12′, 61 men, one 24-pdr. Hzr., two 12-pdr. Hzrs., two Martin boilers, two osc. engines, 7 kts., single screw, 112 tons coal, bark rig, one stack.

Juniata

Wooden screw-sloop built at Philadelphia Navy Yard in 1862. 1,934 tons, 205′ x 38′, one 100-pdr. MLR, one XI″ SB, four 30-pdr. MLR, four 24-pdr. Hzrs., two Martin, one aux. boilers, hor. engine, single screw, 9 kts., bark rig, one stack. Sold in 1891.

K-3, K-4, K-7, K-8

Steel submarines built in 1914, *K-4* by Moran Bros. at Seattle, Wash., others by Union Iron Works at San Francisco, Cal. 392 tons surface, 521 tons submerged, 153′ x 17′ x 13′, four 18″ torpedo tubes, 28 men, two eight-cylinder Nlseco Diesel engines, 480 BHP, twin screws, 14.1 kts. surface, two Electric Dynamic Co. motors, 680 HP, 10.6 kts. submerged. All stricken in 1930.

Kearsarge

Wooden screw-sloop built at Portsmouth Navy Yard in 1861. 1,550 tons, 199′ (pp) x 33′ x 16′, four IX″ SB, two 8″ MLR, one 60-pdr. MLR, 180 men, two Martin boilers, hor. engine, 843 IHP, single screw, 11.1 kts., 165 tons coal, bark rig, one stack. Wrecked in West Indies in 1894.

Lackawanna

Wooden screw-sloop built at New York Navy Yard in 1861. 2,526 tons, 234′ x 38′ x 16′, one 150-pdr. MLR, two XI″ SB, four IX″ SB, two

24-pdr. Hzrs., two Martin boilers, one aux., two hor. engines, single screw, 10.5 kts., bark rig, one stack. Sold in 1887.

Lancaster

Wooden screw-sloop built at Philadelphia Navy Yard in 1858. 3,250 tons, 236′ (pp) x 46′ x 19′, twenty-four IX″ SB, two XI″ SB, two 30-pdr. MLR, two Martin boilers, two hor. engines, 733 IHP, single screw, 9.6 kts., 288 tons coal, 3-masted ship rig, one stack.

Lawrence

Steel destroyer built by Fore River Engine Co. at Weymouth, Mass., in 1903. 400 tons, 246′ x 22′ x 6′, seven 6-pdr. RF, two 18″ torpedo tubes, 78 men, four mod. Normand boilers, two tr. exp. engines, 8,400 IHP, twin screws, 28.41 kts., 108 tons coal, one mast, four stacks. Sold in 1920.

Levant

Wooden sloop-of-war built at New York Navy Yard in 1838. See *Cyane* for characteristics. Missing with all hands on passage from Hilo to Panama in 1860.

Lexington

Wooden sloop-of-war built at New York Navy Yard in 1825. See *Fairfield* for characteristics. Employed as storeship after 1840; sold in 1860.

Macedonian

Wooden frigate built in England for Royal Navy; captured by USS *United States* in October 1812 and commissioned in USN. 1,325 tons (om), 156′ (pp) x 40′ x 18′ (dh), twenty-eight long 18-pdrs., sixteen 32-pdr. carronades, 362 men. Broken up at Norfolk in 1835.

Marblehead

Steel unprotected cruiser built by City Point Works at Boston, Mass., in 1892. 2,000 tons, 257′ x 37′ x 17′, nine 5″/40, six 6-pdrs., 250 men, three DE, two SE boilers, two tr. exp. engines, 5,400 IHP, twin screws, 17 kts., 200 tons coal, schooner rig, two stacks. Sold in 1921.

Marietta

Composite gunboat built by Union Iron Works at San Francisco, Cal., in 1897. 990 tons, 190′ x 34′ x 12′, six 4″/40, four 6-pdrs., 163 men, two B&W boilers, two tr. exp. engines, 1,054 IHP, twin screws, 13.02 kts., 229 tons coal, schooner rig, one stack. Sold in 1920.

Marion

Wooden gunboat built at Portsmouth Navy Yard in 1875. 1,900 tons, 216′ (pp) x 37′ x 17′, one 8″ MLR, six IX″ SB, one 60-pdr. BLR, two

20-pdr. BLR, 194 men, ten cyl. boilers, hor. comp. engine, 735 IHP, single screw, 11.25 kts., 135 tons coal, bark rig, one stack.

Maryland (later Frederick)

Steel armored cruiser built by Newport News S.B. Co. at Newport News, Va., in 1905. See California (San Diego) for characteristics. Sold at Mare Island in 1929.

Massachusetts (later Farallones)

Wooden merchant vessel built by Samuel Hall at Boston, Mass.; acquired by War Department in 1847; transferred to USN in 1849. 750 tons (om), 178' x 32' x 20' (dh), two Ericsson engines, single screw, 3-masted ship rig. Engines and boilers removed, rigged as sailing bark, renamed, and employed as a storeship during Civil War. Sold in 1866.

Milwaukee

Steel first-class cruiser built by Union Iron Works at San Francisco, Cal., in 1906. See Charleston (II) for characteristics. Wrecked near Humboldt Bay, Cal., 13 January 1917.

Merrimack

Wooden screw-frigate built at Boston Navy Yard in 1855. 4,636 tons, 257' (wl) x 51' x 23', twenty-four IX" SB, fourteen 8" shell guns, two X" SB, four Martin boilers, two hor. engines, 1,294 IHP, single screw, 8.87 kts., 3-masted ship rig, one stack. Burned at Norfolk Navy Yard in 1861, raised and converted to ironclad ram CSS Virginia in 1862, blown up to prevent capture in May 1862.

Mohican

Wooden gunboat built at Mare Island Navy Yard in 1883. See Marion for characteristics. Sold in 1922.

Mohongo

Iron double-ender side-wheel gunboat built by Z. Secor at Jersey City, N.J., in 1863. 1,370 tons, 255' x 35', two 100-pdr. MLR, four IX" SB, two 20-pdr. MLR, two 24-pdr. Hzrs., two main, two superheat boilers, inc. engine, 9 kts., two masts, one stack. Sold in 1870.

Monadnock (I)

Iron and wood double-turret monitor built at Boston Navy Yard in 1864. 3,400 tons, 257' x 53' x 13', four XV" SB, vertical water tube boilers, four Ericsson engines, twin screws, 6.5 kts. Broken up in 1875.

Monadnock (II)

Iron monitor built by Continental Iron Works at Vallejo, Cal., and completed by Mare Island Navy Yard in 1896. Some of material from

Monadnock (I) used in construction. 3,990 tons, 262′ x 55′ x 15′, four 10″/30, two 4″/40, five 6-pdrs., 9″ armor belt, 229 men, four SE boilers, two hor. tr. exp. engines, 2,163 IHP, twin screws, 11.63 kts., 386 tons coal, one mast, one stack. Sold in 1923.

Monongahela

Wooden screw-sloop built at Philadelphia Navy Yard in 1862. 1,378 tons, 227′ x 38′ x 15′, engines removed after Civil War; employed as a sailing storeship. Ten 8″ SB. Burned at Guantanamo, Cuba, in 1908.

Monterey

Steel monitor built by Union Iron Works at San Francisco, Cal., in 1893. 4,084 tons, 261′ x 59′ x 15′, two 12″/35, two 10″/30, six 6-pdrs., 13″ armor belt, 231 men, four B&W boilers, two tr. exp. engines, 5,244 IHP, twin screws, 13.6 kts., 206 tons coal, one mast, one stack. Sold in 1922.

Narragansett

Wooden screw-sloop built at Boston Navy Yard in 1859. 1,235 tons, 188′ (pp) x 30′ x 10′, one XI″ SB, four 32-pdrs., two Martin boilers, two hor. engines, single screw, bark rig, one stack. Sold at Mare Island in 1883.

Nero

Steel collier built by J. L. Thompson & Son at Sunderland, Eng.; acquired by USN in 1898. 6,360 tons, 320′ x 41′ x 22′, two SE, one aux. boilers, tr. exp. engine, 1,000 IHP, single screw, 9 kts., 300 tons bunker coal, 3,500 tons cargo coal, schooner rig, one stack. Sold in 1922.

New Orleans

Steel protected cruiser, sheathed with teak below waterline, built at Elswick, Eng., for Brazil in 1897; acquired by USN in 1898. See *Albany* for characteristics. Sold at Mare Island in 1929.

New York (later Saratoga, later Rochester)

Steel armored cruiser built by William Cramp & Sons at Philadelphia, Pa., in 1891. 8,150 tons, 380′ (wl) x 64′ x 28′, four 8″/45, ten 5″/50, 4″ armor belt, 525 men, twelve B&W boilers, four tr. exp. engines, 16,500 IHP, twin screws, 21 kts., 750 tons coal, two masts, three stacks. Stricken in 1933, hulk intentionally sunk in 1941.

Nipsic

Wooden gunboat built at Washington Navy Yard in 1879. 1,375 tons, 185′ (pp) x 35′ x 14′, one 60-pdr. MLR, one XI″ SB, four IX″ SB, eight SE boilers, hor. comp. engine, 839 IHP, single screw, 10.7 kts., 132 tons coal, bark rig, one stack.

North Carolina

Wooden ship-of-the-line built at Philadelphia Navy Yard in 1820. 2,633 tons (om), 196′ (pp) x 53′ x 21′ (dh), armament probably same as that of *Ohio,* 820 men. Sold in 1867.

Nyack

Wooden gunboat built at New York Navy Yard in 1863. 836 tons, 179′ x 30′, one 100-pdr. MLR, two IX″ SB, one 30-pdr. BLR, two 24-pdr. Hzrs., two Martin boilers, hor. engine, single screw, 12 kts., 3-masted ship rig, one stack. Sold at Mare Island in 1883.

Ohio

Wooden ship-of-the-line built at New York Navy Yard in 1820. 197′ (pp) x 53′, thirty long 42-pdrs., thirty long 32-pdrs., twenty-six 42-pdr. carronades. Sold at Boston in 1883.

Omaha

Wooden screw-sloop built at Philadelphia Navy Yard in 1869. See *Alaska* for characteristics. Sold in 1915.

Onward

Wooden merchant vessel purchased at New York in 1861 for use as sailing storeship. 874 tons (om), 159′ x 35′ x 20′ (dh), one 30-pdr. MLR, eight 32-pdrs., 3-masted ship rig. Sold at Callao, Peru, in 1884.

Oregon

Steel battleship built by Union Iron Works at San Francisco, Cal., in 1896. 10,288 tons, 351′ x 69′ x 24′, four 13″/35, eight 8″/35, four 6″/30, 18″ armor belt, 473 men, four DE boilers, two tr. exp. engines, 11,111 IHP, twin screws, 16.79 kts., 1,425 tons coal, one mast, two stacks. Lent to state of Oregon as relic 1922; requisitioned by USN for scrap during World War II; hulk used as ammunition barge; sold to Japanese scrap firm in 1956; broken up in Japan 1957.

Ossipee

Wooden screw-sloop built at Portsmouth Navy Yard in 1861. 1,240 tons, 207′ x 38′ x 16′, one 100-pdr. MLR, one XI″ SB, three 30-pdr. MLR, six 32-pdrs., one 12-pdr. SB, one 12-pdr. MLR, two Martin boilers, two hor. engines, single screw, 10 kts., bark rig, one stack. Sold in 1891.

Paul Jones

Steel destroyer built by Union Iron Works at San Francisco, Cal., in 1902. 420 tons, 250′ x 23′ x 6′, two 3″/50, five 6-pdr. RF, two 18″

torpedo tubes, 78 men, four Thornycroft boilers, two tr. exp. engines, 8,000 IHP, twin screws, 28.91 kts., 168 tons coal, one mast, four stacks. Sold in 1920.

Peacock

Wooden sloop-of-war built by Adam & Noah Brown in New York in 1813. 119' (pp) x 32', twenty 32-pdr. carronades, two long 12-pdrs., 185 men. Broken up at New York in 1828.

Pennsylvania (later *Pittsburgh*)

Steel armored cruiser built by William Cramp & Sons at Philadelphia, Pa., in 1905. See *California (San Diego)* for characteristics. Sold in 1931.

Pensacola

Wooden screw-sloop built at Pensacola Naval Station in 1862. 3,000 tons, 231' (pp) x 44' x 19', twelve IX" SB, two 80-pdr. BLR, two 60-pdr. BLR, two hor. engines, 680 IHP, single screw, 9 kts., 285 tons coal, 3-masted ship rig, one stack. Stricken in 1911.

Perry

Steel destroyer built by Union Iron Works at San Francisco, Cal., in 1902. See *Paul Jones* for characteristics. Sold in 1920.

Petrel

Steel gunboat built by Columbian Iron Works at Baltimore, Md., in 1889. 890 tons, 188' x 31' x 12', four 4"/40, two 3-pdr. RF, 139 men, four SE boilers, hor. comp. engine, 1,045 IHP, single screw, 11.4 kts., 193 tons coal, 3-masted schooner rig, one stack. Sold in 1920.

Philadelphia

Steel protected cruiser built by William Cramp & Sons at Philadelphia, Pa., in 1890. 4,410 tons, 327' (pp) x 49' x 20', twelve 6"/30, four 6-pdr. RF, four DE boilers, two hor. tr. exp. engines, 8,815 IHP, twin screws, 19.68 kts., 525 tons coal, schooner rig, two stacks. Sold in 1926.

Pike (later *A-5*)

Steel submarine built by Union Iron Works at San Francisco, Cal., in 1903. See *Grampus* for characteristics. Stricken in 1922; expended as a target.

Pinta

Iron tug built by Reany, Son & Archbold at Chester, Pa., in 1865. 550 tons, 137' (pp) x 26' x 11', four 12-pdr. Hzrs., one Gatling gun, 190 IHP, 8.5 kts., 111 tons coal, schooner rig, one stack.

Portsmouth

Wooden sloop-of-war built at Portsmouth Navy Yard in 1843. 1,022 tons (om), 152′ (pp) x 38′ x 17′ (dh), eighteen medium 32-pdrs., four 8″ shell guns, 210 men. Sold in 1915.

Potomac

Wooden frigate built at Washington Navy Yard in 1822. See *Brandywine* for characteristics. Sold at Philadelphia in 1877.

Powhatan

Wooden side-wheel sloop built at Norfolk Navy Yard in 1847. 3,765 tons, 254′ x 45′ x 18′, sixteen IX″ SB, two inc. engines, 1,172 IHP, 10.6 kts., 630 tons coal, bark rig, one stack. Sold in 1887.

Preble (I)

Wooden sloop-of-war built at Portsmouth Navy Yard in 1839. See *Dale* for characteristics. Burned at Pensacola in 1863.

Preble (II)

Steel destroyer built by Union Iron Works at San Francisco, Cal., in 1902. See *Paul Jones* for characteristics. Sold in 1920.

Princeton

Composite gunboat built by J. H. Dialogue at Camden, N.J., in 1898. 1,010 tons, 204′ x 36′ x 12′, six 4″/40, four 6-pdr. RF, 156 men, two SE boilers, tr. exp. engine, 923 IHP, single screw, 10.64 kts., 226 tons coal, barkentine rig, one stack. Sold in 1919.

Raleigh

Steel protected cruiser built at Norfolk Navy Yard in 1894. 3,183 tons, 306′ x 42′ x 18′, eleven 5″/40, six 3-pdr. RF, 307 men, eight B&W boilers, two tr. exp. engines, 8,159 IHP, twin screws, 21.12 kts., 575 tons coal, schooner rig, two stacks. Sold in 1921.

Ranger (later *Rockport,* later *Nantucket*)

Iron gunboat built by Harlan & Hollingsworth at Wilmington, Del., in 1876. See *Alert* for characteristics. Loaned to state of Massachusetts for use as schoolship in 1909; sold in 1940.

Raritan

Wooden frigate built at Philadelphia Navy Yard in 1843. See *Brandywine* for characteristics. Burned at Norfolk Navy Yard in 1861.

Relief

Wooden storeship built at Philadelphia Navy Yard in 1836. 468 tons (om), 109′ (pp) x 30′ x 12′ (dh), four 18-pdrs., two 12-pdrs. Sold in 1865.

Resaca

Wooden screw-sloop built at Portsmouth Navy Yard in 1865. 1,129 tons, 216′ x 31′ x 12′, one 150-pdr. MLR, six 32-pdrs., three 24-pdr. Hzrs., hor. engine, single screw, 11 kts., bark rig, one stack. Sold at Mare Island in 1872.

Richmond

Wooden screw-sloop built at Norfolk Navy Yard in 1860. 2,700 tons, 225′ (pp) x 43′ x 17′, twelve IX″ SB, one 8″ MLR, one 60-pdr. BLR, two hor. engines, 692 IHP, single screw, 9.5 kts., 265 tons coal, 3-masted ship rig, one stack. Sold in 1919.

Rowan

Steel torpedo boat built by Moran Bros. at Seattle, Wash., in 1899. 210 tons, 170′ (wl) x 17′ x 6′, four 1-pdr. RF, two 18″ torpedo tubes, 38 men, three Mosher boilers, two tr. exp. engines, 3,200 IHP, twin screws, 27.07 kts., 63 tons coal. Sold in 1918.

Saginaw

Wooden side-wheel gunboat built at Mare Island Navy Yard in 1859. 508 tons, 155′ long, 4.5′ draft, one 50-pdr. MLR, one 32-pdr. SB, two 24-pdr. MLR, 50 men, two boilers, two inc. osc. engines, 8 kts., 100 tons coal, brig rig, one stack. Wrecked on Ocean Island in 1870.

St. Lawrence

Wooden frigate built at Norfolk Navy Yard in 1847. See *Brandywine* for characteristics. Sold at Norfolk in 1875.

St. Louis (I)

Wooden sloop-of-war built at Washington Navy Yard in 1828. See *Fairfield* for characteristics. Sold in 1860.

St. Louis (II)

Steel first-class cruiser built by Neafie & Levy at Philadelphia, Pa., in 1906. See *Charleston* (II) for characteristics. Sold in 1930.

St. Mary's

Wooden sloop-of-war built at Washington Navy Yard in 1844. 958 tons (om), 150′ (pp) x 37′ x 16′ (dh), sixteen medium 32-pdrs., six 8″ shell guns. Sold in 1908.

San Francisco (later *Yosemite*)

Steel protected cruiser built by Union Iron Works at San Francisco, Cal., in 1891. See *Philadelphia* for characteristics. Sold in 1937.

Saranac

Wooden side-wheel sloop built at Portsmouth Navy Yard in 1850. 2,200 tons, 233′ x 38′ x 17′, six VIII″ SB, two boilers, two inc. engines, 605 IHP, 11 kts., bark rig, one stack. Wrecked in Seymour Narrows in 1875.

Saturn

Iron collier built by Harlan & Hollingsworth at Wilmington, Del.; acquired by USN in 1898. 6,220 tons, 297′ x 40′ x 22′, 39 men, four SE, one aux. boilers, tr. exp. engine, 1,500 IHP, single screw, 11 kts., 386 tons bunker coal, 2,400 tons cargo coal, schooner rig, one stack. Sold in 1922.

Savannah

Wooden frigate built at New York Navy Yard in 1842. See *Brandywine* for characteristics. Sold at Norfolk in 1883.

Shark

Wooden schooner built at Washington Navy Yard in 1821. See *Dolphin* for characteristics. Wrecked at mouth of Columbia River in 1846.

Shenandoah

Wooden screw-sloop built at Philadelphia Navy Yard in 1862. 1,375 tons, two XI″ SB, two IX″ SB, one 60-pdr. MLR, two 24-pdr. Hzrs., two 12-pdr. MLR, two Martin, one aux. boilers, two hor. engines, 12 kts., barkentine rig, one stack. Sold in 1887.

Southampton

Wooden sailing ship built or purchased at Norfolk in 1845, converted steamer hull. 567 tons (om), 152′ (pp) x 27′ x 16′ (dh), two 42-pdr. carronades, 45 men. Sold in 1855.

South Dakota (later *Huron*)

Steel armored cruiser built by Union Iron Works at San Francisco, Cal., in 1907. See *California* (*San Diego*) for characteristics. Sold in 1929.

Stewart

Steel destroyer built by Gas Engine & Power Co. at Morris Heights, N.Y., in 1902. Four Seabury boilers; see *Paul Jones* for other characteristics. Sold in 1920.

Supply

Wooden sailing vessel purchased at New York in 1846 for use as a storeship. 547 tons (om), four 24-pdr. carronades. Sold at New York in 1884.

Suwanee

Iron double-ender side-wheel gunboat built by Reany, Son & Archbold at Chester, Pa., in 1863. See *Mohongo* for characteristics. Wrecked in Shadwell Passage in 1868.

Tennessee (later *Memphis*)

Steel armored cruiser built by William Cramp & Sons at Philadelphia, Pa., in 1906. 14,500 tons, 504′ x 73′ x 25′, four 10″/40, sixteen 6″/50, twenty-two 3″/50, four 21″ torpedo tubes, 5″ armor belt, 974 men, sixteen B&W boilers, two tr. exp. engines, 27,430 IHP, twin screws, 22.16 kts., 1,974 tons coal, two masts, four stacks. Wrecked by tidal wave at Santo Domingo in 1916.

Trenton

Wooden screw-frigate built at New York Navy Yard in 1876. 3,900 tons, 253′ (pp) x 48′ x 20′, ten 8″ MLR, eight cyl. boilers, hor. comp. engine, 2,813 IHP, single screw, 12.8 kts., 350 tons coal, 3-masted ship rig, one stack. Wrecked in hurricane at Apia in 1889.

Truxtun

Steel destroyer built by Maryland Steel Co. at Sparrow's Point, Md., in 1902. See *Paul Jones* for characteristics. Sold in 1920.

Tuscarora

Wooden screw-sloop built at Philadelphia Navy Yard in 1861. 997 tons, one XI″ SB, six 68-pdrs., one 100-pdr. MLR, two 30-pdr. MLR, 202 men, two Martin, one aux. boilers, two hor. engines, 9 kts., 200 tons coal, 3-masted ship rig, one stack. Sold in 1883.

United States

Wooden frigate built by Joshua Humphreys at Philadelphia, Pa., in 1797. See *Constitution* for characteristics. Burned at Norfolk Navy Yard in 1861; raised and broken up in 1865.

Vandalia (I)

Wooden sloop-of-war built at Philadelphia Navy Yard in 1828. See *Fairfield* for characteristics. Broken up at Portsmouth in 1870.

Vandalia (II)

Wooden gunboat built at Boston Navy Yard in 1875. See *Marion* for characteristics. Wrecked in hurricane at Apia in 1889.

Vanderbilt

Wooden side-wheel steamer built for Cornelius Vanderbilt in 1855; presented to War Department in 1861; transferred to USN in 1862.

3,360 tons, 250′ x 38′ x 21′, two 100-pdr. MLR, twelve IX″ SB, one 12-pdr. Hzr., four return tube boilers, one beam engine, 14 kts., hermaphrodite brig rig, two stacks. Sold at Mare Island in 1873; converted to sailing vessel *Three Brothers;* coal hulk at Gibraltar until broken up in 1930.

Vincennes

Wooden sloop-of-war built at New York Navy Yard in 1826. See *Fairfield* for characteristics. Sold at Boston in 1867.

Wachusett

Wooden screw-sloop built at Boston Navy Yard in 1862. 1,032 tons, 201′ x 34′ x 14′, three 100-pdr. MLR, four 32-pdr. SB, two 30-pdr. MLR, one 12-pdr. MLR, two Martin, one aux. boilers, two hor. engines, single screw, 11.5 kts., bark rig, one stack. Sold at Mare Island in 1887.

Warren

Wooden sloop-of-war built at Boston Navy Yard in 1826. See *Fairfield* for characteristics. Sold at Panama in 1863.

Washington (later Seattle)

Steel armored cruiser built by New York S. B. Co. at Camden, N.J., in 1906. See *Tennessee* for characteristics. Sold in 1946.

Wateree

Iron double-ender side-wheel gunboat built by Reany, Son & Archbold at Chester, Pa., in 1862. See *Mohongo* for characteristics. Wrecked by tidal wave at Arica, Chile, in 1868.

West Virginia (later Huntington)

Steel armored cruiser built by Newport News S. B. Co. at Newport News, Va., in 1905. See *California (San Diego)* for characteristics. Sold in 1930.

Wheeling

Composite gunboat built by Union Iron Works at San Francisco, Cal., in 1897. See *Marietta* for characteristics. Stricken after World War II.

Whipple

Steel destroyer built by Maryland Steel Co. at Sparrow's Point, Md., in 1902. See *Paul Jones* for characteristics. Sold in 1920.

Wisconsin

Steel battleship built by Union Iron Works at San Francisco, Cal., in 1901. 11,552 tons, 374′ x 72′ x 24′, four 13″/35, fourteen 6″/40 RF,

14″ armor belt, 711 men, eight SE boilers, two tr. exp. engines, 12,609 IHP, twin screws, 17.17 kts., 1,413 tons coal, two masts, two stacks abeam. Sold in 1922.

Wyoming

Wooden screw-sloop built at Philadelphia Navy Yard in 1859. 997 tons, two XI″ SB, one 60-pdr. MLR, three 32-pdrs., two vertical tubular, one aux. boilers, two hor. engines, 10.5 kts., 3-masted ship rig, one stack. Sold in 1892.

Wyoming (later *Cheyenne*)

Steel monitor built by Union Iron Works at San Francisco, Cal., in 1901. 3,225 tons, 255′ x 50′ x 13′, two 12″/40, four 4″/50, 8″ armor belt, 222 men, four B&W boilers, two tr. exp. engines, 2,452 IHP, twin screws, 11.8 kts., 340 tons coal, one mast, one stack. Stricken in 1937.

Yorktown (I)

Wooden sloop-of-war built at Norfolk Navy Yard in 1839. See *Dale* for characteristics. Wrecked in Cape Verde Islands in 1850.

Yorktown (II)

Steel gunboat built by William Cramp & Sons at Philadelphia, Pa., in 1889. Six 6″/30, four 3-pdr. RF, see *Concord* for other characteristics. Sold in 1921.

Bibliography

Most of the manuscript material which forms the basis for this work is found in the National Archives in Washington, D.C. Of much less importance are the manuscripts of the Naval Historical Foundation, deposited in the Library of Congress, and of the New-York Historical Society. There are additional journals and letters of officers and men of the Pacific Squadron and Fleet in many public and private collections throughout the country, but few of these were consulted.

The Naval Records Collection of the Office of Naval Records and Library (ONRL), deposited in the National Archives, contains the official papers relating to the Pacific Station during the entire period of its existence, and so is the most valuable group of manuscripts. The following paragraphs contain a brief description of, and guide to, this material.

The correspondence of the Navy Department is included under several different headings. Since the practice of binding letters and documents into sizable volumes was followed for many years, much of the material pertaining to the nineteenth century is bound and partially indexed. However, some of the divisions are very general; for example, the volumes included under the heading Letters to Officers, Ships of War, March 1798—September 1868, contain letters from the Navy Department to officers serving afloat without regard to station or rank. Thus a familiarity with the names of officers and ships and the periods during which they served on a station is essential to a selection of those pertinent.

Later the ONRL began to store all papers in trays or file boxes according to their nature. The various Subject Files indicate trays of manuscripts as does the heading General Correspondence of the Office of the Secretary. The Area Files, on the other hand, are stored in larger file boxes.

Reports and dispatches from the commanders in chief of the Pacific Squadron are contained in Letters from Officers Commanding Squadrons, Pacific Squadron, February 1841—November 1886. All letters and dispatches were sent in duplicate during most of the nineteenth century, and many of the same letters are in the Area Nine File. The Area Files collectively are described as "Loose Papers Assembled from both Official and Private Sources and Combined to form a New Series, 1648-1910." Area Nine includes "The Pacific Ocean east of Longitude 180° with tributary waters. Also the Arctic Ocean tributary to the Bering Strait." The Area Nine File is the sole source of letters from the commanders in chief for the period prior to 1841 and the years 1886-1910. The

250

afore-mentioned Pacific Squadron Letters are much more complete for the period which they cover. After 1910, the official reports of the commanders in chief, Pacific Fleet, are found in the Subject File, 1911-1925, OX, Pacific Fleet Reports.

Extremely important collateral information is contained in the collection of Logs, Journals, and Diaries of Officers of the United States Navy at Sea and in the group of Letter Books of Officers of the United States Navy at Sea, March 1778—July 1908. In both collections it is necessary to choose the relevant volumes by name of officer or vessel.

Additional material relating to the Pacific Station is included among the Letters from Officers Commanding Expeditions and the volumes of correspondence of the Board of Navy Commissioners. The latter was an important administrative agency during the period of its existence, 1815-1842.

The immense collection of logbooks contained in the Records of the Bureau of Naval Personnel is useful mainly for substantiating matters of fact; the very number of volumes makes it impractical to use all of those which pertain to a period of more than a century. The same remark applies to the medical journals included in the Records of the Bureau of Medicine and Surgery, and to the many volumes which comprise the Records of Courts-Martial and Courts of Inquiry in the Records of the Office of the Judge Advocate General.

The documents of the Naval Historical Foundation in the Manuscript Division, Library of Congress, consist mainly of private papers of naval officers. Several of these collections are relevant to this study, and the Charles G. Ridgely Collection is especially valuable because it includes that officer's journal of his cruise to the Pacific Ocean in the USS *Constellation*.

A few of the journals and letter books located in the Manuscript Section of the New-York Historical Society pertain to the Pacific Station. While hardly comparable to the larger collections cited above, these manuscripts were of real value.

It is obvious that the manuscript collections hereafter cited do not exhaust the sources. A systematic search would reveal much more pertinent data, but the only serious lack of reliable sources was encountered with regard to war plans and similar strategic proposals. Unfortunately, the records of the General Board were unavailable to historians when this study was written, and the Secret and Confidential Files: War Plans, Information and Data, 1896-1923, have not yet been declassified.

PRIMARY SOURCES

Manuscripts

The National Archives, War Records Branch, Navy Section
Area Nine File, 1814-1910
Board of Navy Commissioners
    Letters to the Secretary of the Navy, April 1815—August 1842
    Letters to Officers, April 1815—July 1842
Confidential Letters Sent, February 1813—March 1822, January 1840
Confidential Letters Sent, September 1843—December 1879
General Correspondence of the Office of the Secretary
    Pacific Fleet, 27383

Pacific Reserve Force, 28365
Pacific Torpedo Fleet, 27793
Pacific Torpedo Flotilla, 27368
Letter Books of Officers of the United States Navy at Sea, March 1778—July 1908
 Correspondence of Commander Guert Gansevoort, commanding USS *Decatur,* October 1855—March 1856
 Letters sent by Commo. Isaac Hull, commanding USS *United States,* November 1823—March 1827
 Correspondence of Lieutenant James Charles P. deKrafft, October 1841—January 1861
 Correspondence of Rear Admiral William Mervine, July 1836—August 1868
 Correspondence of Commander John B. Montgomery, commanding USS *Portsmouth,* October 1844—November 1848
 Letters sent by Actg. Rear Admiral George F. Pearson, commanding Pacific and South Pacific Squadrons, February–December 1866
 Correspondence of Commo. Robert F. Stockton, commanding USS *Congress,* 1845-47
 Correspondence of Capt. Daniel Turner, commanding USS *Constitution,* January 1839—November 1841
Letters from the Board of Navy Commissioners, January 1827—August 1842
Letters from Officers commanding Expeditions
 Correspondence relating to the Cruises of *Cyane, Franklin, Ontario, Peacock,* and *United States,* January 1818—May 1827
 Letters from M. Comdt. William B. Finch, commanding the *Vincennes*—July 1829—April 1830
Letters from Officers commanding Squadrons
 Pacific Squadron, February 1841—November 1886
Letters to Officers commanding Squadrons or Vessels, September 1861—May 1886
Letters to Officers, Ships of War, March 1798—September 1868
Logs, Journals, and Diaries of Officers of the United States Navy at Sea
 Journal of a Cruise in the United States' Frigate *Brandywine,* David Deacon, Esq., Commander, and in the U.S. Schooner *Boxer,* Hugh N. Page, Esq., Commander. [April 1834–February 1837. Possibly kept by Midshipman James W. Read.]
 Journal of U.S. Ship *Portsmouth,* J. B. Montgomery, Esq., Commander, from May 12, 1845, to October 5, 1846. [Probably kept by Midshipman Stanwix Gansevoort.]
 Journal and Correspondence of Captain James Biddle, Commanding USS *Ontario,* October 4, 1817—April 23, 1819.
 Cany, Charles E., Captain's Clerk, Captain's Log of U.S. Flagships *California, Saranac,* and *Richmond,* commanded by Captain J. C. P. deKrafft, North Pacific Squadron [November 1872—February 1875].
 Journal of Naval Cadet C. E. Courtney on USS *Newark* and other Ships, 1899-1903.
 Craven, Tunis A. M., Lieutenant, Journal and Observations of Events, during a Cruise in the U.S. Ship *Dale* of 16 guns [June 1846—April 1848].

Journal kept by Lieutenant Tunis Augustus M. Craven aboard USS *Dale,* commanded by Commander John Rudd—August 3, 1848—August 19, 1849.

Dornin, Thomas A., Private Journal on board USS *Brandywine* 1826-28, Cruise in USS *Vincennes* 1829-30, Remarks on board USS *Falmouth* 1831-34, Extracts from Log of U.S. Merchant Ship *Lausanne,* on which Captain Dornin took passage from New York to join the Pacific Squadron, to assume command of U.S. Schooner *Shark* October 1841, Extract from Log of USS *Shark* 1841-42, Extract from Log of USS *Portsmouth* 1851-52.

Dornin, Thomas A., Commander, Journal on board USS *Portsmouth,* 1852-1855.

Gamble, William P., Journal of a Cruise in the U.S. Ship *Fairfield,* Elie A. F. [La] Vallette, Esqr., commanding [January 1834—August 1835].

Private Remarks of Lieutenant Charles Gauntt, of the U.S. Ship *Macedonian,* John Downes, Esqr., Commander, made during a Cruise in the Pacific Ocean in the Years 1818.19.20.21.

Journal kept by Cadet Midshipman A. W. Grant aboard USS *Lackawanna,* September 24, 1878—September 3, 1880, and aboard USS *Iroquois,* April 12, 1882—January 27, 1883.

Harrell, Abram Davis, Midshipman, Journal of a Cruise in the Pacific in the U.S. Line of Battle Ship *North Carolina,* Bearing the Broad Pendant of Com. Henry E. Ballard, under Command of T. O. Selfridge, Esq., 1837-38 & 39.

Journal kept by Midshipman Philip C. Johnson, Jr., aboard the *Savannah* and the *Ohio,* on a voyage from Boston to Monterey, California, December 14, 1846—November 14, 1848.

Log of Captain William Mervine, commanding U.S. Ships *Cyane* and *Savannah,* July 26, 1845, to November 16, 1846.

Extracts from Journal of William H. Meyers, Gunner on board USS *Cyane* 1841-1843 on a Cruise to the Pacific and Return.

Journal of Cadet Midshipman Albert P. Niblack, USN, 1880-1882 on board USS *Lackawanna* and USS *Adams.*

Journal of the USS *Charleston,* G. C. Remey, Captain commanding [December 1889—March 1892].

Reynolds, William, Commander, Remark Book of USS *Lackawanna* for the Cruise commencing 7th May 1866.

Journal of Midshipman Stephen C. Rowan, USS *Vincennes* 1825-1827.

Selfridge, Thomas O., Jr., Midshipman, Journal of the Cruise of USS *Independence* in the Pacific Ocean, 1854-1856.

Sharp, William, Midshipman, Remarks and Occurrences on board the U.S. Frigate *United States,* November 3, 1843, to January 18, 1845.

Taylor, Fitch W., the Reverend, The Razee. [Journal kept by the Chaplain of USS *Independence,* ca. 1854.]

Journals and notebooks of Lieutenant Henry A. Wise, USN, Cruise of USS *Independence* from Boston to the Pacific Ocean, September 19, 1846—March 2, 1849.

Office of the Secretary (including Chief of Naval Operations) Confidential Correspondence, 1917-1919 (declassified)

Records of the Bureau of Medicine and Surgery
  Medical Journal of USS *Independence,* December 25, 1847—September 26, 1848
Records of the Bureau of Naval Personnel
  Smooth Log of USS *Savannah,* September 23, 1844—June 28, 1846
Records of the Office of the Judge Advocate General
  Records of Courts Martial and Courts of Inquiry, Vols. XVII and LX
Secret and Confidential Correspondence of the Office of the Secretary, 1919-1926 (declassified)
Subject File, 1775-1910
  VP, Protection of Individuals and Property Abroad
Subject File, 1911-1927
  IA, Pacific Fleet Circulars
  ICA, Campaign Orders, Pacific Fleet
  IMA, Movement Orders, Pacific Fleet
  IPA, Operations Orders, Pacific Fleet
  ISA, Sailing Orders, Pacific Fleet
  IZA, Orders, Pacific Fleet
  OS, Ship Movements
  OX, Pacific Fleet Reports
Translations of Messages Sent in Cipher, October 1888—January 1910

The Library of Congress, Manuscript Division

Silas Casey Collection
Bladen Dulany Collection
William F. Fullam Collection
Henry C. Kane Collection
Charles G. Ridgely Collection
Thomas O. Selfridge Collection
Thomas H. Stevens Collection

The Library of the University of California at Los Angeles

Journal kept by Thomas Lancey of the Cruise of the *Dale,* June 6, 1846—March, 1849. Typescript from the original 3 vols. in the Cowan Collection.

Los Angeles Public Library

High Lights from the Log of the *Savannah,* 1845-1846, by William P. Toler. Typewritten abstract from the original in the Los Angeles Public Library.

New-York Historical Society, Manuscript Section

Caspar F. Goodrich Papers
Two private letters from Commodore Isaac Hull to Secretary of the Navy S. L. Southard, 31 January 1826 and 1 September 1826
Isaac Hull Letter Book No. 1, 25 October 1823—2 July 1827
Isaac Hull Letter Book No. 2, 25 October 1823—7 November 1827
Isaac Hull Order Book, 24 November 1823—29 April 1827
Journal kept by Midshipman J. L. Parker during the Pacific Cruise of the USS *Potomac,* August 1831—June 1833
William T. Swinburne Correspondence

Miscellaneous

Private letters of Samuel Francis DuPont

Letter from Admiral Arthur J. Hepburn, USN (Ret.), to author, 28 November 1955

BOOKS

Allen, Gardner W. (ed.). *The Papers of Isaac Hull.* Boston: The Boston Athenaeum, 1929.

American Naval Policy as Outlined in Messages of the Presidents of the United States since 1790. Washington: Government Printing Office, 1922.

American State Papers, Naval Affairs. 4 vols. Washington: Gales and Seaton, 1834-61.

Anderson, Charles R. (ed.). *Journal of a Cruise to the Pacific Ocean, 1842-1844, in the Frigate* United States. Durham: Duke University Press, 1937.

Bowen, Harold G., Vice Admiral, USN (Ret.). *Ships, Machinery, and Mossbacks.* Princeton: Princeton University Press, 1954.

Clark, Charles E., Rear Admiral, USN (Ret.). *My Fifty Years in the Navy.* Boston: Little, Brown and Co., 1917.

Coontz, Robert E., Rear Admiral, USN (Ret.). *From the Mississippi to the Sea.* Philadelphia: Dorrance and Co., 1930.

Dana, Richard H., Jr. *Two Years Before the Mast,* with a supplement by the author and introduction and additional chapter by his son. Boston and New York: Houghton Mifflin Co., 1911.

Daniels, Josephus. *The Wilson Era: Years of War and After, 1917-1921.* Chapel Hill: University of North Carolina Press, 1946.

Dewey, George, Admiral of the Navy, USN. *Autobiography.* New York: Charles Scribner's Sons, 1913.

Evans, Holden A. *One Man's Fight for a Better Navy.* New York: Dodd, Mead and Co., 1940.

Evans, Robley D., Rear Admiral, USN. *A Sailor's Log.* New York: D. Appleton and Co., 1901.

Fiske, Bradley A., Rear Admiral, USN (Ret.). *From Midshipman to Rear Admiral.* New York: The Century Co., 1919.

Franklin, Samuel R., Rear Admiral, USN (Ret.). *Memories of a Rear Admiral.* New York: Harper and Bros., 1898.

Halsey, William F., Fleet Admiral, USN, and Bryan, J., III. *Admiral Halsey's Story.* New York: McGraw Hill Book Co., 1947.

Hammond, George P. (ed.). *The Larkin Papers.* 5 vols. Berkeley: University of California Press, 1951-55.

Mahan, Alfred T., Rear Admiral, USN (Ret.). *From Sail to Steam.* New York: Harper and Bros., 1907.

Maxwell, R. T. *A Visit to Monterey in 1842,* ed. John H. Kemble. ("Early California Travels Series," Vol. XXV.) Los Angeles: Glen Dawson, 1955.

Melville, Herman. *White Jacket; or, The World in a Man-of-War.* New York: Harper and Bros., 1850.

Mercier, Henry J. *Life in a Man-of-War; or, Scenes in "Old Ironsides" during her Cruise in the Pacific.* By a Foretop-man. Philadelphia: 1841.

Naval Investigation, 1920. 2 vols. Washington: Government Printing Office, 1921.

Paulding, Hiram, Lieutenant, USN. *Journal of a Cruise of the United States Schooner* Dolphin, *among the Islands of the Pacific Ocean; and a Visit to the Mulgrave Islands, in Pursuit of the Mutineers of the Whale Ship* Globe. New York: G. & C. & H. Carvill, 1831.

Register of the Commissioned, Warrant, and Volunteer Officers of the Navy of the United States, including Officers of the Marine Corps and Others, 1821-1923.

Regulations, Circulars, Orders, and Decisions, for the Guide of Officers of the Navy of the United States. Washington: C. Alexander, 1851.

Reynolds, J. N. *Voyage of the United States Frigate* Potomac, *under the Command of Commodore John Downes, during the Circumnavigation of the Globe, in the Years 1831, 1832, 1833, and 1834.* New York: Harper and Bros., 1835.

Rodman, Hugh, Rear Admiral, USN (Ret.). *Yarns of a Kentucky Admiral.* Indianapolis: Bobbs-Merrill Co., 1928.

Rules of the Navy Department regulating the Civil Administration of the Navy of the United States. Washington: Globe Office, 1832.

Ruschenberger, W. S. W. *Three Years in the Pacific; Including Notices of Brazil, Chile, Bolivia, and Peru.* By an officer of the USN. Philadelphia: Carey, Lea & Blanchard, 1834.

Schley, Winfield S., Rear Admiral, USN (Ret.). *Forty-five Years under the Flag.* New York: D. Appleton and Co., 1904.

Secretary of the Navy. *Annual Reports, 1823-1924.*

Ships' Data: U.S. Naval Vessels. Washington: Government Printing Office, 1893-1923.

Warriner, Francis. *Cruise of the United States Frigate* Potomac *Round the World During the Years 1831-1834.* New York: Leavitt, Lord & Co., 1835.

Wiley, Henry A., Rear Admiral, USN (Ret.). *An Admiral from Texas.* New York: Doubleday, Doran & Co., 1934.

Wilkes, Charles, Lieutenant, USN. *Synopsis of the Cruise of the U.S. Exploring Expedition, during the Years 1838, '39, '40, '41, and '42;* delivered before the National Institute on June 20, 1842. Washington: Peter Force, 1842.

———. *Narrative of the United States Exploring Expedition.* Philadelphia: Lea & Blanchard, 1845. 5 vols.

Wise, Henry A., Lieutenant, USN. *Los Gringos.* New York: Baker and Scribner, 1849.

Young, Lucien, Lieutenant, USN. *The* Boston *at Hawaii; or, Observations and Impressions of a Naval Officer during a Stay of Fourteen Months in those Islands on a Man-of-War.* Washington: Gibson Bros., 1898.

PERIODICALS

Duvall, Robert C. "Extracts from the Log of the U.S. Frigate *Savannah* Kept by Robert Carson Duvall," *California Historical Society Quarterly,* III (1924), 105-25.

Rowan, Stephen C., Lieutenant, USN. "Recollections of the Mexican War," ed. George W. Tyler, *U.S. Naval Institute Proceedings,* XLV (1919), 539-59.

Stapler, John, Lieutenant, USN. "Gunboats," *U.S. Naval Institute Proceedings,* XLII (1916), 861-72.

Taussig, J. K., Vice Admiral, USN (Ret.). "We Chopped Wood," *U.S. Naval Institute Proceedings*, LXX (1944), 639-43.

NEWSPAPERS

Los Angeles Times, 1920-23.
New York Times, 1920-23.

SECONDARY SOURCES

BOOKS

Albion, Robert G., and Pope, Jennie B. *Sea Lanes in Wartime: The American Experience, 1775-1942*. New York: W. W. Norton and Co., 1942.

Appleton's Cyclopaedia of American Biography, ed. James G. Wilson and John Fiske. 6 vols. New York: D. Appleton & Co., 1888-89.

Bailey, Thomas A. *A Diplomatic History of the American People*. 4th ed. New York: Appleton-Century-Crofts, 1950.

Bancroft, Hubert H. *The History of California*. 7 vols. San Francisco: A. L. Bancroft and Co. and The History Co., 1884-90.

Bayard, S. J. *A Sketch of the Life of Com. Robert F. Stockton*. New York: Derby and Jackson, 1856.

Bennett, Frank M., Passed Assistant Engineer, USN. *The Steam Navy of the United States*. Pittsburgh: Warren and Co., 1896.

Bradley, Harold W. *The American Frontier in Hawaii: The Pioneers, 1789-1843*. Stanford: Stanford University Press, 1942.

Bywater, Hector C. *Sea-Power in the Pacific*. Boston and New York: Houghton Mifflin Co., 1921.

Callahan, James M. *American Foreign Policy in Mexican Relations*. New York: The Macmillan Co., 1932.

Chadwick, French E., Rear Admiral, USN (Ret.). *Relations of the United States and Spain: The Spanish-American War*. 2 vols. New York: Charles Scribner's Sons, 1911.

Chapelle, Howard I. *The History of American Sailing Ships*. New York: W. W. Norton and Co., 1935.

————. *The History of the American Sailing Navy*. New York: W. W. Norton and Co., 1949.

Clinard, Outten J. *Japan's Influence on American Naval Power*. Berkeley: University of California Press, 1947.

Cole, Allan B. (ed.). *Yankee Surveyors in the Shogun's Seas: Records of the United States Surveying Expedition to the North Pacific Ocean, 1853-1856*. Princeton: Princeton University Press, 1947.

Cox, Isaac J. *Nicaragua and the United States*. Boston: World Peace Foundation, 1927.

Cutler, Carl C. *Greyhounds of the Sea: The Story of the American Clipper Ship*. Annapolis: U.S. Naval Institute, 1961.

Dahlgren, Madeleine Vinton. *Memoir of John A. Dahlgren*. Boston: James R. Osgood and Co., 1882.

Denny, Harold N. *Dollars for Bullets, The Story of American Rule in Nicaragua*. New York: The Dial Press, 1929.

The Dictionary of American Biography, ed. Allen Johnson and Dumas Malone. 20 vols. New York: Charles Scribner's Sons, 1928-37.

Dulles, Foster R. *America in the Pacific: A Century of Expansion.* Boston and New York: Houghton Mifflin Co., 1932.

Ellicott, John M., Lieutenant, USN. *The Life of John Ancrum Winslow, Rear Admiral, United States Navy.* New York: G. P. Putnam's Sons, 1902.

Emmons, George F., Lieutenant, USN. *The Navy of the United States from the Commencement, 1775-1853, with a Brief History of each Vessel's Service and Fate as Appears upon Record.* Washington: Gideon and Co., 1853.

Hamersly, Thomas H. A. (ed.). *General Register of the United States Navy and Marine Corps.* Washington: 1882.

Henderson, Daniel. *The Hidden Coasts.* New York: William Sloane Associates, 1953.

Historical Transactions, 1893-1943. New York: The Society of Naval Architects and Marine Engineers, 1945.

Hittell, Theodore H. *History of California.* 4 vols. San Francisco: N. J. Stone and Co., 1897.

Howe, M. A. DeWolfe. *George von Lengerke Meyer: His Life and Public Services.* New York: Dodd, Mead and Co., 1920.

Jane, Fred T. (ed.). *Jane's Fighting Ships.* London: Sampson, Low and Marston, 1906, 1914, and 1922.

Kemble, John H. *The Panama Route, 1848-1869.* (University of California Publications in History, Vol. XXIX.) Berkeley: University of California Press, 1943.

Knox, Dudley W., Captain, USN. *A History of the United States Navy.* New York: G. P. Putnam's Sons, 1936.

Krafft, Herman F., and Norris, Walter B. *Sea Power in American History.* New York: The Century Co., 1920.

Longstaff, F. W. *Esquimault Naval Base: A History of Its Work and Its Defences.* Victoria, B. C.: The Victoria Book and Stationery Co., Ltd., 1941.

Lott, Arnold S., Lieutenant Commander, USN. *A Long Line of Ships.* Annapolis: U.S. Naval Institute, 1954.

Maclay, Edgar S. *A History of the United States Navy from 1775 to 1901.* 3 vols. New York: D. Appleton and Co., 1901.

Mahan, Alfred T., Captain, USN. *The Interest of America in Sea Power, Present and Future.* Boston: Little, Brown and Co., 1898.

Mitchell, Donald W. *History of the Modern American Navy.* New York: Alfred A. Knopf, 1946.

Millington, Herbert. *American Diplomacy and the War of the Pacific.* New York: Columbia University Press, 1948.

Morison, Samuel E. *By Land and By Sea.* New York: Alfred A. Knopf, 1954.
———. *The Maritime History of Massachusetts, 1783-1860.* Boston: Houghton Mifflin Co., 1921.

Neeser, Robert W. *A Statistical and Chronological History of the United States Navy.* 2 vols. New York: The Macmillan Co., 1909.

Nevins, Allan. *Frémont, The West's Greatest Adventurer.* 2 vols. 2nd ed. New York: Harper and Bros., 1928.

O'Gara, Gordon C. *Theodore Roosevelt and the Modern American Navy.* Princeton: Princeton University Press, 1942.

Paullin, Charles O. *Diplomatic Negotiations of American Naval Officers, 1778-1883.* Baltimore: The Johns Hopkins Press, 1912.

Pomeroy, Earl S. *Pacific Outpost: American Strategy in Guam and Micronesia.* Stanford: Stanford University Press, 1951.
Pratt, Fletcher. *The Navy: A History.* New York: Garden City Publishing Co., 1941.
————. *Preble's Boys.* New York: William Sloane Associates, 1950.
Pratt, Julius W. *Expansionists of 1898: The Acquisition of Hawaii and the Spanish Islands.* Baltimore: The Johns Hopkins Press, 1936.
Rensch, Hero E. and Ethel G. *Historic Spots in California: The Southern Counties.* Stanford University: Stanford University Press, 1932.
Rogers, Fred B. *Montgomery and the* Portsmouth. San Francisco: John Howell, 1958.
Rydell, Raymond A. *Cape Horn to the Pacific.* Berkeley and Los Angeles: University of California Press, 1952.
Scroggs, William O. *Financiers and Filibusters: The Story of William Walker and His Associates.* New York: The Macmillan Co., 1916.
Sherman, Edwin A. *The Life of the Late Rear Admiral John Drake Sloat.* Oakland: Carruth and Carruth, 1902.
Sprout, Harold and Margaret. *The Rise of American Naval Power, 1776-1918.* Princeton: Princeton University Press, 1939.
————. *Toward a New Order of Sea Power: American Naval Policy and the World Scene, 1918-1922.* Princeton: Princeton University Press, 1940.
Stevens, Sylvester K. *American Expansion in Hawaii, 1842-1898.* Harrisburg: Archives Publishing Co. of Pennsylvania, 1945.
Stuart, Charles B., Engineer-in-Chief, USN. *The Naval and Mail Steamers of the United States.* 2nd ed. New York: Charles B. Morton, 1853.
Wright, E. W. (ed.). *Lewis and Dryden's Marine History of the Pacific Northwest.* Portland: Lewis and Dryden Printing Co., 1895.

PERIODICALS

Adams, E. D. "English Interest in the Annexation of California," *American Historical Review,* XIV (1909), 744-63.
Albion, Robert G. "Distant Stations," *U.S. Naval Institute Proceedings,* LXXX (1954), 265-73.
Anderson, Bern, Rear Admiral, USN (Ret.). "The Impact of Rapid Communications on the Employment of Naval Forces," *U.S. Naval Institute Proceedings,* LXXVII (1951), 1157-67.
Bailey, Thomas A. "The United States and Hawaii during the Spanish-American War," *American Historical Review,* XXXVI (1931), 552-60.
Belknap, Charles, Lieutenant, USN. "The Naval Policy of the United States," *U.S. Naval Institute Proceedings,* VI (1880), 375-91.
Bradley, Harold W. "Hawaii and the American Penetration of the Northeastern Pacific, 1800-1845," *Pacific Historical Review,* XII (1943), 277-86.
Brandt, John H. "The Navy as an Indian Fighter," *U.S. Naval Institute Proceedings,* LVI (1930), 691-96.
Churchill, William. "Seumanutafa and Fa'atulia," *U.S. Naval Institute Proceedings,* XXXIV (1908), 601-3.
Cole, Allan B. "The Ringgold-Rodgers-Brooke Expedition to Japan and the North Pacific, 1853-1859," *Pacific Historical Review,* XVI (1947), 152-62.

Daley, R. F., Second Lieutenant, USMC. "The Attack on Quallah-Battoo," *U.S. Naval Institute Proceedings,* LXXIX (1953), 767-71.

Dillingham, Walter F. "Pearl Harbor," *U.S. Naval Institute Proceedings,* LVI (1930), 403-10.

Dyer, Brainerd. "Confederate Naval and Privateering Activities in the Pacific," *Pacific Historical Review,* III (1934), 433-43.

Earle, Edward M. "The Navy's Influence on our Foreign Relations," *Current History,* XXIII (1926), 648-55.

Ellison, Joseph W. "The Partition of Samoa: A Study in Imperialism and Diplomacy," *Pacific Historical Review,* VIII (1939), 259-88.

Farenholt, A., Surgeon, USN. "The U.S.S. *Independence:* An Appreciation," *U.S. Naval Institute Proceedings,* XL (1914), 129-34.

Feipel, Louis N. "The Wilkes Exploring Expedition. Its Progress through Half a Century: 1826-1876," *U.S. Naval Institute Proceedings,* XL (1914), 1323-50.

————. "The United States Navy in Mexico, 1821-1914," *U.S. Naval Institute Proceedings,* XLI (1915), 33-52, 489-97, 889-903, 1159-72, 1527-34, 1993-2002, and XLII (1916), 171-82.

Gilbert, Benjamin F. "French Warships on the Mexican West Coast," *Pacific Historical Review,* XXIV (1955), 25-37.

Glass, Henry, Commander, USN. "Naval Administration in Alaska," *U.S. Naval Institute Proceedings,* XVI (1890), 1-19.

Gleaves, Albert, Captain, USN. "An Officer of the Old Navy: Rear-Admiral Charles Steedman, USN (1811-1890)," *U.S. Naval Institute Proceedings,* XXXIX (1913), 197-210.

Gudde, Erwin G. "Mutiny on the Ewing," *California Historical Society Quarterly,* XXX (1951), 39-47.

Hannay, David. "Sea Power in the Pacific," *Edinburgh Review,* CCXXXIV (July–October 1921), 122-35.

Hardy, Osgood. "The *Itata* Incident," *Hispanic American Review,* V (1922), 195-226.

Hayden, Everett. "The Samoan Hurricane of March, 1889," *U.S. Naval Institute Proceedings,* XVII (1891), 283-87.

Hunt, Ridgely, Lieutenant, USN. "Naval Might," *U.S. Naval Institute Proceedings,* XXXVIII (1912), 7-68.

Hussey, John A. "The Old State House at Benicia," *California Historical Society Quarterly,* XVII (1938), 260-71.

————. "The Origin of the Gillespie Mission," *California Historical Society Quarterly,* XIX (1940), 43-58.

Lewis, Charles L. "Our Navy in the Pacific and the Far East Long Ago," *U.S. Naval Institute Proceedings,* LXIX (1943), 857-64.

Livermore, S. W. "American Strategy Diplomacy in the South Pacific, 1890-1914," *Pacific Historical Review,* XII (1943), 33-51.

Maclay, Edgar S. "An Early 'Globe-Circling' Cruise," *U.S. Naval Institute Proceedings,* XXXVI (1910), 481-500.

Neeser, Robert W. "The Navy's Part in the Acquisition of California, 1846-1848," *U.S. Naval Institute Proceedings,* XXXIV (1908), 267-76.

————. "The Ships of the United States Navy, 1776-1915," *U.S. Naval Institute Proceedings,* XLI (1915), 1185-96.

O'Laughlin, J. C. "The American Fighting Fleet, Its Strategic Disposition," *Cassier's Magazine,* XXIV (Sept., 1903), 375.

Paullin, Charles O. "Naval Administration under the Naval Commissioners, 1815-1842," *U.S Naval Institute Proceedings,* XXXIII (1907), 597-641.

————. "Naval Administration, 1842-1861," *U.S. Naval Institute Proceedings,* XXXIII (1907), 1435-70.

————. "Early Voyages of American Naval Vessels to the Orient," *U.S. Naval Institute Proceedings,* XXXVI (1910), 429-63, 707-34, 1073-99, and XXXVII (1911), 239-75, 389-417.

————. "A Half Century of Naval Administration in America, 1861-1911," *U.S. Naval Institute Proceedings,* XXXVIII (1912), 1309-36; XXXIX (1913), 165-95, 735-60, 1217-67, 1469-1508; and XL (1914), 111-28, 419-29, 673-87, 1059-71.

Richards, David K. "The Beginning of Pearl Harbor, July, 1909—December 7, 1941," *U.S. Naval Institute Proceedings,* LXX (1944), 537-45.

Westcott, Allan. "Captain 'Mad Jack' Percival," *U.S. Naval Institute Proceedings,* LXI (1935), 313-19.

Wheeler, Gerald E. "Naval Aviation's First Year," *U.S. Naval Institute Proceedings,* LXXXVII (May 1961), 89-95.

MANUSCRIPT

Bradley, Udolpho T. "The Contentious Commodore—Thomas ap Catesby Jones of the Old Navy." Unpublished Ph.D. dissertation, History Department, Cornell University, 1933.

General Index

Acapulco, Mexico, 22, 82, 113, 119, 122

Adams, John Quincy, U.S. President, 51

Africa Station, 7, 114

Alaska, 131, 136, 137, 154, 162, 191, 199

Aleutian Islands, 106, 136, 162, 165, 166

Amapala, Honduras, 186

American Fur Company, 3

Anglo-Japanese Alliance, 189, 196

Antarctica, 52

Apia, Samoa, 136, 139, 140, 141, 169

Appomattox, surrender at, 122

Apra, Guam, 192

Arica, Chile, 21, 30, 132

Armistice of 1918, 188, 189

"Armored Cruiser Squadron," 169

Armstrong, James, officer, USN, 63, 64, 69, 70

Asiatic Fleet, 170

Asiatic Squadron, 128, 130, 136, 139, 152, 155, 158, 159, 162, 164, 170

Asiatic Station, 126

Aspinwall, New Granada, 105, 109, 113, 114, 119. See also Colón

Associated Chambers of Commerce of the Pacific Coast, 181

Astoria, Oregon, 3

Atlantic & Pacific telegraph line, 116

Atlantic Fleet, 162, 169, 170, 172, 179, 190, 191, 195, 197
round-the-world cruise, 167, 168

Auckland, New Zealand, 139, 141

Aulick, John H., officer, USN, 57, 58, 60

Auranco (Arauco?), Chile, 29

Australia, 127, 133, 134, 157

Auxiliary Naval Force, 153

Aviation experiments, 170

Bahia Blanca, Argentina, 184

Bahia, Brazil, 183

Balboa, Canal Zone, 183

Balch, George B., officer, USN, 137

Ballard, Henry E., officer, USN, 26, 47, 48, 49, 50, 51, 54, 100

Balmacedo, José, Chilean President, 144

Baltimore incident, 145, 146

Baltimore, Maryland, 9

Bancroft, George, U.S. Secretary of the Navy, 70, 71, 72, 75, 76, 77, 80, 81, 87, 88, 89, 91

Barbary states, 5

Baring Bros. & Company, 11

Barker, Albert S., officer, USN, 153

Barron, James, officer, USN, 33, 34

Bartlett, John R., officer, USN, 153

Bay of Panama, 197

Beardslee, Lester A., officer, USN, 136, 150, 151, 152

Bear Flag Republic, 77

Bell, Charles H., officer, USN, 116, 117, 118, 119, 120

Benevedes, Vicente, Spanish naval officer, 29

Benham, Andrew E. K., officer, USN, 144

Benicia, California, 97, 104

Benson, William S., officer, USN, 177, 181, 182

Bering Sea, 147, 166

Berlin Agreement of 1889, 156

Berlin, conference at, 140, 142

Biddle, James, officer, USN, 3, 4, 5, 6, 17, 34, 87, 88, 89, 90, 91

Biddy, Jonathan, enlisted man, USN, 99

Black, John, enlisted man, USN, 99

Black, Peter, enlisted man, USN, 99

Blaine, James G., U.S. Secretary of State, 146
Blockade, 4, 17, 22, 31, 32, 35, 36, 49, 50, 82, 86, 87, 88, 89, 91, 115, 118, 120
Blount, James H., 149
Board of Navy Commissioners, 11, 32, 41, 45, 58, 59
Board on Organization, 143
Bolivar, Simon, 35
Boston, Massachusetts, 1, 17, 25, 59
Bouet, E. C., French naval officer, 119, 120
Boutwell, Edward B., officer, USN, 108
Branch, John, U.S. Secretary of the Navy, 41, 42
Brazil Squadron, 45
Brazil Station, 7, 114
Bremerton, Washington, 152, 167, 173, 175, 193
British Guiana-Venezuela boundary controversy, 150
Brooke, John M., officer, USN, 107
Brown, George, U.S. Commissioner to Hawaii, 71, 72
Brown, George, officer, USN, 142, 143, 144, 145, 146, 148, 150
Brown, Thomas, officer, USN, 33
Bryan, H. F., officer, USN, 194
Buchanan, James, U.S. Secretary of State, 77
Buenos Aires, Argentina, 184, 185
Bureau of Navigation, 147, 157
Bureau of Steam Engineering, 118
Burton, Henry S., officer, USA, 88, 94
Butler, Smedley D., officer, USMC, 172
Bywater, Hector C., 195, 196

Cahuenga, surrender at, 85
Caldwell, Charles H. B., officer, USN, 135
Callao, Peru, 2, 4, 10, 21-25, 30, 31, 35, 38, 39, 40, 42, 44, 47-50, 57, 61-63, 64, 67, 68, 70, 96, 125, 127, 135, 145, 153
Canton, China, 1, 43

Cape Flattery, 126
Cape of Good Hope, 1, 2, 41, 43, 53, 58, 106
Cape Henry, 20
Cape Horn, 1, 2, 4, 19, 20, 25, 27, 30, 34, 47, 50, 52, 58, 59, 89, 95, 108, 110, 134
Cape San Lucas, 76
Cape San Roque, 18
Cape Verde Islands, 18
Caperton, William B., officer, USN, 176, 177, 181, 182, 183, 184, 185, 191
Caribbean Sea, 5, 6, 40, 118, 150, 194
Carlisle, J. M., 100
Caroline Islands, 53
Casey, Silas, officer, USN, 158
Cassin, Stephen, officer, USN, 33
Castro, José, Mexican army officer, 79, 81
Cavite, Philippine Islands, 164, 165
Chagres, Panama, 8, 9, 105
Charleston, South Carolina, 124
Charleston Navy Yard, 25
Chauncey, Isaac, officer, USN, 58
Chesapeake Bay, 181
Chimbote Bay, Peru, 146
China trade, 1, 2
Chincha Islands, 106, 125
Cholera, 132
Civil War, 54, 113-123, 126, 129, 130, 135, 154, 178
Clark, Charles E., officer, USN, 153
Claxton, Alexander, officer, USN, 54, 55, 56, 57, 58, 59
Cleveland, Grover, U.S. President, 149, 150, 155
Cochrane, Lord, 5, 22, 23, 24, 25, 28, 29
Collins, Napoleon, officer, USN, 134
Colón, 158, 159
Columbia River, 3, 5, 6, 10, 32, 53, 73, 74, 93, 98, 168
Columbia Valley, 73
Commesford, Henry, enlisted man, USN, 99
Conception, Chile, 61
Cone, Hutchinson I., officer, USN, 168

Confederate States of America, 113, 115, 117, 119, 124
Confederate States Navy, 114, 121
Conference on limitation of armament, 196
Conner, David, officer, USN, 75
Coolie trade, 136
Coos Bay, Oregon, 168
Coquimbo, Chile, 21, 23, 25
Corinto, Nicaragua, 172, 186
Costa Rica, 109
Court of St. James, 147
Coxe, Richard S., 34
Crane, William M., officer, USN, 33
Crowninshield, Arent S., officer, USN, 157
Crowninshield, Benjamin W., U.S. Secretary of the Navy, 17
Cuba, 158
Curtis, I. W., officer, USMC, 72
Curtiss, Glenn, 170
Czarnicke, enlisted man, USN, 155

Dallas, Alexander J., officer, USN, 65, 66, 67, 68, 69, 70
Daniels, Josephus, U.S. Secretary of the Navy, 173, 181, 190, 196
Davenport, Henry K., officer, USN, 121
Davis, Charles H., officer, USN, 109
Dayton, James H., officer, USN, 164
Decatur, Stephen, officer, USN, 6, 17
Democratic party, 190
Denby, Edwin, U.S. Secretary of the Navy, 197
Denman, Joseph, British naval officer, 125
Depot of Charts and Instruments, 52
Desertion, 15, 21, 40, 50, 95, 96, 97, 98, 100, 118, 130
Dewey, George, officer, USN, 133, 152, 154, 155, 156
Diáz, Adolfo, Nicaraguan President, 172
Dickerson, Mahlon, U.S. Secretary of the Navy, 47
Dobbin, James C., U.S. Secretary of the Navy, 103, 107, 127

Dornin, Thomas A., officer, USN, 63, 103
Downes, John, officer, USN, 1, 6, 17-25, 27, 28, 43, 44, 45, 46, 51, 100, 198, 199
Dueling, 25, 27, 59, 60
Dulany, Bladen, officer, USN, 101, 102, 103, 104, 106
Duntze, John A., British naval officer, 86
Dupetit-Thouars, Admiral, French naval officer, 67
DuPont, Samuel F., officer, USN, 81

East India Squadron, 70, 87
East India Station, 7, 43, 44, 67, 90, 114
East Indies, 23
Eberle, Edward W., officer, USN, 197
Eleventh Fleet, 168
Elliott, Jesse D., officer, USN, 33
El Salvador, 154
Ely, Eugene, 170
Emergency Fleet Corporation, 187
Esquimalt, British Columbia, 136, 150, 151
European Squadron, 147
European Station, 126
Evans, Holden A., officer, USN, 161
Evans, Robley D., officer, USN, 146

Farragut, David G., officer, USN, 104, 107, 108, 118
Finch, William B., officer, USN, 40
Fiji Islands, 53, 105
Filibusters, 102, 103, 109, 110
Forrest, French, officer, USN, 57
Forsyth, John, U.S. Secretary of State, 63
Fort Montgomery, 78
Fort Sumter, 124
Frémont, John C., officer, USA, 77, 78, 79, 81, 82, 85, 91, 92
Friendship incident, 43
Fullam, William F., officer, USN, 175, 176, 177, 180, 181, 182, 185, 186, 187, 188, 191
Fur trade, 1, 2

Galápagos Islands, 37
Gansevoort, Guert, officer, USN, 107
Gauntt, Charles, officer, USN, 18, 19, 21
Geisinger, David, officer, USN, 90
General Board, 196
General Order Ninety-four, 197, 198
Gentlemen's Agreement of 1907-8, 166
Ghent, Treaty of, 3, 4
Gherardi, Bancroft, officer, USN, 148
Gibson, William, officer, USN, 99
Gillespie, Archibald H., officer, USMC, 78, 79, 81, 83, 85, 91
Glass, Henry, officer, USN, 161
Gleaves, Albert, officer, USN, 185
Golden Gate, 8, 96, 114, 122, 153
Goodrich, Caspar F., officer, USN, 162
German High Seas Fleet, 180, 181
Graham, William A., U.S. Secretary of the Navy, 100, 101
Grand Fleet (British), 180, 181
Gray, Robert, master mariner, 1, 3
Greer, James A., officer, USN, 143, 144
Gregory, Francis H., officer, USN, 42
Guadalupe Hidalgo, Treaty of, 90, 102
Guam, 58, 189, 196
Guano, 106, 125
Guayaquil, Ecuador, 21, 31
Guaymas, Mexico, 89, 176
Guise, Admiral, Peruvian naval officer, 31, 35, 36
Gulf of California, 61, 82, 97
Gulf of Mexico, 40, 75
Gunn, William E., officer, USN, 153

Halford, William, enlisted man, USN, 133
Hall, William, enlisted man, USN, 99
Hamilton, John R., officer, USN, 112
Hampton Roads, Virginia, 51, 52, 106, 116, 125, 183

Harber, Giles B., officer, USN, 164
Hardy, Sir Thomas, British naval officer, 28
Harrison, Benjamin, U.S. President, 146
Havana, Cuba, 133, 152
Hawaiian Islands, 2, 30, 37, 40, 57, 58, 63, 66, 67, 71, 72, 74, 79, 94, 96, 111, 127, 131, 133, 138, 151, 156, 158, 165, 199
annexation of, 155
Hawaiian Republic, 149, 155
Hawaiian Revolution, 148, 149
Hayes, Rutherford B., U.S. President, 135
Henley, John D., officer, USN, 33
Herbert, Hilary A., U.S. Secretary of the Navy, 151
Heywood, Charles, officer, USN, 88
Hilo, Hawaii, 111
Hoff, Henry K., officer, USN, 115
Hogg, Thomas E., officer, CSN, 121
Hogan, Michael, U.S. Consul, 39
Hollins, George N., officer, USN, 69
Home Station, 7, 75
Honduras, 109
Hong Kong, 106, 152
Honolulu, Hawaii, 37, 38, 40, 53, 66, 71, 72, 96, 133, 136, 138, 139, 141, 142, 144, 148, 150, 152, 154, 155, 156, 187
Howard, Thomas B., officer, USN, 174, 175
Howison, Neil M., officer, USN, 74
Huacho, Chile, 24
Hubbard, John, officer, USN, 170
Hudson, William L., officer, USN, 52
Huerta, Victoriano, 174
Hughes, Aaron K., officer, USN, 143
Hugunin, Daniel C., officer, USN, 84
Hull, Isaac, officer, USN, 33, 35, 36, 37, 38, 39, 68
Hull, Mrs. Isaac, 35
Humboldt Bay, California, 168, 177, 178
Hunt, William, officer, USN, 111
Hunters Point Dry Dock, 167
Hydrographic Office, 52

Imperial Japanese Navy, 187, 189, 196
Impressment, 4, 15, 21, 40
Influenza epidemic of 1918, 191
Iquique, Chile, 145
Irwin, John, officer, USN, 150
Isherwood, Benjamin F., officer, USN, 118
Isthmus of Panama, 8, 22, 23, 105, 108, 109, 115, 123, 133, 134, 158
Isthmus of Tehuantepec, 105

Jackson, Andrew, U.S. President, 44, 46, 51
Johnston Island, 141
Jones, Hilary P., officer, USN, 197, 198, 199
Jones, Jacob, officer, USN, 39, 40, 41, 68
Jones, Meriwether P., officer, USN, 64
Jones, Thomas ap Catesby, officer, USN, 36, 38, 39, 41, 51, 59-70, 76, 80, 89, 90, 91, 94, 95-98, 99-101, 104, 109, 138
Juan Fernández Islands, 30
Judd, Dr. G. P., Hawaiian official, 72

Kamehameha III, King of Hawaii, 38
Kane, Henry C., British naval officer, 141
Kauai Island, 133
Kautz, Albert, officer, USN, 156
Kearny, Lawrence, officer, USN, 67, 68
Kearny, Stephen W., officer, USA, 84, 85, 91, 92
Kendrick, John, master mariner, 1
Kennon, Beverly, officer, USN, 35, 36
Kilpatrick, Judson, U.S. diplomat, 125
Kimberly, Lewis A., officer, USN, 138, 139, 141, 142
Kurile Islands, 106

La Mesa, Battle of, 85
La Paz, Lower California, 73, 88, 94, 114
Larkin, Thomas O., U.S. Consul, 74, 77

LaVallette, Elie A. F., officer, USN, 89
León, Nicaragua, 172
Lewis and Clark Expedition, 3
Liliuokalani, Queen of Hawaii, 148, 149, 150
Lima, Peru, 4, 22, 23, 24, 33, 35, 36, 48, 56, 63, 69
Liverpool, England, 123
Long Beach, California, 162, 193
Long, John C., officer, USN, 109, 110
Long, John D., U.S. Secretary of the Navy, 152, 153, 156
Los Angeles, California, 66, 81, 82, 83, 84, 197
Louis Philippe, King of France, 62
Lower California, 63, 81, 86, 87, 103, 114, 182
Luce, Stephen B., officer, USN, 138

MacArthur, Arthur, Jr., officer, USN, 159, 160
MacDonald, John D., officer, USN, 197
McArthur, William P., officer, USN, 99
McCann, William P., officer, USN, 145
McCauley, Charles S., officer, USN, 99, 101
McDougal, David, officer, USN, 117, 122
McKinley, William, U.S. President, 155
Macao, China, 1, 41, 43
Madeira, 52
Magdalena Bay, Mexico, 161, 167
Magruder, George A., officer, USN, 101
Mahan, Alfred T., officer, USN, 138, 146, 149, 162, 165
Malietoa, King of Samoa, 139, 142, 156
Managua, Nicaragua, 172
Manchuria, 166
Manila Bay, Battle of, 154, 155, 156
Manila, Philippine Islands, 53, 133
Manua Islands, 157
Manzanillo, Mexico, 90, 174

"Marching through Georgia," 149
Mare Island, California, 104, 107, 108, 109, 114, 115, 116, 117, 118, 119, 122, 126, 127, 128, 129, 136, 138, 142, 144, 152, 154, 155, 159, 160, 161, 162, 168, 170, 173, 176, 187, 192, 193
Marquesas Islands, 37, 38, 40, 57, 62
Marshall, John, U.S. Chief Justice, 32
Mason, John Y., U.S. Secretary of the Navy, 68, 86, 88, 90, 94
Maximilian, Emperor of Mexico, 117
Maxwell, Dr. R. T., 68
Mazatlán, Mexico, 63, 73, 74, 75, 76, 82, 86, 90, 96, 103, 120, 187
Meade, Richard W., officer, USN, 138
Measles, 94, 183
Mediterranean Sea, 3, 5, 30
Mediterranean Squadron, 6, 29
Mediterranean Station, 3, 114
Mervine, William, officer, USN, 74, 78, 81, 82, 83, 106, 107, 108, 109
Metcalf, Victor H., U.S. Secretary of the Navy, 163
Mexican War, 75-92, 95, 104
Mexico City, Mexico, 64, 82
Meyer, George von L., U.S. Secretary of the Navy, 172, 173, 176, 180
Micheltorena, Manuel, Mexican army officer, 66, 70
Midway Islands, 132
Miller, Joseph N., officer, USN, 152, 153, 154, 155, 156
Miller, Thomas, British naval officer, 110
Missroon, John S., officer, USN, 78
Mitchell, John K., officer, USN and CSN, 114
Mollendo, Peru, 25
Molokai Island, 136
Monroe Doctrine, 124
Monterey, California, 2, 5, 57, 63, 64, 65, 68, 70, 73, 74, 75, 76, 77, 78, 79, 81, 82, 84, 87, 89, 92, 96, 99
Montevideo, Uruguay, 27, 183, 184
Montgomery, Elliott, 84
Montgomery, John B., officer, USN, 78, 84, 86, 90, 110, 111, 112, 113, 114, 115, 118

Montgomery, William H., officer, USN, 84
Mulgrave Islands, 37
Mullan, Dennis W., officer, USN, 139, 141
Mumps, 183
Murphy, enlisted man, USN, 155
Murray, Alexander, officer, USN, 135

Nantucket, Massachusetts, 2
Naval Academy Practice Squadron, 181
Naval Observatory, 52
Naval Overseas Transport Service, 187, 191
Naval War College, 138, 195
New Bedford, Massachusetts, 2
New Orleans, Louisiana, 114, 118
New York Navy Yard, 108
New York, New York, 17, 30, 39, 41, 47, 50, 53, 59, 109
New York Times, 196
New York Volunteers, 88, 91
New Zealand, 53, 60, 158
Nicaraguan revolution of 1911, 171, 172
Nicholas, John S., officer, USN, 63
Nootka Sound, 1
Norfolk, Virginia, 18, 59, 106
North Atlantic Squadron, 148, 158
North Atlantic Station, 126
North Island, 170, 193
North Pacific Sealing Convention, 148
North Pacific Squadron, 127, 130, 131, 134, 135
North Pacific Station, 127, 128
North West Company, 3, 4
Nukahiva, 67
Núñez, Méndez, Spanish naval officer, 125 126

Oahu, 66, 73
Ocean Island, 132
Office of Naval Intelligence, 146
Oregon, 32, 60, 62, 70, 71, 75, 77, 93, 98, 107
Oregon Bill, 71
Oregon Territory, 32, 58

Pacific Fleet, formation of, 164, 190, 191
Pacific Mail Steamship Company, 103, 105, 120, 154, 155
Pacific Northwest, 98, 107, 193, 199
Pacific Reserve Fleet, 173, 175, 176, 177, 179, 182
Pacific Station, limits of, 58, 170
Page, Hugh N., officer, USN, 73
Pago Pago, Samoa, 138, 139, 157, 169
Palau Islands, 58
Palo Alto, Battle of, 75
Panama, 22, 23, 30, 31, 42, 57, 61, 63, 64, 65, 67, 70, 76, 80, 96, 99, 102, 105, 108, 110, 111, 113, 114, 115, 119, 120, 123, 127, 131, 138, 139, 153, 155, 158, 161, 162
Panama Canal, 159, 167, 172, 179, 180, 190, 195
Panama City, Panama, 158
Panama Railroad Company, 105
Parker, Foxhall A., officer, USN, 70
Patrol Force, Pacific Fleet, 182, 183, 185, 186
Paulding, James K., U.S. Secretary of the Navy, 57, 58
Paulet, Lord George, British naval officer, 66, 72
Pearl Harbor, Hawaii, 72, 138, 148, 179, 186, 193, 196
Pearson, George F., officer, USN, 120, 121, 122, 123, 127
Percival, John, officer, USN, 37, 72, 74
Perry, M. Calbraith, officer, USN, 100
Pezuela, Don Joaquin de, Viceroy of Peru, 28
Philippine insurrection, 158
Philippine Islands, 154, 155, 189, 196
Picaroons, 3, 7, 40
Pichilinque, Mexico, 186
Planning Committee, 189, 190
Point Argüello, 99
Point Conception, 99
Political asylum, 28, 29
Polk, James K., U.S. President, 78, 80, 81, 85, 86, 94
Port Hueneme, California, 188
Porter, David, officer, USN, 3, 17, 38

Porter, David D., officer, USN, 135
Preble, George H., officer, USN, 135
Preston, William B., U.S. Secretary of the Navy, 97, 110, 114
Prevost, John B., U.S. diplomat, 4
Pribilof Islands, 147
Privateers, 36, 113, 115, 117, 154
Puerto Rico, 158
Puget Sound, 53, 73, 87, 98, 107, 136, 150, 153, 154, 168, 199
Puget Sound Naval Station, 152
Puget Sound Navy Yard, 173, 187, 192, 193

Quallah-Battoo, Sumatra, 43, 44
Queen, Walter W., officer, USN, 133
Quilca, Chile, 30
Quinteros Bay, 145

Ramsay, William, officer, USN, 36
Read, George C., officer, USN, 33
Renshaw, James, officer, USN, 33
Resaca de la Palma, Battle of, 75
Reynolds, Alfred, officer, USN, 173
Reynolds, William, officer, USN, 131
Ridgely, Charles G., officer, USN, 6, 25, 27, 28, 30, 59, 60
Ringgold, Cadwallader, officer, USN, 106
Rio de Janeiro, Brazil, 4, 25, 47, 50, 52, 59, 106, 183, 184
Rio de la Plata, 27, 183, 184, 185
Rio Grande, 74
Ripple Rock, 133
Robeson, George M., U.S. Secretary of the Navy, 129, 135
Robinson, Jeremy, U.S. Consul, 34
Rodgers, Christopher R. P., officer, USN, 135, 136
Rodgers, George W., officer, USN, 33
Rodgers, John (I), officer, USN, 32, 41, 45
Rodgers, John (II), officer, USN, 106, 124, 125
Rodman, Hugh, officer, USN, 191, 192, 194
Roosevelt, Theodore, U.S. Assistant Secretary of the Navy, 152, 153;

U.S. President, 159, 166, 167, 171, 180
Rose Island, 157
Rowan, Stephen C., officer, USN, 81
Royal Hawaiian band, 149
Royal Navy, 34, 140, 189, 191
Russian America, 32
Russo-Japanese War, 166

Sacramento, California, 84
Sacramento River, 53
Samoa, 52, 105, 138, 139, 142, 156, 157, 199
Samoan hurricane of 1889, 140
Sampson, William T., officer, USN, 156
San Blas, Mexico, 22, 90
San Diego, California, 81, 82, 84, 86, 126, 144, 154, 160, 161, 168, 170, 171, 176, 186, 193
Sandwich Islands, 58. *See also* Hawaiian Islands
San Fernando, California, 85
San Francisco Bay, 63, 70, 88, 95, 96, 103, 159, 167, 170
San Francisco, California, 53, 72, 73, 75, 76, 78, 79, 83, 96, 97, 100, 104, 107, 109, 113, 114, 115, 116, 117, 119, 121, 122, 123, 130, 133, 135, 139, 142, 145, 146, 147, 148, 150, 152, 153, 154, 158, 162, 166, 167, 168, 186
San Gabriel River, Battle of, 85
San José del Cabo, Lower California, 88, 91
San Lucas, Lower California, 88
San Martín, General José de, 28
San Pablo Bay, 159
San Pascual, Battle of, 85
San Pedro, California, 81, 83, 84, 186, 193
Santa Barbara, California, 81
Santa Fe, New Mexico, 84
Santiago, Chile, 20, 30
Santiago de Cuba, Battle of, 156
Sausalito, California, 70
Savaii Island, 157
Schley, Winfield S., officer, USN, 145, 146

Schoonmaker, Cornelius M., officer, USN, 141
Scurvy, 96
Sealing, 2, 147, 148
Seattle Post-Intelligencer, 163
Seattle, Washington, 107
Sebree, Uriel, officer, USN, 169
Selfridge Expedition, 133
Selfridge, Thomas O., officer, USN, 48
Semmes, Raphael, officer, CSN, 119
Seward, William H., U.S. Secretary of State, 126
Seymour, Sir George, British naval officer, 71, 75, 76, 79, 92
Seymour Narrows, 133
Shadwell Passage, 132
Shirley, Paul, officer, USN, 119
Shubrick, Thomas B., officer, USN, 60
Shubrick, W. Branford, officer, USN, 87, 88, 89, 90, 91, 94, 100
Sicard, Montgomery, officer, USN, 132, 133
Simpson, Edward B., officer, USN, 135
Sitka, Alaska, 131, 132, 133, 136, 137, 153
Slave trade, 7
Sloat, John D., officer, USN, 42, 70, 71, 72, 73, 74, 75, 76, 77, 78, 79, 80, 82, 91, 92, 100, 104
Society Islands, 40, 52, 57
Solomon Islands, 157
Southard, Samuel L., U.S. Secretary of the Navy, 8, 33, 34, 36, 38, 40, 42
South Atlantic Squadron, 145
South Atlantic Station, 126, 134, 145
South Carolina, 60, 112
Southerland, William H. H., officer, USN, 172
South Pacific Squadron, 127, 130, 131, 134
South Pacific Station, 127, 128
Spanish-American War, 152-56, 160, 186
Special Service Squadron of 1865, 124, 125, 126
Special Service Squadron of 1892, 148
Special Service Squadron of 1920, 194

Spence, Robert T., officer, USN, 33
Squadron of Evolution, 143, 194
Stevens, John L., U.S. diplomat, 148, 149
Stewart, Charles, officer, USN, 6, 29, 31, 32, 33, 34, 35, 68, 100
Stewart, Mrs. Charles, 30
Stockton, Robert F., officer, USN, 74, 79, 80, 81, 82, 83, 84, 85, 86, 87, 88, 91
Strait of Magellan, 106, 119, 125, 148, 153, 167
Strait of Shimonoseki, 118
Stribling, Cornelius K., officer, USN, 63, 69, 96
Sucre, Antonio José de, Peruvian army officer, 31
Suez Canal, 167
Sugar cane, 41
Suisun Bay, 99
Sulu Archipelago, 53
Sutter's Fort, 77, 95
Swinburne, William T., officer, USN, 164, 169
Sydney, Australia, 52

Taft, William H., U.S. President, 171, 172
Tahiti, 38, 40, 62, 67, 71, 138
Talcahuano, Chile, 61
Tamasese, 139
Tampico, Mexico, 174
Taylor, Zachary, officer, USA, 82
Texas, 77, 180
Thatcher, Henry K., officer, USN, 127, 131
Thomas, Richard, British naval officer, 62, 63, 66
Thompson, Charles C. B., officer, USN, 33, 41, 42
Thompson, Smith, U.S. Secretary of the Navy, 32
Tilley, Benjamin F., officer, USN, 157
Tonga Islands, 157
Torpedo Flotilla, 161
Toucey, Isaac, U.S. Secretary of the Navy, 108

Tracy, Benjamin F., U.S. Secretary of the Navy, 143, 146
Transport and Cruiser Force, 185
Tuamotu Archipelago, 52, 53
Tudor, William, U.S. diplomat, 35
Tumbes River, 21
Turner, Daniel, officer, USN, 54, 55, 57, 58, 60
Tutuila, Samoa, 157

Unalaska, Alaska, 147, 153
Union Iron Works, 115, 121, 151
United States
    Congress, 71, 150, 155
    Exploring Expedition, 52, 53, 54, 59
    Fishery Commission, 154
    Fleet, established, 197
    House of Representatives, 32
    Naval Militia, 153
    Naval War College, 138, 195
    Revenue Cutter Service, 136, 148
    Senate, 105, 138, 149
    State Department, 12, 138, 152
    Surveying Expedition to the North Pacific Ocean, 106, 107
United States Mail Steamship Company, 105
Upolu Island, 157
Upper California, 63, 64, 76, 81, 82, 86, 91
Upshur, Abel P., U.S. Secretary of the Navy, 56, 60, 61, 65

Vallejo, California, 192
Valparaiso, Chile, 2, 3, 4, 5, 8, 10, 20-25, 27, 28, 29, 30, 32, 33, 39, 42, 47, 48, 50, 61, 66, 67, 68, 87, 96, 106, 111, 117, 125, 127, 132, 136, 138, 145, 146
Van Buren, Martin, U.S. diplomat, 43
Vancouver Island, 73, 136
Vanderbilt, Cornelius, 109
Veracruz, Mexico, 174
Vigilance Committee, 107
Vigilantes, 135
Virginius affair, 133

Wadsworth, Alexander S., officer, USN, 33, 46, 47
Walker, Sir Baldwin, British naval officer, 86
Walker, William J., 103, 109
Walla Walla Indians, 83, 84
War of the Pacific, 137, 138, 146
War Plan Green, 179, 180, 194
War Plan Orange, 179
War Plans Portfolio, 179
Warrington, Lewis, officer, USN, 58, 100
Washington, D.C., 64, 87, 100, 101, 135, 147, 149, 196
Washington Island, 62
Washington Territory, 98, 107
Washington's Birthday, 20, 44
Welles, Gideon, U.S. Secretary of the Navy, 114, 115, 117, 118, 119, 125, 126, 127
Werden, Reed, officer, USN, 134, 135
West Africa, 157
Western Board of Inspection and Survey, 160

West India Station, 7
West Indies, 3, 6
Whaling, 2, 3, 8, 38, 40, 57, 58, 70, 105, 106, 122, 123, 126
Wilkes, Charles, officer, USN, 52, 53, 54, 117
Willamette River, 53
Willamette Valley, 73
Williams, Clarence S., officer, USN, 191
Wilson, Azariel, chaplain, USN, 23
Wilson, Woodrow, U.S. President, 174
Wiltse, Gilbert C., officer, USN, 148, 149
Winters, enlisted man, USN, 155
Woodbury, Levi, U.S. Secretary of the Navy, 43, 45
Woods, Stanley, officer, USN, 160
World War I, 174, 180-88, 189

Yellow fever, 131, 132
Yellow Serpent, Indian chief, 84
Yerba Buena, California, 78
Yukon River, 153

Ship Index

This index of ships' names includes only those appearing in the text of this book. In Appendix III will be found the complete list of ships composing the U.S. Naval Forces on Pacific Station from 1818 to 1915, and Appendix IV will give the characteristics of all the ships which served on Pacific Station.

Abarenda, USS, 157, 158
Active, U.S. Coast Survey Ship, 107
Active, USS, 155
Adams, USS, 135, 139, 142, 148
Adler, SMS, 140, 141
Alabama, CSS, 118
Alabama, USS, 167
Alaska, USS, 135
Albany, USS, 165, 181
Albatross, USS, 154, 155
Alert, USS, 138, 141, 147
Alexander Agassiz, U.S. merchant-man, 187
Alliance, USS, 148
Andrew Jackson, U.S. merchantman, 9
Andromache, HMS, 23, 24
Annapolis, USS, 172
Aquila, U.S. merchantman, 122
Ariel, U.S. merchantman, 118, 119
Asheville, USS, 194

Badger, USS, 156
Baltimore, USS, 145, 146, 148, 152
Bennington, USS, 150, 154, 156, 161
Birmingham, USS, 192
Boston, USS, 67
Boston, USS (2nd), 148, 149, 159, 162, 163
Boxer, USS, 49
Brandywine, USS, 39, 41, 46, 47
Brutus, USS, 187

California, USS (armored cruiser), 172. *See also San Diego*

California, USS (battleship), 187, 192, 198
Calliope, HMS, 140, 141, 142
Camanche, USS, 122, 126
Carysfort, HMS, 66
Charleston, USS, 142, 143, 144, 145, 148, 150, 154
Charleston, USS (2nd), 163, 165
Chattanooga, USS, 176
Cherub, HMS, 3
Cheyenne, USS (ex-*Wyoming*), 177, 178, 185, 186
Chicago, USS, 162, 163, 185, 191
Cleveland, USS, 194
Clio, HMS, 110
Collingwood, HMS, 71, 79
Colorado, U.S. merchantman, 122
Colorado, USS, 177. *See also Pueblo*
Columbia, U.S. merchantman, 1, 3
Columbus, U.S. merchantman, 103
Columbus, USS, 87, 88, 89
Congress, USS, 74, 79, 81, 83, 88, 89, 90
Constance, HMS, 86
Constellation, USS, 25, 27, 28, 29, 30, 67
Constitution, U.S. merchantman, 140
Constitution, USS, 54, 55, 56, 70, 72, 74
Conway, HMS, 29
Corwin, USRC, 154
Creole, HMS, 28
Cyane, USS, 61, 62, 63, 64, 65, 69, 73, 74, 76, 77, 79, 80, 82, 88, 90, 91, 113, 114, 119, 131

Dacotah, USS, 127
Dale, USS, 57, 61, 62, 63, 64, 88
Davis, USS, 160
Decatur, USS, 106, 107, 115
DeKalb, USS, 183
Denver, USS, 191, 194
Des Moines, USS, 194
Dolphin, USS, 6, 29, 30, 32, 33, 34, 37, 38, 39, 41, 42
Dolphin, USS (2nd), 194
Dublin, HMS, 62, 63

Eber, SMS, 140, 141
Edith, USS, 98, 99
Empress of China, U.S. merchantman, 1
Enterprise, USS, 12, 49, 50
Erie, USS, 67, 69, 73, 88, 90
Esmeralda, Chilean warship, 145
Essex, USS, 1, 3, 17, 19
Ewing, U.S. Coast Survey schooner, 99

F-1, USS, 187
Falmouth, USS, 42, 49, 99, 101
Fama, Mexican merchantman, 64
Farallones, USS (ex-Massachusetts), 120, 127
Farragut, USS, 160
Fenimore Cooper, USS, 106, 107
Fisgard, HMS, 86
Flying Cloud, U.S. merchantman, 8, 9
Flying Fish, USS, 52
Fortune, USS, 160
Fox, USS, 160
Franklin, USS, 6, 29, 30, 31, 33, 34
Frederick, USS (ex-Maryland), 182, 183, 185
Fredonia, USS, 127, 132
Friendship, U.S. merchantman, 43

Galveston, USS, 194
Ganges, HMS, 111
General Brown, U.S. merchantman, 28
Georgia, U.S. whaler, 50
Globe, U.S. whaler, 37
Grampus, USS, 159
Grant, USRC, 154
Guerrière, USS, 41, 42

H-3, USS, 177, 178
H. N. Carlton, U.S. merchantman, 136
Hopkins, USS, 182
Hornet, USS, 6
Huntington, USS (ex-West Virginia), 182

Icarus, HMS, 151
Imogene, HMS, 49
Imperieuse, HMS, 151
Independence, USS, 87, 88, 90, 94, 108, 109, 116, 144
Iowa, USS, 158, 159
Iroquois, USS, 138, 142, 143
Iroquois, USS (2nd), 155
Itata, merchantman, 144, 145

J. M. Chapman, U.S. merchantman, 119
Jamestown, USS, 127, 131, 136
John Adams, USS, 108
John Hancock, USS, 106, 107
Juno, HMS, 78

Lackawanna, USS, 127, 131, 135
Lady Washington, U.S. merchantman, 1
Lancaster, USS, 110, 113, 115, 116, 117, 120, 121
Lautaro, Chilean frigate, 24
Lawrence, USS, 185
Levant, USS, 73, 74, 76, 77, 80, 81, 111, 112, 178
Lexington, USS, 49
Liberdad, Mexican schooner, 82
London, merchantman, 38
Louisa, U.S. merchantman, 24

McCulloch, USCGC, 188
Macedonian, U.S. merchantman, 22
Macedonian, USS, 1, 6, 15, 17, 18, 19, 20, 21, 22, 23, 24, 25, 26, 47, 51, 198
Macedonian, USS (2nd), 51
Machias, USS, 191
Maine, USS, 152
Maine, USS (2nd), 167

Malek Adhel, Mexican brig, 82
Marblehead, USS, 162, 185
Marietta, USS, 153
Marion, USS, 147
Maryland, USS (armored cruiser), 177. *See also Frederick*
Maryland, USS (battleship), 197, 198
Massachusetts, USS, 98, 106, 107, 110. *See also Farallones*
Merrimack, USS, 109, 110. *See also* CSS *Virginia*
Michigan, USS, 190
Milwaukee, USS, 163, 165, 176, 177, 178, 181
Mohican, USS, 127, 129, 130
Mohican, USS (2nd), 138, 139, 141, 143, 147, 148, 152, 154, 156
Mohongo, USS, 121, 127
Monadnock, USS, 125, 126
Monadnock, USS (2nd), 151, 153, 154
Monocacy, USS, 130
Monongahela, USS, 140, 141
Monterey, USS, 146, 150, 151, 154

Naniwa, HIJMS, 152
Nanshan, USS, 187
Narragansett, USS, 113, 120, 133, 138
Nebraska, USS, 167
New Orleans, USS, 177
New York, USS, 159. *See also Saratoga*
Niagara, USS, 194
Nipsic, USS, 139, 140, 141
North Carolina, USS, 26, 46, 47, 48, 49, 50, 51
Numancia, Spanish warship, 125
Nyack, USS, 127, 133

Ocean Express, merchantman, 129
Ohio, USS, 90, 96
Olga, SMS, 140, 141
Omaha-class cruisers, 192
Omaha, USS, 134, 135
Ontario, USS, 1, 3, 4, 5, 6
Onward, USS, 128, 134, 135
Oregon, USS, 151, 152, 153, 158, 173, 185, 186, 191, 192
Osprey, HMS, 136

Ossipee, USS, 131
Owen Glendower, HMS, 28

Paul Jones, USS, 160, 163
Peacock, USS, 33, 35, 36, 38, 39, 40
Peacock, USS (2nd), 51, 52, 53, 73
Pearl, U.S. merchantman, 30
Pembroke, U.S. merchantman, 118
Pennsylvania, USS (armored cruiser), 170. *See also Pittsburgh*
Pennsylvania, USS (battleship), 197, 199
Pensacola, USS, 127, 135, 145
Perry, USRC, 154
Perry, USS, 160, 185
Peruvian, U.S. schooner, 30, 34
Philadelphia, USS, 150, 155, 156
Phoebe, HMS, 3
Pike, USS, 159
Pinta, USS, 137
Pittsburgh, USS (ex-*Pennsylvania*), 173, 182, 183, 185
Porpoise, USS, 52, 53, 106
Portsmouth, USS, 73, 76, 78, 84, 86, 88, 89, 90, 103
Potomac, USS, 19, 42, 43, 44, 45, 46, 199
Powhatan, USS, 125, 127
Preble, USS, 89, 90, 101
Preble, USS (2nd), 160, 162, 163
Princeton, USS, 162, 163
Pueblo, USS (ex-*Colorado*), 182, 183, 185

Raccoon, HMS, 4
Raleigh, USS, 181
Rampart, U.S. merchantman, 24
Ranger, USS, 134, 143, 148
Raritan, USS, 101
Relief, USS, 52, 57
Resaca, USS, 127, 131
Richmond, USS, 134, 135
Robinson Crusoe, schooner, 30
Royal Arthur, HMS, 151
Rush, USRC, 154

Sacramento, USS, 194
Saginaw, USS, 118, 120, 122, 127, 132, 133
St. Lawrence, USS, 101

St. Louis, USS, 41, 42, 57
St. Louis, USS (2nd), 165
St. Mary's, USS, 101, 109, 110, 113, 114
Salem, USS, 192
Salvador, U.S. merchantman, 121
San Diego, USS (ex-*California*), 181, 182, 185, 186
San Francisco, USS, 145, 148
San Jacinto, USS, 117
Saranac, USS, 111, 113, 114, 119, 120, 122, 127, 133
Saratoga, USS (ex-*New York*), 185, 186
Savannah, USS, 68, 69, 70, 73, 74, 75, 76, 77, 81, 82, 83, 84, 88, 96, 98, 99, 101
Sea Gull, USS, 52
Shark, USS, 57, 61, 62, 63, 67, 70, 73, 87
Shenandoah, CSS, 122, 123, 126
Solace, USS, 168
South Carolina, USS, 190
South Dakota, USS, 169, 182, 183, 185
Steuben, USS, 183
Suwanee, USS, 121, 122, 127, 132

Tacoma-class cruisers, 162
Tacoma, USS, 191, 194
Tennessee, USS, 169
Thetis, USS, 142, 147, 148
Trent, British mail steamer, 117
Trenton, USS, 139, 140, 141, 142
Tuscarora, USS, 125, 127, 133

United States, USS, 17, 33, 36, 37, 38, 39, 59, 60, 61, 62, 63, 66, 69

Vandalia, USS (2nd), 138, 140, 141, 142
Vanderbilt, USS, 125, 127
Vicksburg, USS, 185, 187
Vigilant, USS, 155, 156
Vincennes, USS, 39, 40, 41, 46, 52, 53, 58, 106, 107
Virginia, CSS (ex-USS *Merrimack*), 116
Virginius, Cuban merchantman, 133

Wachusett, USS, 136, 138
Warren, USS, 73, 74, 82, 84, 88, 99, 104, 110, 115, 120
Washington, USS, 169
Wateree, USS, 119, 120, 121, 127, 132
Waterwitch, U.S. schooner, 30, 34
West Virginia, USS, 176. *See also Huntington*
Wheeling, USS, 154
Wisconsin, USS, 158, 159, 167
Wyoming, USS, 111, 112, 113, 114, 117
Wyoming, USS (2nd), 159, 161. *See also Cheyenne*
Wyoming, USS (3rd), 197

Yorktown, USS, 57, 60, 61, 63
Yorktown, USS (2nd), 146, 148, 150, 156, 163, 165, 182, 185